The American Revolution, State Sovereignty, and the American Constitutional Settlement, 1765–1800

The American Revolution, State Sovereignty, and the American Constitutional Settlement, 1765–1800

Aaron N. Coleman

LEXINGTON BOOKS
Lanham • Boulder • New York • London

Published by Lexington Books
An imprint of The Rowman & Littlefield Publishing Group, Inc.
4501 Forbes Boulevard, Suite 200, Lanham, Maryland 20706
www.rowman.com

Unit A, Whitacre Mews, 26-34 Stannary Street, London SE11 4AB

British Library Cataloguing in Publication Information Available

The hardback edition of this book was previously catalogued by the Library of Congress as follows:

Library of Congress Cataloging-in-Publication Data

Names: Coleman, Aaron N., author.
Title: The American Revolution, state sovereignty, and the American constitutional settlement, 1765–1800 / Aaron N. Coleman.
Description: Lanham, Maryland : Lexington Books, an imprint of the Rowman & Littlefield Publishing Group, 2016. | Includes bibliographical references and index.
Identifiers: LCCN 2015046068 (print) | LCCN 2015047627 (ebook)
Subjects: LCSH: Constitutional history--United States--18th century. | States' rights (American politics)--History--18th century.
Classification: LCC Kf4541.C55 2016 (print) | LCC KF4541 (ebook) | DDC 342.7302/909033--dc23
LC record available at http://lccn.loc.gov/2015046068

ISBN: 978-1-4985-0062-3 (cloth: alk. paper)
ISBN: 978-1-4985-0064-7 (pbk: alk. paper)
ISBN: 978-1-4985-0063-0 (electronic)

∞™ The paper used in this publication meets the minimum requirements of American National Standard for Information Sciences Permanence of Paper for Printed Library Materials, ANSI/NISO Z39.48-1992.

Printed in the United States of America

To Alex and Lorelei, and, especially, Emily.

Contents

Acknowledgments

In my attempt to research and write this book, I have incurred more debts than I can ever begin to repay. From elementary and high school history teachers, like Mr. Jeff Castle, Frank Baldridge, and Larry Fitzpatrick, I learned the foundations of the American Revolution. At Cumberland College (now University of the Cumberlands), I received one of the finest history undergraduate educations any future historian could want. Drs. Eric Wake, Oline Carmical, Al Pilant, and Bruce Hicks exposed me to the discipline and art of the historian, and the importance of excellent teaching in the classroom. It is my hope that this book is a testament to the education they gave me. At the University of Louisville, I met and studied with two of the finest scholars and gentleman I have ever known, Dr. Thomas Mackey and Dr. Gary L. Gregg, II. Dr. Mackey's constant demand "for paper" and excellence allowed me to develop my skills in ways I did not think possible. I am proud to call him my friend, and most thankful that he is still agreeing to read my "paper," including parts of this book, and offer the insightful and thoughtful remarks as only he can. With Dr. Gregg, I found a true brother-in-arms—the number of conversations I had with him on the general theme of this book helped me sharpen my thoughts.

My time at the University of Kentucky where I completed my PhD was invaluable. It was there that I met and worked with Lance Banning. In my sophomore year of college, I read *The Jeffersonian Persuasion*. That masterwork was the first to expose me to a world where politics and political ideas interplayed and affected each other. I was drawn especially to the interpretative battles over the Constitution during that pivotal decade. From that moment, I wanted to study the American founding, and the interchange of politics and ideas, under Professor Banning. My work with Professor Banning will always remain a highlight of my life. He was everything a scholar should be, gracious, friendly, and extremely demanding. His untimely passing was a blow to everyone who knew him, but his legacy will endure. I am not sure he would agree with everything in this book, but I do know he would have appreciated it.

Also at UK, I found a cadre of classmates and professors who contributed in some way to this book. Dr. Daniel Blake Smith deserves special thanks. Not only did he graciously take me on as his student after Professor Banning's untimely passing, but he offered valuable and important feedback to what became chapter 2 of this book. Also at UK, I became fast friends with Michael Schwarz and David Hollingsworth, two of the most gifted historians I have ever worked with. Mike's critical contribution to my thinking about the nature of Federalist denunciations of the Kentucky and Virginia Resolutions made its way into this book. Dave Hollingsworth is among my closest and dearest friends. His close friendship and willingness to poke fun at me is matched by critical editing skills and mastery of the early republic. All have been incalculable to me as I have written this book.

Additionally, this book could not have been completed without the help of Ms. Hannah Wilks Martin, Mr. Joey Fiefhaus, and Ms. Chole Sharp. Hannah was my work-study assistant at Kentucky Christian University and she was critical to the initial stages of this research project. Hannah did most of the photocopying, book collecting, and cataloguing that made this whole project easier to research. Joey and Chole played the same role, but in its final stages, while at my current position at the University of the Cumberlands. A big thanks to all their hard work. At the same time, I also want to thank the library staff at Kentucky Christian University and University of the Cumberlands. Mrs. Naulyen Enders, Heidi Wineland, and Elizabeth Couns at KCU, and Mrs. Jan Wren at UC, helped me track down books, articles, and put in numerous interlibrary loans for me. I am grateful for their hard work and dedication. Without it, this book could not have been completed. Additionally, I must thank Dr. John Wineland, my fellow history colleague at KCU, and Drs. Barry A. Vann and Jennifer Simpson, my departmental colleagues at UC, for their untiring support and willingness to listen to me drone on daily about this project and my progress. All three are great colleagues and friends. Finally, Mrs. Shirley Stephens and Mrs. Debbie Wood, our program's administrative assistants and gatekeepers, deserve special thanks. I am not sure how they endured my endless talk about this book, but they did. I appreciate their listening, encouragement, and friendship.

I also would like to thank the editors and reviewers at the *Journal of the Historical Society*. Parts of chapters 1 and 2 were taken from my article, "Debating the Nature of State Sovereignty: Nationalists, State Sovereigntists, and the Treaty of Peace (1783)," which they published in the fall of 2012. It is reused here with their permission and thanks. Thanks also goes to Peter Haworth, editor of *Anamensis*. Elements of chapters 1 and 2 are also taken from a forthcoming piece in that journal. Peter also served as my co-chair for a panel on state sovereignty we hosted at the 2011 Annual Meeting of Political Scientists. I thank all the participants of that panel for their feedback and thoughts. Other elements of this book, particularly those surrounding the drafting of the Burke Amendment and the Tenth Amendment, were presented at various conferences since 2010. I thank all those conferences and my fellow panelists.

No other historian and friend has been more important to the development and completion of this book than Adam Tate. I met Adam at a conference in Princeton in the summer of 2009, and since then he has been my dear friend and fellow traveler. The origins of this book, and its shape and development, all came out of the hours of conversation he and I have had over the years. Adam is the only person to have read the entirety of this book. His keen intellect, penetrating analysis, and excellent editing skills, all of which far outstrip my own, saved me from not only many mistakes but also influenced my thoughts on this topic in profound ways. In many ways, and although he is too humble to admit it, this book is as much his effort as it is mine. It was his encouragement and pushing me to write that helped make this book a reality.

My biggest debts and thanks, however, go to my family. My parents, Jerry and Sue, gave me the books, time, devotion, and guidance as only two excellent parents can. It is from my Dad that I received my love of history. Hearing him talk about my grandfather's military experience fighting in the battles of Guadalcanal and Bougainville, and meeting General Douglas McArthur, sparked my interest in knowing the events of the past. Their unconditional love and support have always been there—even when I told them I wanted to be a historian. I love them more than I can express and thank them for their continual support and encouragement. My children, Alex and Lorelei, are the sources of my greatest happiness. While young, both understood that Daddy was working on a book, and that it was time consuming. Although they helped by getting books from a shelf or files out the file cabinet—and accompanying me on the occasional trip to the library—their biggest and most important service came in the best way that kids can: by being an important reminder that there are things more significant than even the founding. To my wife, Emily, goes both my love and the most important thanks. Only her love outmatched her support, patience, and encouragement over the course of writing this book. As the vice president of student services, her own job is of the most demanding type, yet she still found the time to sit and listen to my worries and fears about completing this project, and to take the kids to visit their grandparents and aunts and uncles while I stayed home to write. How she was able to do all of that, and still be patient with me, is a testament to the wonderful wife and mother she is. I love her dearly and thank her for the sacrifices that made this book possible. It is to her and our kids that this book is dedicated.

Aaron N. Coleman
June 10, 2015

Introduction

Many Americans today assume that the federal government has always been the predominant governmental authority in the American constitutional system. Few realize that debates over the nature of sovereignty and federalism are as old as the founding itself. Many take it for granted that the Constitution of 1787 established a powerful national government charged with addressing any issue of national importance. That the Revolutionary generation established something fundamentally different would surprise them. Yet, that was exactly what happened. The founders did not establish a powerful centralized government possessed of a grand purpose. Instead, they established a decentralized federal order rooted in the idea of state sovereignty. To borrow from the historian of ideas, Michael Oakeshott, the founders did not establish a teleocratic system, a government designed to carry out specific philosophical objectives. Rather, they created, again borrowing from Oakeshott, a nomocratic order, or one "defined by an established way of conducting their business than by a set of goals."[1] Why they chose a constitutional order based upon state sovereignty is the primary purpose of this book.

In trying to answer the question of why the founders established state sovereignty as the bedrock of their constitutional order, the book argues two points. First, that federalism and state sovereignty became near synonymous terms during the founding period. When the concept of federalism was mentioned, more often than not, they meant it as a system where state sovereignty remained its foundation. Second, it argues that the idea of popular sovereignty at the time of the founding was not tied to the broader notion of a national popular sovereignty. In fact, most Americans of that era rejected the idea of a national popular sovereignty. Instead, they articulated it in the phrase "the people of the several states." The difference was historically and constitutionally significant. Historically, Americans had anchored their self-government to their distinct historical experiences. This meant, then, they viewed liberty and self-governing from a distinctively localist perspective. This localist view, in turn, led to two important constitutional ideas. First, that popular sovereignty existed on the state, not national, level. Secondly, they embraced the idea that state government best defended republican self-government and protected liberty. At the same time, the idea of popular sovereignty resting with the people of the several states helps to distinguish between the ideas of power and sovereignty, two terms scholars too often use interchangeably. Sovereignty, while meaning the final and absolute decision-making, also carried with it the notion of legitimacy. Governments could only exercise its powers if they had the legitimate authority—sovereignty—to wield that power. This distinction helps explain why the Constitution of 1787 was not a fundamental change to an already settled order and why political battles between the Federalists and Republicans in the decade following the Constitution's ratification were so significant. Since most Americans considered the Constitution as ratified by the people of the several states, they believed this gave the general government a limited sovereignty; it could wield only those powers enumerated within the document. Any exercise of authority outside those powers was illegitimate and a violation of sovereignty they invested with the states and a direct threat to their liberty.

The idea that the founders placed sovereignty in the states and not the federal government runs counter to the prevailing understanding of scholars of the Revolution and of the Constitution. Historians, political scientists, and legal scholars have not ignored the topics covered in this book—discussions of the imperial crisis, the ratification of the Constitution, and the political battles of the 1790s remain well-ploughed fields—but they have often misinterpreted the constitutional dimensions that underpin the context, assumptions, implications, and reasoning made by the participants of those events. The result has been an incomplete picture of the constitutional thought of the founding era. This oversight can be attributed, in part, to scholars' preoccupation with political ideas. Starting in the mid-1960s with the work of Bernard Bailyn, Gordon Wood, and J. G. A. Pocock, scholars began to take seriously the political ideas of the Revolutionary period. What they discovered was a rich and complicated world of political ideas, often labeled as republican, commonwealth, Whig, or Country Opposition, that stretched from the writings of antiquity and renaissance Florence to English polemicists and theorists of the seventeenth and eighteenth century. Eventually, as these scholars revealed, republican ideas found a receptive home in colonial America. Republican theorists taught their readers that liberty thrived best when practiced under a republican form of government. Yet, at the same time, liberty was fragile and succumbed easily to the polar threats of democratic licentiousness and arbitrary tyranny. The key, then, to the proper practice of republican government and liberty rested upon a virtuous citizenry willing and able to supplant their own self-interest to that of the larger common good. The virtue demanded by republican government faced its own persistent threats in the form of administrative corruption and patronage. Only through a periodic return to first principles could a people stave off this corruption and preserve their virtue.[2]

The appeal and near-universal influence of these ideas to Revolutionary Americans cannot be denied. In colonial America, these ideas helped shape the American perception of and response to Britain's tightening of imperial control as well as influencing the immediate post-war period. As Lance Banning demonstrated, these ideas persisted past the adoption of the Constitution and shaped the political formation of the Jeffersonians.[3] At the same time, the explorations of the "republican synthesis" led scholars of multiple disciplines to explore the intellectual world of Revolutionary America. The resulting explosion of interdisciplinary work on the intellectual interplay between republican ideology and religion, law, and politics widened and deepened scholars' understanding of the founding period.[4] At the same time, however, this focus on republican thought overlooked, or downplayed, the significance of the state sovereignty in American constitutional thought. Too often, scholars equated Americans' political ideas surrounding republicanism with their thoughts on how it operated on a national level. The result was a noticeable absence of discussion of Revolutionary Americans' thoughts on state sovereignty.

The second reason for why scholars have overlooked state sovereignty scholars rests on their nationalist viewpoint. As constitutional scholar Akhil Amar admits, most academics writing on the founding have viewed the period through nationalist lenses.[5] Influenced by the expansion of federal power—the presidency and federal courts especially—during the Civil War, the New Deal, and the Great Society, scholars too often read modern exercises of national power back into the past.[6] As such, these scholars approach the question of sovereignty's location from a distinctly nationalist stance. The great progressive scholar Merrill Jensen noted this interpretive problem over seventy years ago, pointing to how scholars "have accepted a tradition established by the Federalist Party [of 1787]" while refusing to "consider that the Federalist Party was organized to destroy a constitution." Thus, it was wise Federalists, looking to lodge power in a national government that could bypass untrustworthy state majorities, who established a constitutional settlement of a powerful national government. In doing so, they supposedly solved the theoretical issue of how to maintain republican government and liberty over an extended territory.[7]

One does not have to return to the Progressive interpretation of the early republic to appreciate Jensen's point. Too often interpretations of the founding overlook what Americans of the period actually said about their constitutionalism, and how they attempted to put those ideas into practice. Scholars often assume the correctness of the Federalist/Nationalist account. A contextual approach—one that is less concerned with the broader ideological trajectory of the period—can better unpack the intellectual and constitutional assumptions of Americans of the founding era. It can also tell a different narrative, one grounded more broadly in the history of the early republic. Jensen's point, which is just as relevant today as it was in 1940, is that rather than allowing the context of the arguments and events to demonstrate how most Americans approached and applied the issue of sovereignty, nationalist scholars often reinforce the ideology of those who advocated for national government, namely the Nationalists of the 1780s and Federalists of the 1790s. Scholars, then, often downplay or struggle assessing evidence that might suggest a significant number of Americans held contrary views.

While many scholars agree with Gordon Wood's assertion that questions of sovereignty remained "the most important theoretical question" throughout the period, they often use the term sovereignty to mean both legitimacy and the exercise of power, thus obstructing the issue.[8] Foremost among these scholars is historian Jack Rakove. He notes how Revolutionary Americans assumed the existence of at least some form of quasi-sovereign power for the colonial governments. The Continental Congress' initial exercise of powers traditionally associated with sovereignty, he argues, blurred what this sovereignty meant in the practical sense. Adding to the haze covering sovereignty's repository was how the people and colonies/states seem to have blessed congressional actions while simultaneously asserting state sovereignty. Americans, he presumed, gave only cursory attention to the question of sovereignty as they were busy fighting the Revolution. To Rakove, therefore, the question of the true divisions of responsibility and authority between the states and the Confederation Congress rested a great deal more on a mixture of expediency and pragmatism than reasoned thinking or historical traditions. As he wryly put it, the Americans of the founding period made a "hash out of sovereignty."[9]

If state sovereignty resulted only from "the pragmatic division of sovereignty between Union and state"—as the most convenient wartime choice—and was not a fundamental aspect of American constitutionalism, once the over-arching concern of winning the war was removed, this pragmatic arrangement could be remedied and settled properly.[10] This is why the "hash of sovereignty," from the nationalist historians' point of view, became even more indiscernible with the Articles of Confederation. To most scholars, the Articles attempted too much in terms of national governance while providing too little in way of national authority. In giving the Congress the power to fight and win a war against the world's most powerful nation, the Articles denied them the independent authority to raise funds for the effort. National governance became especially problematic, according to these scholars, because of Article II of the Articles of Confederation, which noted that "each state retains its sovereignty, freedom, and independence, and every power, jurisdiction, and right, which is not by this Confederation expressly delegated to the United States, in Congress assembled." Most scholars dismiss this provision, believing that Article II was "satisfactory only in the theoretical sense" and an unnecessary restatement of the obvious. Richard B. Morris, for example, forcefully denies the importance of state sovereignty. To him, it seemed that "a review of the evidence makes it clear that a national government was in operation before the formation of the states" and that in declaring independence from Britain, the Continental Congress "acted for the people rather than as the agent of thirteen separate states."[11]

For some scholars state sovereignty represented something more problematic than simply a restatement of the obvious or an unimportant mark on the path of nation building; it represented a constitutional failure of the Revolution. As Peter Onuf has written, "constitutional articulation of a radically decentered [*sic*] post-imperial regime" that thirteen separate sovereigns represented and Article II protected "stood in counterpoint to the realities of federal state formation." State sovereignty, he has further argued, "did not represent the logical culmination of the resistance movement, but rather the unintended consequence of its failure." As such, "independence was a means toward union, not an end in itself."[12] According to this argument, state sovereignty was an accident of the Revolution, a sad acknowledgment that the Revolution did not live up to its ideals, or, worse, a "noxious" "fiction" in that the states were never truly sovereign. To assert otherwise made a mockery of the Revolution's intent.[13] During the writing and ratification debates over the Constitution the problem of sovereignty continued to rear its head. With the notable exception of the Federalist argument against a Bill of Rights, most nationalist historians adopt the Federalist argument that the Constitution was superior to the Articles. Siding with the Federalist argument forces Nationalist historians to downplay once again the plausibility of the counterarguments.

Nationalist historians do note that proponents of state sovereignty won some concessions in the Constitution, particularly in the Senate. Nevertheless, the Constitution ultimately achieved Nationalists' objectives, albeit in an imperfect form. The survival of federalism and some acknowledgment of state sovereignty in the Tenth and Eleventh Amendments represents something of a dilemma for the Nationalist historians. To downplay the importance of those two amendments, and how they represent at a continuation of the state sovereignty under the new Constitution, scholars have claimed that a different federalism emerged out of Philadelphia in 1787. The evidence of this alteration of federalism often rests from an over-reliance on the *Federalist Papers*, especially *Federalist 10* and *39*. This new federalism differed in style and substance from the Articles since the Constitution operated directly upon the people, bypassed the states in many questions of governance, prohibited some state actions, and gave only slight acknowledgment of state sovereignty. Nationalist historians celebrate this conception of federalism as the unique American contribution to political theory and history.[14] In many ways, though, what nationalist historians celebrate is what federalism has become since the 1930s rather than what it was in 1787. This new federalism, supposedly unique and worthy of adulation from its creation in 1787, nevertheless still accommodated the "stubborn realities" and "misgivings about the capacities of state government."[15] Maintaining these misgivings led to what Edward Purcell, Jr. has called a "doubly blurred, fractionated, instrumental, and contingent" constitutional system.[16] As we will see, the only group that considered state sovereignty a "stubborn reality" at the Convention were the Nationalists. Indeed, and as this book demonstrates, there was no significant alteration to federalism that sprang out of 1787, and contrary to what other scholars have argued, the Constitution maintained a "single and true balance in the federal structure" based upon sovereignty of the states.[17] The Tenth and Eleventh Amendments ensured that.

Not surprisingly, nationalist historians review the ratification of the Constitution and adoption of the Bill of Rights through a Federalist lens.[18] Opponents of the Constitution, under this interpretation, were "men of little faith," conservatives who failed to embrace national popular sovereignty and clung desperately to state—and their own—power. The one real contribution the Constitution's opponents made to American governance, scholars admit, was their demands for a Bill of Rights. Yet, a close examination of this celebration reveals that it was not for the reasons that opponents demanded one in 1788, but for how twentieth and twenty-first century federal courts, via the unsubstantiated doctrine of incorporation, have cherry-picked through the first eight amendments to curb the power of the states.[19] Missing from most of this analysis is the Tenth Amendment. Even those works that do review the amendment often do so for the purposes of dismissing the amendment. Legal scholar Charles Lofgren notes that ambiguities riddle the amendment. This vagueness, he adds, is "worthwhile to attempt to clarify," only "so far" as it is "susceptible to clarification of its origins and 'original understanding.'" In the end, though, Lofgren acknowledges the continual importance of the states in American governance but concludes the Tenth Amendment is ultimately unimportant to the constitutional structure.[20] Charles Hobson and Eugene W. Hickock have explored the historical background to the amendment perhaps more than any other scholars have. Although he is careful in exploring the historical background and origins of the Tenth Amendment, Hobson, working from the idea that a "new federalism" emerged during the ratification debates, notes that the amendment is "in one sense superfluous" because the Constitution's opponents had forced a clarification of federalism at the ratification debates. To Hickock, the amendment "states in bold terms the fundamental demarcation of governing power that was at the very center of the debate over the constitution." While Hickok explains the purpose of the Tenth Amendment, he does not cover how the Tenth Amendment could accomplish such a cumbersome and debatable task.[21] As we will see, the American of the founding era considered the Tenth Amendment much more important than modern scholars do.

Not all nationalist-leaning scholars have rejected the importance of state sovereignty in the constitutional thought of the founders. The works of Jack P. Greene and Forrest McDonald provided two notable exception. Greene's work, which focused predominantly on the colonial period, explored the contextual workings of the imperial constitutional relationship. He found that the imperial constitutional structure was one of negotiation between center and periphery. Under this scheme, authority between the imperial center and its peripheral settlements remained fluid, unsettled, and in constant negotiation. Since colonial Americans conceived the structure of their political order in these terms, Americans carried this idea of negotiation with them in declaring independence and establishing their own American union.[22] McDonald offered a grittier understanding of the founding. Instead of seeing the founders as idealistic political philosophers, McDonald revealed them as players in a world of hardnosed politics, where political and economic self-interest mixed with pragmatic wheeling and dealing. McDonald did not ignore intellectual history, however. His most famous, and arguably most important, work, *Novus Ordo Seclorum*, explored the deep intellectual context in which the Constitution's framers operated. McDonald's context, moreover, was not attached solely to the realm of political theory. Instead, it covered how Anglo-Americans understood the legal, political, and economic ideas of their era as well as their understanding of English history and rights, and the immediate political contexts surrounding the internal workings of the Constitutional Convention. McDonald's analysis led him to conclude that the framers certainly designed a more powerful central government, but one contrived for only those specific purposes contained within its enumeration of powers; it contained no teleology beyond that. This limited nature of the federal government, moreover, derived from the American belief that liberty and private property remained best protected when tied to local governance. McDonald followed up on these conclusions in his work *Imperium in Imperio: States' Rights and the Union, 1776–1876*. There, McDonald traced the American attempt to establish a divided government. Once again, he demonstrated that Americans preferred the local to the general. Yet, and in a point nationalist-minded scholars often overlook, McDonald noted that the American preference for state governments was not an inherent endorsement of weak government. On the contrary, most Americans expected and demanded strong and robust state governments that would fuel economic growth and innovation. They feared a centralized government would threaten liberty and protect special economic interests.[23]

Recent works have also challenged nationalistic treatments of federalism and state sovereignty but have not dived deep enough into the context of the period. David Hendrickson's *Peace Pact* has explained how viewing state sovereignty as a failure of the Revolution ignores the context of the period. Americans perceived the states as sovereign entities and even adopted international norms in dealing with each other. Quite often during the Revolutionary period, he notes, "the supremacy contended for [Congress] was an avowedly limited sovereignty, reaching to these objects, largely external, of which the faith of the confederated states was pledged."[24] In other words, the states were sovereign in all ways save those related to foreign relations with a nation, war and peace. Rather than a failure of the Revolution, state sovereignty was what Americans expected to emerge from the Revolutionary War. In fact, he argues that the Constitution, in reality, was a peace pact, a treaty of sorts among sovereign entities meant to maintain a union, rather than a consolidated nation-state. Yet, Hendrickson, like those his work challenges, dismisses Article II of the Articles of Confederation noting that "in fact, [it] was supremely unimportant and simply restated the intention of the congress with the respect to the sources and limits of its authority."[25] He even accepts the idea that the Bill of Rights "wrote down the construction that the Federalists had placed upon the Constitution in the state ratifying convention, above all the doctrine that everything not given to the federal government was reserved to the states, but it left ample room for argument over the line of partition." In a work that seeks to curb those who "exaggerate the significance of the national idea in the ear of revolution and constitution building," this is a puzzling way to dismiss the constitutional significance of the Tenth Amendment.[26]

Even more recently, Alison LaCroix has attempted to identify the ideological origins of American federalism.[27] She traces the origins of federalism to seventeenth-century and early eighteenth-century law of nations thinkers such as Grotius, Pufendorf, and Vattel. Federalism in the Revolutionary period was as much a question of ideological approach as it was implementation as a constitutional and political principle. "The organizing principle" behind federalism was "divided authority," although some Americans would have placed a stronger emphasis on "divided" or "authority," depending on their view. LaCroix focuses her attention on two periods, the imperial crisis of the 1760s and 1770s and the Judiciary Acts of 1789 and 1801. This narrow approach led her to conclude that debates over legislative sovereignty in the 1760s and 1770s between Parliament and colonies resulted in Americans accepting "legislative layers." With the Constitution of 1787, this question of layers gave way to issues of jurisdiction. "The period between 1787 and 1802," LaCroix writes, "witnessed a transformation in American constitutional discourse from the language of legislative power and sovereignty to that of judicial power and jurisdiction."[28] Of vital importance to this transformation was Article III of the Constitution and the supremacy clause. When combined with Section Twenty-Five of the 1789 Judiciary Act, these three provisions empowered the court to render decisions upon state actions.

By rooting federalism in an ideology that predates the Revolution, LaCroix's work has added greatly to our understanding of federalism.

Her explanation that questions of jurisdiction started to overshadow issues of sovereignty is thought provoking. Yet, in important ways, her argument is problematic. Her argument that Americans accepted federalism because of the writings of continental Europeans ignores the practical experience with divided government that characterized colonial American constitutional development. At the same time, her work oddly stops with the Revolutionary War and resumes with the Constitutional Convention. Missing from her analysis is the Articles of Confederation and Article II; she mentions neither. She devotes only a few pages to the Articles noting that, rather than a "working-out of a vision of multilayered authority," they "represented a strategy for resistance and defense."[29] She accepts the nationalist idea that pragmatism ruled the drafting of the Articles, and her complete silence on Article II is repeated when she fails to mention how the Tenth Amendment might fit into her argument of the shift from sovereignty to jurisprudence. Had she devoted analysis to Article II of the Articles of Confederation and the Tenth Amendment, its origins, purpose, and use in the 1790s, she could have seen that sovereignty remained the fundamental constitutional question of the era.

The one scholar that explicitly rejected any notions of nationalism at the founding was M. E. Bradford. In his powerfully argued *Original Intentions: On the Making and Ratification of the United States Constitution*, Bradford wove constitutionalism into the intellectual story of the American founding and argued for the nomocratic nature of the Constitution. The framers and, more importantly, the ratification conventions, having a shared repugnancy towards "tyranny established and imposed in the name of 'good causes,'" did not adopt the document for the teleological purposes of redesigning American society. They sought a limited and procedural document intended only to bring government under the rule of law. This nomocratic objective meant that Constitution did not, and could not, address the wide range of issues that a diverse society faced. Each state that ratified the Constitution, Bradford showed, did so for their own specific reasons, resulting in thirteen separate understandings and intentions attached to the document. Thus, the Constitution provided only the process and outline for how these diverse groups could resolve their difference; it did not provide the answer.[30]

The works of Greene, McDonald, and, especially, Bradford, have influenced the writing of this book. What it attempts is a contextual, historical approach that blends legal, ideological, and political developments that allow the reader to appreciate the choices in front of Americans at the time. Instead of imposing a modern, nationalistic, and teleological framework on the past, it allows the reader to see the arguments as they emerge from the circumstances of the Revolutionary era. In reconstructing how Americans believed state sovereignty their most potent weapon in defending their liberty against centralized power, the book answers

the late Pauline Maier's contention that "it now takes historical imagina-
tion to understand how people could have understood the preservation
of the rights of the states as a way of protecting individual rights."[31]

***

*The American Revolution, State Sovereignty, and the American Constitutional
Settlement, 1765–1800* is organized in two sections, "Establishing the Revolutionary Settlement" and "Defending the Revolutionary Settlement."
Section one, which covers chapters 1–4, traces the historical origins of
state sovereignty and the American belief that state sovereignty protected
liberty. Starting with the constitutional development of the colonies, the
section traces the idea of state sovereignty through to the imperial crisis,
the drafting and implementation of Article II of the Articles of Confederation, and the writing and ratification of the Constitution. Chapter 1 provides an overview of the English development of sovereignty residing in
King-in-Parliament as well as colonial constitutional development. It explains how Americans during the imperial crisis rejected the Blackstonian notion of King-in-Parliament's sovereignty, which maintained that
Parliament was the "supreme, irresistible, absolute uncontrolled authority" in the British constitutional system. Rather, the colonies, drawing
upon their constitutional experiences, argued in favored of an imperial
federalism rooted in King-in-Colonial-Assembly. In this arrangement, the
colonies and Parliament would divide power. The colonial assemblies
would handle their own internal affairs while Parliament maintained authority over issues concerning the larger British Empire. When Parliament refused to relent, and made increasingly stark attempts to assert
their authority, Americans in the 1770s responded by denying Parliament
had any sovereignty over them whatsoever, and that its authority over
the empire resulted from the consent of the colonies. By the time
Americans declared independence, they had a well-articulated argument
for the importance of colonial—now state—sovereignty to their liberty.
Thus, the American embracement of state sovereignty was far from accidental or purely pragmatic.

Chapters 2 and 3 focus on the drafting of the Articles of Confederation
and the immediate post-war years. Chapter 2 pays special attention to the
arguments behind the acceptance of Article II of the Articles of Confederation, sometimes known as the Burke Amendment. The amendment stated that "each state retains its sovereignty, freedom, and independence,
and every power, jurisdiction, and right, which is not by this confederation expressly delegated to the United States, in Congress assembled."
One of the book's most important contributions is the focus on the Burke
Amendment's singular importance to the constitutional history of the
Revolutionary era. The amendment solidified state sovereignty as the

most integral part of the American constitutional settlement. This claim is contrary to all other works that discuss Articles of Confederation. Through a detailed recounting of the political events between 1780 and 1784, the importance of the Burke Amendment and the insistence of many that the amendment allowed state interposition to protect individual liberty will become clear. The debates between the Nationalists, who desired a more centralized confederation, and the "State Sovereigntists" over the Treaty of Paris provide rarely explored context for the question of a constitutional settlement. Rather than viewing the 1780s as a struggle between "cosmopolitans" and "localists" or lamenting the failures of Nationalists to secure a stronger national government via implied powers, the chapter argues that these political battles, at their core, were fundamental disputes over the constitutional settlement of the American Revolution. Yet, as chapter 3 notes, by 1787 most Americans, no matter their constitutional positions, believed the confederation was in serious trouble. The chapter explains those difficulties and how the Nationalists used those problems to advocate for a new constitutional settlement centered upon federal power. When they finally succeeded in gathering a convention of the states to consider revising the Articles, the Nationalists overplayed their hand by underestimating the American attachment to state sovereignty. As the chapter argues, it was the actions of the advocates of state sovereignty, and their ability to secure state sovereignty, that actually preserved the convention and secured the Constitution. Indeed, the Constitution that emerged from Philadelphia represents, at best, only a partial resettlement of the constitutional order.

Chapter 4 focuses on the ratification debates. The Anti-Federalists consistently complained that the proposed government would "swallow" the states into a great consolidated government. The Anti-Federalists worried that the lack of a Burke Amendment-type of statement in the Constitution threatened the liberty of all Americans. Yet, as the chapter details, the Federalists made repeated promises that since the Constitution created a limited government of limited powers neither state sovereignty nor liberty was in danger. In order to fulfill those promises, the Federalists made the momentous decision to accept an amendment to the Constitution that preserved state sovereignty. The promises for a limited government and provision protecting state sovereignty helped secure the Constitution's ratification.

Chapters 5–8 fall under the second section, "Defending the Settlement." This section examines the first decade under the Constitution and reveals how central state sovereignty remained to the political developments of the period. The section also demonstrates that, despite their promises, the Federalists almost immediately began to push for Blackstonian sovereignty for the general government. The one exception, as detailed in chapter 5, was the Judiciary Act of 1789. Chapter 5 also notes that the first hint at the Federalists' backtracking on their promises came with the drafting of the Bill of Rights, and the Tenth Amendment in particular. Chapter 6 explores how the economic program of Alexander Hamilton represented the actual breaking of the Federalists' promises made during ratification. Hamilton's program, and the arguments made in Congress defending it, centered upon the idea that the federal government was wholly sovereign and the states as little more than ancillaries of the federal government. Chapter 7 follows the growing division between the Federalists and the recently organized Republican Party. In realizing that the Federalists had broken their promises on preserving state sovereignty as the foundation of the constitutional order, the Republicans, particularly James Madison and John Taylor of Caroline, took to the presses to warn the public of the dangers posed by the centralizing policies and arguments of the Federalists. The Federalist threat could be stopped, they argued, only by returning to state sovereignty. The chapter also details the first major victory of state sovereignty in the 1790s, the Eleventh Amendment. A clear rejection of the Federalists' arguments for a national popular sovereignty, the Eleventh Amendment reaffirmed state sovereignty in an undeniable fashion. The eighth and final chapter explores the constitutional battle over the Alien and Sedition Acts. When the crisis with France escalated to a quasi-war in 1798, the Federalists passed these two measures on the grounds that the federal government possessed the common law. This common law, particularly the common law right to self-defense, they argued, superseded any stated limitations in the Constitution. The chapter concludes with the Republican counterattack, focusing chiefly on the famous Kentucky and Virginia Resolutions of 1798. Most examinations of the Resolutions assert that Thomas Jefferson and James Madison invented interposition in response to the Alien and Sedition Acts. Yet, as the book demonstrates, the idea of interposition was not new to Jefferson or Madison. It was a well-established idea embedded in the very nature of state sovereignty. Although historians make much out of how most of the other states denounced the resolutions, the chapter argues that the condemnation was more a reflection of the political climate surrounding the French Revolution and the quasi-war with France than of the idea itself. Finally, it was the election of 1800 and the Republican ascendency that ended the Federalists' centralizing threat and secured state sovereignty and the Revolution's constitutional settlement. A postscript provides an overview of the continuations of that settlement into the nineteenth century.

NOTES

1. Michael Oakeshott, *Lectures in the History of Political Thought*, Terry Nardin and Luke O'Sullivan, eds. (Exeter: Imprint Academics, 2005), 479–85; Oakeshott, "The Rule of Law," in *On History and Other Essays* (Indianapolis: Liberty Fund, 1999), 129–78; and *On Human Conduct* (Oxford: Oxford University Press, 1975). The quote is from M. E.

Bradford, *Original Intentions: On the Making and Ratification of the United States Constitution* (Athens: University of Georgia Press, 1993), 33.

2. Bernard Bailyn, *Ideological Origins of the American Revolution* (Cambridge, MA: Harvard University Press, 1967; 1991); Gordon Wood, *Creation of the American Republic, 1776–1787* (Chapel Hill: University of North Carolina Press, 1970); J. G. A. Pocock, *The Machiavellian Moment: Florentine Political Thought and the Atlantic Tradition* (Princeton, NJ: Princeton University Press, 1975), 423–50. Also see Caroline Robbins, *The Eighteenth-Century Commonwealthman: Studies in the Transmission, Development, and Circumstance of the English Liberal Thoughts from the Restoration of Charles II until the War with the Thirteen Colonies* (Cambridge, MA: Harvard University Press, 1959; reprint, Indianapolis: Liberty Fund, 2004).

3. Lance Banning, *The Jeffersonian Persuasion: Evolution of a Party Ideology* (Ithaca, NY: Cornell University Press, 1978).

4. Excellent examples of the interdisciplinary approaches include George W. Carey, *In Defense of the Constitution* (Indianapolis, IN: Liberty Fund, 1997); Barry Alan Shain, *The Myth of American Individualism* (Princeton, NJ: Princeton University Press, 1996); Gary L. Gregg, ed. *Vital Remnants: America's Founding and the Western Tradition* (Wilmington, DE: ISI Books, 1999); and Randy E. Barnett, *Restoring the Lost Constitution: The Presumption of Liberty* (Princeton, NJ: Princeton University Press, 2005).

5. Akhil Amar, *The Bill of Rights: Creation and Reconstruction* (New Haven, CT: Yale University Press, 2000), 3–4.

6. See, for example, Samuel Beer's contention that his New Deal liberalism and his inability to "escape the immense formative influence of the Civil War upon the American political mind" influenced the interpretation of his book, *To Make a Nation: The Rediscovery of American Federalism* (Cambridge, MA: Harvard University Press, 1993), vii–xi, quote on viii. Also, Jack Rakove has explained how that idea of state sovereignty, as applied directly via the Tenth Amendment, is, "[f]or a Madisonian like myself, who happens to think that the national government has indeed played a crucial role in enlarging rather than limiting fundamental rights and liberties, . . . not a happy thought." Jack Rakove, "American Federalism: Was there an Original Understanding?" in Mark Killenbeck, ed., *The Tenth Amendment and State Sovereignty: Constitutional History and Contemporary Issues* (Lanham, MD: Rowman & Littlefield, 2001), 129. This is not to claim that these works are illegitimate or lack important insights; far from it. Rather, it should cause readers, historians especially, to approach their interpretations with some hesitation.

7. Merrill Jensen, *The Articles of Confederation: An Interpretation of the Social-Constitutional History of the American Revolution, 1774–1781* (Madison: University of Wisconsin Press, 1940; 1970), 3.

8. Gordon Wood, *Creation of the American Republic, 1776–1787* (Chapel Hill: University of North Carolina Press, 1970), 354.

9. Jack Rakove, *Beginning of National Politics: An Interpretative History of the Continental Congress* (New York: Knopf, 1978); "American Federalism: Was there an Original Understanding?" and "Making a Hash of Sovereignty Parts I and II in *Green Bag* 2 and 3 (1998 and 1999): 35–44 and 51–59.

10. Rakove, "American Federalism: Was there an Original Understanding?," 110.

11. Richard B. Morris, *The Forging of the Union, 1781–1789* (New York: Harper, 1987), 77; and "The Forging of the Union Reconsidered: A Historical Refutation of State Sovereignty Over Seabeds," *Columbia Law Review* 74 (1974): 1088. For an even more intensely nationalist view see Curtis P. Nettles, "The Origins of the Union and the States," *Proceedings of the Massachusetts Historical Society* 62 (1963): 68–83. Although this book does not address the finer points of the works mentioned here, it is nevertheless a direct challenge to this nationalist viewpoint.

12. Peter Onuf, *The Mind of Thomas Jefferson* (Charlottesville: University of Virginia Press, 2007), 65–98; Onuf, "Federalism, Democracy, and Liberty in the New American Nation," in Jack P. Greene, ed., *Exclusionary Empire: English Liberty Overseas, 1600–1900* (Cambridge: Cambridge University Press, 2009), 132–159.

13. Peter Onuf, "James Madison's Extended Republic," *Texas Tech Law Review* 21 (1990): 2376; Jack P. Greene, *Peripheries and Center: Constitutional Development in the Extended Polities of the British Empire and the United States, 1607–1788* (Athens: University of Georgia Press, 1986), 180.

14. Wood, *Creation,* 525 and 545. Rakove, *Original Meanings, 161–203.* Martin Diamond, "What the Framers Meant by Federalism," and Harry Jaffa, "The Case for a Stronger National Government," both in Robert A. Goldwin, ed., *A Nation of States: Essays on the American Federal System* (Chicago: Rand McNally, 1961): 24–41 and 106–124.

15. Rakove, *Original Meanings,* 162.

16. Edward A. Purcell, Jr., *Originalism, Federalism, and the American Constitutional Enterprise* (New Haven, CT: Yale University Press, 2007), 6–7.

17. Ibid., 9.

18. An important and recent exception to this is Pauline Maier, *Ratification: The People Debate the Constitution, 1787–1788* (New York: Knopf, 2010). For the "men of little faith" see Cecila M. Kenyon, "The Anti-Federalists on the Nature of Representative Government," *William and Mary Quarterly* 12 (January 1955): 3–45.

19. Raoul Berger, *Government by Judiciary: The Transformation of the Fourteenth Amendment* (Cambridge, MA: Harvard University Press, 1977; reprint, Indianapolis: Liberty Fund, 1997).

20. Walter Berns, "The Meaning of the Tenth Amendment," in Goldwin, ed., *A Nation of States:* 126–148. Charles A. Lofgren, "The Origins of the Tenth Amendment: History, Sovereignty, and the Problem of Constitutional Intention," in Ronald K. L. Collins, ed., *Constitutional Government in America: Essays and Proceedings from Southwestern University Law Review's First West Coast Conference on Constitutional Law* (Durham, NC: Carolina Academic Press, 1980): 332. The same is true in the work by Leonard Levy. His *Original Intent and the Framers' Constitution* (New York: Macmillian, 1988) and *Origins of the Bill of Rights* (New Haven, CT: Yale University Press, 2001) make no mention of federalism or the Tenth Amendment.

21. Charles Hobson, "The Tenth Amendment and the New Federalism of 1789," in Jon Kukla, ed., *The Bill of Rights: A Lively Heritage* (Richmond: Library of Virginia, 1988): 153–63; Eugenge W. Hickock, "The Original Understanding of the Tenth Amendment," in Eugene W. Hickock, ed., *The Bill of Rights: Original Meanings and Current Understandings* (Charlottesville: University Press of Virginia, 1991): 455–64.

22. Jack P. Greene, ed., *Exclusionary Empire: English Liberty Overseas, 1600–1900* (Cambridge: Cambridge University Press, 2009); *The Constitutional Origins of the American Revolution* (Cambridge: Cambridge University Press, 2010).

23. Forrest McDonald, *Novus Ordo Seclorum: The Intellectual Origins of the Constitution* (Lawrence: University Press of Kansas, 1987); *Imperium in Imperio: States' Rights and the Union* (Lawrence: University Press of Kansas, 2000).

24. David Hendrickson, *Peace Pact: The Lost World of the Founding* (Lawrence: University Press of Kansas, 2003), 154.

25. Ibid., 134.

26. Ibid., ix.

27. Alison LaCroix, *The Ideological Origins of American Federalism* (Cambridge, MA: Harvard University Press, 2010).

28. Ibid., 180.

29. Ibid., 128.

30. Bradford, *Original Intentions,* quote on 36.

31. Maier, *Ratification,* 467.

I

Establishing the Revolutionary Settlement

ONE

King-in-Colonial-Assembly

The Background to State Sovereignty

The nearly 170 years that marked the founding of Jamestown to the battle of Lexington and Concord established the foundations of the constitutional settlement that emerged from the Revolution. For most of this period, the colonies were largely self-governing and never had to grapple with the question of where sovereignty rested within the imperial structure. In seventeenth-century England, however, questions of sovereignty tore apart their constitutional order. Ironically, the English constitutional settlement of 1688, which placed sovereignty in the hands of an omnipotent Parliament, was the singular issue that tore the colonies from the mother country. When the colonies finally addressed the question of sovereignty within the imperial structure, they had two general options from which to draw their responses. Sovereignty resided in either King-in-Parliament or with King-in-Colonial-Assembly. Drawing upon their own colonial experiences with divided government, colonial Americans made a constitutional and ideological argument for a decentralized imperial constitution with sovereignty divided between Parliament and the colonies. Their choice of this second of the two options brought controversy, conflict, and, ultimately, independence. By 1775, Parliament's increasingly aggressive attempts to assert sovereignty over the colonies led to the colonial abandonment of divided sovereignty and instead to the argument that sovereignty rested with King-in-Colonial-Assembly.

***

Questions of sovereignty dominated the constitutional history of seventeenth-century England. When the Stuart dynasty claimed that all sovereignty rested within their kingly powers and prerogatives, they butted against traditional English constitutional thought that the English common law limited and confined kingly authority.[1] Best expressed in the thirteenth-century writings of Henri de Bracton, Sir John Fortesque's *De Laudibus Legum Angliae,* and Sir Edward Coke's *Institutes*, these writers held that royal power was "restrained by political law," and, while under no man, was under "God and the law."[2] Coke added to this formula by noting that the ancient constitution of England was one where custom and long usage was the primary determinant of what was legal and right.[3] This afforded the king some of his prerogative authority, but only those powers that had long been in use. Otherwise, the common law confined the powers of the king. Under the ideas of Fortesque and Coke, then, only the laws to which they had consented governed the English people. That consent, moreover, came from both the customary common law and the institution of Parliament. Englishmen believed that this combination kept them free from the despotism of continental Europe.[4]

When Charles I prorogued Parliament in 1629 and embarked upon a period of governing through prerogative, he threatened the very foundations of English liberty. When Parliament asserted that sovereignty rested with it and the ancient constitution, the resulting civil war, beheading of Charles I, and the English Republic, destroyed the constitutional foundations those actions were intended to preserve.[5] Although the restoration of the Stuarts in 1660 reestablished the English constitutional system, the growth and power of Parliament was noticeable. In 1688, when relations between king and Parliament broke down once again over questions of sovereignty, Parliament forced James II to abdicate the throne in a "Glorious Revolution," and replaced him with the dual monarchy of William and Mary. The ascendency of Parliament was complete. Gone was the idea that the ancient constitution confined the actions of the king or parliament. Instead, a new English constitutional settlement emerged: King-in-Parliament.[6]

As the eighteenth-century progressed, the idea that sovereignty rested permanently with Parliament became orthodox, at least in England. The idea of the customary constitution persisted and maintained a hold on English constitutionalism and English politicians like William Pitt and Edmund Burke, but, by the mid-eighteenth century, notions that Parliament was sovereign began eclipsing it.[7] No one expressed this idea better than Sir William Blackstone. In his *Commentaries on the Law of England*, published in 1765, the English jurist argued that in all governments "there is and must be in all of them a supreme, irresistible absolute, uncontrolled authority, in which the *jura summi imperii*, or the rights of sovereignty, reside."[8] With this formula, Blackstone echoed the ideas of sixteenth-century French legal philosopher Jean Bodin. In his *Six Books on the Commonwealth,* published exactly two centuries before American independence, Bodin defined sovereignty as the "absolute and perpetual power of a commonwealth," that was "not limited either in power, or in function, or in length in time." This power, while not arbitrary, could not be divided, nor could it be "relinquished or alienated."[9] While Bodin applied this theory of a unified sovereignty to the monarchy, Blackstone linked it to Parliament. The "omnipotence of parliament" was so "transcendent and absolute" that "it can, in short, do everything that is not naturally impossible . . . what they can do, no authority upon earth can undo."[10] It would be this Blackstonian theory of sovereignty that the Americans would challenge during the crisis with Britain.

Eighteenth-century colonial Americans were aware of the growing sovereignty of Parliament. They had celebrated the overthrow of James II in 1688, and welcomed Parliament's ascendancy, believing that Parliament best secured England's liberties.[11] Yet, while English officials assumed that parliamentary sovereignty meant that Parliament could govern the colonies, most colonial Americans never accepted the idea that Parliament's sovereignty in England translated to sovereignty over them. Such an arrangement was foreign to their entire colonial experience.

The general theme of English governance of its North American colonial possessions was one of laxity, or, in the more famous phrase, "salutary neglect."[12] The governing oversight England provided the colonies came directly from the crown. Starting with the establishment of Jamestown in 1607 and continuing through to the start of the Revolution, the colonies could not take measures that were "repugnant" of either English statutory or common law.[13] The other mechanism of control came from the Lords of Trade, which Charles II established in 1679. Although Charles envisioned the Lords of Trade as a sort of ruling overlord for the colonies that would exert strong monarchial control over the colonies, work to consolidate some of the colonies, and stop the growth of proprietary colonies, that vision fell far short of what actually happened. In 1696, the Board of Trade replaced the Lords of Trades. The Board of Trade had two primary functions. Its first and primary function was to advise the crown on issues related to colonial governance. The second role the board played was to review all colonial legislation and either approve or veto it. While this power could have been significant, the board rarely used it. In its seven-decade history, the board rejected only 5.5 percent of all colonial laws.[14]

The one area where England did play an active role in colonial governance was trade. Through the various navigation and mercantile acts, England regulated the nature and extent of colonial trade. They restricted trade to within the empire and limited what items colonial merchants could send to England and the rest of the empire. Although smuggling certainly occurred, particularly with molasses, the colonies obeyed the mercantile system.[15] This acquiescence would be a major obstacle to the Americans once their dispute with Parliament began.

England's lax control over colonial affairs led to several significant constitutional developments that colonial Americans would draw upon in their confrontation with Parliament. First, and most importantly, it provided them with the experience of self-government. As historians Jack P. Greene and Michael Kammen have demonstrated, "between 1620 and 1660, every American colony with a substantial body of settlers adopted some form of elected assembly to pass laws for the polities they were creating."[16] Indeed, by the early eighteenth century all the colonies that existed had powerful colonial assemblies.[17] From the start, these assemblies were the "aggressive spokesman" for their "constituent's rights to the traditional English principles of consensual governance" including the right not to legislate or be taxed without their consent, to initiate legislation for their own governance.[18] For all intents and purposes, and as English commentators noted, the colonial governments by 1750 were reflections of the English government.[19] They had a governor (usually crown appointed), a lower house that mirrored the House of Commons in that it initiated all taxation and appropriation bills, and an upper house that acted like the House of Lords and advised the colonial governors on various issues. The significance of colonial self-government was enormous and had deep reverberations throughout colonial and Revolutionary America. It assured fierce colonial resistance to any attempt by England to intrude upon colonial self-government because it violated the traditional rights of Englishmen.[20] The colonial assemblies represented them and protected their property and not the authority of the far-distant English government.

At the same time, this self-government was made possible through the second important constitutional development, the authority of written documents. Whether in the form of covenants, licenses, proprietary grants, or charters, these documents, despite technical differences between them, provided the instrumentation necessary to establish colonial government. As political scientist Donald Lutz had pointed out, most charters opened with some form of preamble that stated the purpose, history, and legal background that established the reasoning behind each document. From there, these charters sketched out the geographical area over which the charter applied, and framed the nature and powers of the colonial government. Many of these documents also provided a statement of rights or liberties of the inhabitants who lived under them. It was from these documents that the first state constitutions would derive.[21]

Additionally, these various colonial charters provided the colonies with the institutional defense of their self-government. When the threat of revoking colonial self-government appeared, the colonies could refer back to specific clauses within their charters to protect their customary rights. The result was the origins of the American adherence to written protections of their rights as well as the notion that proscribed powers should confine government. In the colonial period, these ideas were only in their infancy, but they would mature into powerful elements of American constitutionalism.[22]

The third significant constitutional development that emerged from Britain's lax oversight was the notion that a division of governmental authority and power could happen. From the start of the colonial experience, Americans demonstrated a familiarity with divided government. Indeed, most of the early settlers of Virginia and Massachusetts brought with them the importance of local attachments and an autonomy that became demonstrable as the population of colonies grew and settlements developed and pushed ever westward.[23] Even had these settlers not brought their English heritage of local governance with them, the geographic diversity between the colonies and from within each colony made local governance a necessity. So powerful was the idea of divided power and local attachment that in Rhode Island, it actually delayed the establishment of a colonial government for several years.[24] In other colonies, the political strength of these local towns was such that when they demanded that colonial governments begin to receive representatives, the colonial governments had little choice but to agree. The result was that for most of the colonial experience, colonial Americans regarded their representatives as little more than "ambassadors from their local districts" who were bound to vote in certain ways by local instructions from the towns.[25]

It is difficult to overstate the weight of local attachment to colonial American constitutional development. Steeped as they were in the basic ideas of English constitutionalism, in particular, the idea that a people must offer consent through their actual representatives before government could legislate and tax, the meaning of local government becomes even more visible. Local government meant representation, and representation breathed constitutional legitimacy into government's actions. The further one moved away from local government, the greater potential it had to be tyrannical. It was from this division of colonial governmental authority that Americans had their first experience with federalism.

Among the first explicit examples of federalism in colonial America was the 1639 Fundamental Orders of Connecticut.[26] The orders stated that in order to "mayntayne the peace and union of a people," it was necessary to "order and dispose of the affayres of the people." As a result, the orders created a new civil society, the "Publike State or Comonwelth" of Connecticut. This "Combination and Confederation" left each town its own independent identity by keeping their own covenant agreements intact. At the same time, the General Court possessed the "supreme power of the Comonwelth," but left the people of Harford,

Wyndsor, and Wethersfield to their own local self-government.[27] Thus, the Fundamental Orders of Connecticut embodied the tenets of what came to be known as federalism: the necessity and foundation of local governance, a respect for the diversity and needs of local areas, and the idea that, on certain particular matters, unity was required.[28] This pattern of federalism repeated itself throughout the colonies in the seventeenth and eighteenth centuries.

Colonial experience with dividing governmental authority influenced the various colonial confederations during colonial American history. From the New England Confederation of 1642 to the Albany Plan of Union in 1754, most of these organizations addressed the need for mutual defense. With one notable exception, the 1685–1688 Dominion of New England, these plans did not touch upon the governing structure of the colonies. Mutual benefit led the colonies to confederate, but their tradition of self-government was too strong to allow the colonies to do more than that. As a result, many of the plans for unification failed to obtain the consent of the colonial assemblies, as in the case of the Albany Plan of Union. Others became defunct shortly after their establishment, as with the New England Confederation.[29] Nevertheless, these attempts at union revealed that any attempt to unite the colonies would have to be for limited purposes only; colonial self-government would be maintained above all else.

By the mid-eighteenth century, then, colonial Americans had an intimate familiarity with self-government, the value of written instruments of government, and dividing the powers of governments amongst various governing bodies. Importantly, these experiences diverged from the constitutional trends occurring in England at the same time. As the colonies grew familiar with actual representation, divided government, and written charters, England was becoming an increasingly centralized state where Parliament's will triumphed over ancient liberties, and all power and authority was drawn into it. Although English towns and localities still maintained local government, it was only by parliamentary grace that they did.[30] Under the Blackstonian sovereignty that formed the foundation of Parliament's power, ancient charters and liberties that formed the basis of local government in England could be altered if Parliament so chose. The vast differences in constitutional development between the colonies and the mother country would prove to be the undoing of the imperial relationship.

***

With the conclusion of the French and Indian War in 1763, England's empire stretched from the Indian Ocean to the Atlantic. Their victory over the French gave England unchallenged dominance in North America and the world's most powerful military. These achievements came with some costs, however. By 1763, England had acquired at debt of £125 million, a staggering sum for the eighteenth century. At the same time, it had to deal with hostile Indians in the newly acquired Northwest Territory as well as Catholic French nationals who remained in Canada. Even though England had an effective fiscal-military system in place to help ease the burden of the debt, English leaders knew that these new responsibilities required action.[31] In particular, they wanted their colonial possessions to help pay for the cost and upkeep of the military presence that was necessary to defend the colonies from Indian attack.

In 1764 and 1765, and again in 1767, prime ministers George Grenville and Charles Townshend submitted plans in the form of the Sugar, Stamp, and Townshend Acts. The Sugar Act lowered the tariff prices of molasses from six pence per gallon to three, thereby undercutting the lucrative smuggling trade, while insuring that the colonial market bought molasses from the British West Indies. The measure also strengthened the authority of customs inspectors in order to catch and detain possible smugglers. While the Sugar Act was an indirect tax, in that if one did not buy molasses or the rum distilled from molasses, they did not pay the tax, the same could not be said of the Stamp and Townshend Acts. Both taxed the colonists directly by forcing them to pay a tax on most paper products, including legal documents, newspapers, and even dice and on other goods such as paint, lead, and paper.[32]

Although both measures stated matter-of-factly that their purpose was for the raising of revenue for "defraying the expenses of defending, protecting, and securing" the colonies, the Stamp and Townshend Acts were more important than just their stated purpose.[33] It was the first time Parliament directly taxed the American colonies. Such an action was not only unprecedented, but it raised the serious constitutional question of how Parliament could directly tax the colonists since they were not represented in Parliament. Taxation and consent through representation was one of the hallmarks of the English Constitution, dating back to *Magna Charta*.[34] Even the rise of parliamentary sovereignty had not erased the power of that ancient idea. Most members of Parliament seemed to have little concern over the issue; many simply assumed that Parliament possessed the sovereign power necessary to tax the colonies. The Grenville administration was not as certain.[35]

Thomas Whately, a member of Grenville's administration, provided the answer. In his extended pamphlet, "The Regulations Lately Made Concerning the Colonies and the Taxes Imposed upon Them," Whately argued that Parliament enacted the Stamp Act in order for the colonies to share in the "[p]reservation of these Advantages and the Protection of the Colonies from future Dangers" presented after the victory in the French and Indian War.[36] England, Whately continued, had "a Right at all Times, she is under a necessity . . . to demand" assistance from the colonies to defray these costs. The Stamp Act was not oppressive; it was not "draining Plantations of money which they can so ill spare." Were Parliament asking them to pay for the entire upkeep of the British military, that would be the "severest Oppression of an American tax."[37] Instead, England was taxing in the "manner most suitable to [colonial] circumstances." Whately then continued by embracing parliamentary sovereignty. "The Right of the Mother Country to impose such a Duty upon her Colonies . . . cannot be questioned," he noted, no "Power can abridge that Authority, or dispense with the Obedience that it due to it." At the same time, he acknowledged that taxation through consent was a "sacred pledged of liberty" that all English subjects were entitled to.[38]

Yet, if Parliament had the right to tax the colonies, and consent was necessary to enact taxation measures, Whately had to address the fundamental constitutional question of colonial representation in Parliament. His answer was both clever and monumentally important. All British subjects, whether Londoners or Colonists, were "virtually represented in Parliament." Every "Member of Parliament sits in the House [of Commons], not as Representative of his own Constituents, but as one of that august Assembly by which all the Commons of Great Britain are represented."[39] All the "Colonies and all British Subjects whatever, have an equal Share in the general Representation of the Commons of Great Britain, and are bound by the Consent of the Majority of that House" even if they "had not particular Representatives there." Therefore, any attempt by the colonies to refer to their colonial governments or charters would not be heard since the "Citizens of London" also have town council and yet pay taxes enacted by Parliament.[40] Despite the differences in legislative powers, the colonies were "on the same footing with the rest." In fact, claimed Whately somewhat darkly, if there was "any inconsistency between a national and a provincial Legislature, the consequence would be the abolition of the latter; for the advantages that attend it are purely local." Thus, the "concurrence" of the colonial assemblies was not necessary since the relationship between Parliament and colonial assembly was not one of equals.[41]

By tying Parliament to all British subjects and not just to those boroughs or districts that actually voted for representatives, Whately tried heading off any colonial objections to the Stamp Act before they could protest. More importantly, virtual representation offered Parliament what it believed was the only constitutional argument available to explain the relationship between the colonies and parliamentary sovereignty. Had Whately admitted that only the colonial assemblies could tax colonists because they actually voted for their representatives, he would be denying the sovereignty of King-in-Parliament and instead admitting that the colonies were, in fact, self-governing entities removed from Parliament's authority. Virtual representation offered the simplest solution to the thorny path of taxation. At the same time, the idea of virtual representation was the logical constitutional outcome of England's century-and-a-half policy of lax oversight of the colonies. Since England had never taxed the colonies directly or had the colonies send representatives, and had, instead, sat back while colonial legislatures developed and grew in power, when the need finally came to acquire revenue from the colonies, it had little choice but to fall back to the idea that Parliament represented all English subjects. Although Whately's exposition on "virtual representation" would be England's primary constitutional argument over the next decade, the American colonies dismissed it immediately. The idea of virtual representation contradicted the "Birthright and Inheritance" of being English subjects. That birthright included all the "essential Rights and Privileges of the *British* Constitution," the most fundamental of which was ensuring that "every Commoner hath a right not to be subjected to law made without his consent."[42] Since Parliament represented only Britain itself and not the entirety of the British Empire, it stood to reason that Parliament's authority did not reach to those "British Dominions" that were "not represented in the grand legislature of the nation."[43] If Parliament's authority did extend to the colonies as Whately and other members of Parliament claimed, why, asked one anonymous author in North Carolina, had England allowed the establishment of colonial assemblies with the power to tax their residents?[44] The question drove at the nature of the constitutional dispute emerging between Parliament and the colonies.

In rejecting the idea of virtual representation, the colonies were also denying the application of the sovereignty of King-in-Parliament over the colonies. Instead, the colonies drew upon their own understanding of the English constitution and their own constitutional development. Adhering to the older, pre-1688 notions of the ancient constitution in which custom equated with authority, the colonies argued that their assemblies, and not Parliament, had always taxed colonial subjects. This "prescription, or long usage" was "understood to give Right." The right of being taxed by the colonial assembly, wrote Aequus, was "sanctified by successive usage, grounded upon a generous reliance on English Faith and Compact, and that usage" was "ratified by repeated authoritative acquiesces."[45] Under this theory of customary usage equating to authority, since the colonies had always taxed their residents with England's permission, only the colonies could continue to do so. This idea of customary constitutionalism tied perfectly with the colonies' arguments in favor of their chartered government and self-government. Parliament was not sovereign over the colonies, colonial Americans argued, because their colonial instruments of government had never acknowledged their authority. Instead, those charters established colonial government to represent colonial residents. It was this actual representation—the actual act of selecting representative—that constitutionally empowered the colonial assemblies to enact taxation measures.

The colonial argument for actual representation went deeper than the issues of taxation and legislation. The colonies were connecting actual representation and the authority of their legislature to the protection of traditional English rights. The corporate authority of the legislature protected the liberties of individuals. Whereas Parliament was the protector of liberty in England, the colonies assigned this role to their individual legislatures. When parliamentary sovereignty and virtual representation threatened the power of the colonial assemblies, it also jeopardized the liberties of individual subjects. Thomas Fitch made this point ably when he noted that:

> [t]he legislative authority of the colonies, will, in part, actually be cut off, a part of the same will be taken out of their own assemblies, even such part as they have enjoyed so long, and esteem most dear; nay, may it not be truly said, in this case, that the assemblies in the colonies will have left no other power or authority, and the people no other freedom, estates or privileges, than what be called a tenancy at will?[46]

The development of this connection between the colonial assemblies, which represented the populace of the entire colony, being used to protect the rights of individuals would have enormous consequences in the establishment of a state sovereignty constitutional order.

The final argument the colonies made against Parliament was the idea of an imperial federalism. The colonies did not enter the debates over the Stamp Act with a preconceived notion of an imperial federalism. Instead, the idea was the natural outgrowth of their conceptions of the English constitution and colonial constitutional experience. If Parliament was not sovereign over the colonies because of customary right, chartered governments, and actual representation, it stood to reason that the responsibilities of government would be divided between Parliament and colonial assemblies. Scholars such as Edmund Morgan have maintained that the Stamp Act dispute was a debate only over whether Parliament's authority to tax extended to internal taxation or if they could only externally tax the colonies as in the case of the Sugar Act. "The issue of the day," Morgan stated, "was taxation" since "Parliament at this time was not attempting to interfere in this department."[47] The dichotomy between external and internal taxation was present, but it became more important only after the Stamp Act had been repealed. At issue in controversy over the Stamp and Townshend Acts was the very nature of Parliament's power, of whether it was sovereign over all the colonies. By turning to their traditional experiences with divided government and arguing for an imperial federalism, the colonies were making a constitutional and legal case that federalism was the proper arrangements for good government. Yet, the colonial argument was much more than an extended lesson over how to structure power. By transforming their constitutional experiences into an ideology of federalism, the colonies were also making a philosophical case that decentralization was the best protection of liberty. This constitutional and philosophical argument for a decentralized imperial federalism could only be realized if colonial assemblies were de facto sovereign. To be sure, Americans throughout the decade of 1764 to 1774 were too diffident to assert that sovereignty resided in the colonial assemblies, but that was the essence of their claim.

The colonial assemblies were sovereign because they represented the people of the colonies. Virginian Richard Bland noted how "British subjects [were] governed only agreeable to laws to which they themselves have some way consented."[48] According to Bland, from the moment of their establishment, the colonies were to "make laws for their own government, suitable to their circumstances; not repugnant to, but as near as might be, agreeable to the laws of England." The colonies were "independent, as to their internal government of the original Kingdom, but united with her, as to their external polity, in the closest and most intricate League and Amity." This self-government allowed the colonies "all the freedom and liberty that the subjects in England enjoy." In other words, a clear division of authority separated Parliament from the colonial assemblies. In another work by Bland, he elaborated more on this federal division between Parliament and colonial assembly. Because the colonies were English, they were entitled to all the rights and liberties of Englishmen. To preserve these traditional rights, they had to "have legal constitutions," which included legislatures that represented the people of the various colonies. The obligation of the colonial legislatures, in turn, was passing laws for the "INTERNAL government." This did not apply just to taxation, but to legislation as well. To Bland, then, Parliament's only responsibility were those issues relating to the "EXTERNAL" issues of governance, although he did not specify what those external issues might be. From there, Bland went on to note that any law that Parliament enacted with the "INTERNAL polity" of the colonies was "arbitrary, as depriving us of our rights, and may be opposed."[49]

Nor was Bland alone in his separation between the powers of the colonial assemblies and Parliament. In Massachusetts, members of their General Court noted that Parliament certainly possessed a "general superintending Power . . . over the whole British Empire" but that authority was "exclusive [of the] right to make laws for our own internal government and taxation." Rather, "it seems necessary that they should exercise this power within themselves." Only through each legislative body possessing authority over their own internal issues could "that equality which ought ever to subsist among all his Majesty's subjects" be carried through the "extended empire."[50] Even more explicit on the existence of an imperial federalism was Rhode Island governor Stephen Hopkins. In all imperial systems, he wrote, there was "many separate governments each of which hath peculiar privileges." The empire of Great Britain was no different. Although there were "matters of a general nature" to which Parliament had the authority to attend to, such as the economic regulation and military protection of the entire empire, nevertheless, no single power of Parliament, "though greater than the other part, is by that superiority entitled to make law for or to tax the lesser part."[51] In other words, just because Parliament had authority over external issues did not grant it authority over all issues. Other colonists elaborated Hopkins' argument by noting that Parliament's oversight and "restrictions on navigation, commerce, or other external regulations" meant the "legislatures of the colonies were left entirely to the internal government" as detailed in their "peculiar constitutions" and "according to the principles of the national constitution."[52] Finally, a young Alexander Hamilton, writing ten years after Bland and the others, echoed these core sentiments by noting that:

> [o]ur Legislatures are confined to ourselves, and cannot interfere with Great Britain. We are best acquainted with our own circumstance, and therefore best qualified to make suitable regulations . . . let every colony attend to its own internal police, and all will be well.[53]

No American better explained this federal imperialism than John Dickinson. In his influential "Letters from a Farmer in Pennsylvania," published in 1767 as a response to the Townshend Acts, Dickinson made the explicit argument for the division between the Parliament and the colonial assemblies. Parliament "unquestionably possesses a legal authority to *regulate* the trade of *Great Britain* and all her colonies," because "such an authority is essential to the relation between a mother country and her colonies; and necessary for the common good of all."[54] Because the colonies were part of a collective whole, the idea of Parliament regulating imperial trade in order to insure those parts would not inflict unintended economic injury upon each other made sense. Parliament's attempt to raise revenue from the colonies was unconstitutional because neither Crown nor Parliament had ever taxed the colonies thereby violating the customary constitutional right of taxation without representation. At the same time, however, the "no taxation without representation" debate was also over internal and external power, and, thus, imperial federalism.

Dickinson's connection between the question of internal and external authority and taxation can be seen further in his careful avoidance in conceding parliamentary sovereignty over the colonies. Throughout the epistles, he embraced a distinctly limited notion of parliamentary authority. According to Dickinson and other advocates of imperial federalism, Parliament could only "preserve the connection" of the empire via the regulation of external affairs. Any action beyond that would be unconstitutional. Dickinson admitted that the colonies were "as much dependent on *Great Britain* as a perfectly free people can be on another."[55] This passage, however, is more revealing than it seems and provides insight into how most colonial Americans perceived the empire. The colonists were Englishmen and by that they possessed all the traditional English liberties, but they maintained only the most general of political relationships with the mother country, namely the external issues of trade. To Dickinson and other advocates of federal imperialism, this minimal dependency upon England preserved liberty. Rather than rely upon an entity three thousand miles away for everything, each colony had its own colonial assemblies managing business particular to their own colony. It was this actual representation that made the federal imperial connection possible and limited Parliament's power over the empire. It also further explains why Americans considered Parliament's taxation scheme tyrannical. A free people, Dickinson wrote, were "not those, over whom government is reasonable and equity exercised, but those who live under a government so constitutionally checked and controlled, that proper provision is made against its being otherwise exercised." [56] Actual representation in the individual colonies regarding issues of "internal business" like taxation provided the appropriate constitutional protection of liberty, whereas a more centralized empire threatened liberty.

Dickinson reserved special scorn over Britain's desire for a consolidated empire. Such an empire, with its uniform laws formulated from unseen and unknown MPs, directly threatened liberty. As he noted in the Ninth Letter, notions that colonial governments could not administer justice or defend themselves was not only absurd but an excuse to "form an idea of a slavery more complete, more miserable, more disgraceful" in order to "bow down our necks, with all the stupid serenity of servitude, to any drudgery, which our lords and masters shall please to command." [57] Dickinson's correlation between consolidated government and the loss of liberty would reverberate throughout the Revolutionary period.

All of this evidence suggests that the colonies were concerned with more than the just the issue of taxation. By advocating for an imperial federal constitution that demarcated the powers of Parliament and colonial assemblies between the external matters of the empire and the internal issues of the colonies, they explicitly rejected the Blackstonian idea of an omnipotent King-in-Parliament. Instead, they made an ideological and nomocratic case for decentralization that allowed for individual self-government but, at the same time, the protection of the whole. When the colonies made repeated references to their external dependency upon Parliament, what they meant was this collective protection.

This imperial federal system, moreover, did not mean the colonies abandoned the British structure. They still considered themselves deeply loyal subjects of the crown. Instead, what they advocated was a constitutional structure best described as King-in-Colonial-Assembly. [58] Because colonial Americans, even while having their own internal government, remained both Englishmen and part of the British Empire, but their allegiance extended to and remained exclusively with the English monarch. As Benjamin Franklin put it to Lord Kames, "private interests and not Parliament established the colonies." These "Adventurers voluntarily engag'd to remain the King's Subjects" and not subjects of Parliament. Since the colonies made laws in "their Assemblies or little Parliaments," with the consent of the colonial governor who represented the crown's person, the colonies "seem[ed] so many separate little States, subject to the same Prince."[59]

The idea of a King-in-Colonial-Assembly was federalism in action. Although colonial Americans like Bland, Hopkins, and Dickinson all denied that Parliament wielded a Blackstonian sovereignty over the colonies, they still acknowledged a limited role for Parliament in the empire. Yet, this role did not relate to sovereignty. In formulating the idea of an imperial federalism, Americans placed sovereignty in the hands of King-in-Colonial-Assembly. This enabled colonial Americans to sidestep the potentially intellectual and practical problems of creating an *imperium-in-imperio*, or sovereignty-within-a-sovereignty. Best expressed by Montesquieu in his 1748 *Spirit of the Laws*, although the idea was present in the classical past, the idea that two competing sovereignties could govern the same space was considered a "solecism" that led to political destruction.[60] Yet, by removing sovereignty from King-in-Parliament and locating it within King-in-Colonial-Assembly, colonial Americans believed they answered the question of where the final authority over the internal affairs of the colonies rested.

For the decade between 1764 and 1774, Americans held to the basic idea that the colonies would handle their own internal affairs while Parliament maintained the empire. England, not surprisingly, abjured all claims that Parliament was not sovereignty. Indeed, in this decade, they demonstrated repeatedly their belief in their own sovereignty. In 1766, and in response to their repealing of the Stamp Act, Parliament passed the Declaratory Act. Short, but powerful, the Declaratory Act was perhaps the best expression of Parliament's constitutional belief during the entire imperial crisis. In the most well-known part of the act, it stated that:

> colonies and plantations in *America* have been, are, and of right ought to be subordinate unto, and dependent upon the imperial crown and parliament of *Great Britain*; and that the King's majesty, by and with the advice and consent of the lords spiritual and temporal, and commons of *Great Britain*, in parliament assembled, had, hath, and of right ought to have, full power and authority to make laws and statutes of sufficient force and validity to bind the colonies and people of *America*, subjects of the crown of *Great Britain*, in all cases whatsoever.[61]

This was the classic statement of sovereignty resting in King-in-Parliament. The measure flatly denied the Americans' division between internal and external authority between colony and Parliament. Instead, Parliament asserted its right to govern all dimensions of colonial affairs in the way it best saw fit, and the colonies could not object. What is often overlooked, however, was how the Declaratory Act did more than just express parliamentary sovereignty, it acted upon the idea. In its second section, the Declaratory Act nullified any official colonial legislature's idea that challenged Parliament's supremacy. "All resolutions, votes, orders, and proceedings, in any of the said colonies or plantations, whereby the power and authority of the parliament of *Great Britain*, to make laws and statutes as aforesaid, is denied, or drawn into question, are, and are hereby declared to be, utterly null and void to all intents and purposes whatsoever."

More important than the Declaratory Act, however, was the battle that occurred in 1766–1768 between New York's colonial assembly and Parliament. The entire controversy revolved around parliamentary supremacy. The dispute derived from the Parliament's passage of the Mutiny Act, which was part of the Townshend Acts. In the measure, Parliament provided a list of supplies that it demanded the colonial assemblies, "at the expense of the province," gather and furnish for British troops who might be stationed within their colonies.[62] This was parliamentary supremacy in action; it dealt directly with the internal affairs of the colonies by requiring the colonial assemblies to pay for the billeting of the troops, with the only method available to pay for the supplies being the raising of taxes. The measure angered the colonies. The Massachusetts General Court declared it contrary to the "very nature of a free constitution" because "if we are but blindly to give as much of our own and of our constituents substance, as may be commanded, or thought fit to expend by those we know not."[63] Put another way, Parliament, who did not represent the colonies, was dictating to the colonies how to raise and spend their money. At the same time, if the colonies did obey Parliament's command it would establish a precedent, or usage, of parliamentary supremacy, thereby creating a serious constitutional dilemma. New York responded by allocating funds to purchase certain parts of Parliament's list of supplies, but declined to pay for others. The message the New York assembly sent was clear. They were "shewing their power to grant only what they should supposed proper" in order to make it "appear a voluntary act of their own, and not done in obedience to an act of [P]arliament."[64]

Parliament was furious. It decided to deliver a message to the colonies that "this country would not tamely suffer her sovereignty to be wrested out of her hands."[65] That message came in the form of the New York Restraining Act of 1767. The measure suspended the New York colonial assembly until it fulfilled Parliament's command to supply "all such necessaries" as required in the Mutiny Act. Until that compliance occurred, New York would not have a colonial government. Parliament followed the Restraining Act by agreeing to a resolution condemning New York for disobeying Parliament's authority.[66]

The colonies understood Parliament's message, and, more important-ly, the implications behind it. John Dickinson, in the first of his *Letters*, noted that it was not "necessary that this suspension should be caused by an act of Parliament." In the common law, it was accepted and well understood that one of the monarch's prerogative power was to pro-rogue the legislature. All that needed to happen, Dickinson claimed, was for the king to act through his royal governor and dissolve the assembly until it agreed to pay. To do that would have confined the issue only to New York and within keeping with the idea of King-in-Colonial-Assem-bly. Instead, Parliament took the extra, and threatening, step of "a parlia-mentary assertion of the supreme authority of the British legislature over the colonies." By expanding the issue to all the colonies, and not just New York, it gave "the suspension a consequence vastly more affecting."[67]

In the end, New York appropriated a sum of money that could be used to supply the troops but never appropriated the money for the specific items listed in the Mutiny Act. For Parliament, who desired to avoid an even deeper confrontation, New York's appropriation was enough for them to agree that the colony met the technicalities of the law. Although the issue of money and supplies was resolved, the larger ques-tion of Parliament's sovereignty in relation to the empire remained. Par-liament's fierce response and bold assertions of its sovereignty worried the colonists. For its part, the New York colonial assembly, upon its first meeting after the controversy, agreed to a series of resolutions that de-fended the idea of King-in-Colonial-Assembly. The most important of those resolutions noted how:

> this colony lawfully and constitutionally has and enjoys an internal legislature of its own, in which the crown, and the people of this colo-ny, are constitutionally represented; and that the power and authority of the said legislature, cannot lawfully or constitutionally be sus-pended, abridged, abrogated or annulled by any power, authority or prerogative whatsoever, the prerogative of the crown ordinarily exer-cised for prorogations and dissolutions only expected.[68]

The constitutional divisions between Parliament and the colonies lin-gered for several years. The issue reached its final and conclusive head in the Tea Act, the Boston Tea Party, and subsequent Coercive Acts. The Tea Act of 1773 was as bold a reflection of parliamentary sovereignty as the Restraining Act. It interfered with the internal elements of colonial affairs by forcing colonists to accept the Dutch East India Company's monopoly on the tea trade and meant they had little choice but to pay the impost tax for the tea. Thus, Britain was imposing its authority on the colonies. When the town of Boston responded with its famous Tea Party in Decem-ber of 1773, Parliament's response was the Coercive Acts of 1774. Four measures in all, the Coercive Acts abolished the Massachusetts government and charter of 1691 and replaced it with a military Governor-General, closed the port of Boston, removed certain trials away from the colony, and forced the quartering of British soldiers in Boston homes.[69] In short, the measures were the most explicit example of parliamentary sovereignty in all of colonial American history.

The measures provoked an important shift in the colonies' constitutional argument. Whereas prior to the Coercive Acts, or Intolerable Acts as the colonies called them, colonial Americans had rested their argument on the division of power between the internal affairs of the colonial assemblies and the external responsibilities of Parliament. They dropped this division altogether and argued that full sovereignty rested solely with the "King, at the head of his respective American Assemblies."[70] In many ways, the colonies had been moving towards this development as early as 1765, but Parliament's actions of the proceeding decade and culminating in the Coercive Acts forced the colonies to admit openly the idea of colonial sovereignty. If the British Empire was to be saved, it had to be saved on colonial Americans' terms. The implications of this shift for the imperial federal argument were substantial and far-reaching.

American defenders of colonial sovereignty placed most of their emphasis on consent. This renewed emphasis on consent allowed colonial Americans to advocate not just for colonial sovereignty, but it also allowed them to explain their previous emphasis on the internal and external divisions of imperial governance. In his influential 1774 pamphlet, "The Considerations on the Nature and Extent of the Legislative Authority of the British Parliament," James Wilson noted how "all the different members of the British empire are distinct states, independent of each other, but connected together under the same sovereign in right of the same crown." This meant that the "legislative authority of each part," including Parliament, was "confined within the local bounds of that part." Only the king, for whom Americans gave their loyalty, and could play an active part in colonial governance, could regulate trade.[71] Thomas Jefferson made a similar, if more aggressive, argument in his "Summary View of the Rights of British-America." Parliament's actions in regulating colonial trade, the young Jefferson argued, was an act of "arbitrary power" designed to admit "uncontrouled power . . . over these states." The "exercise of free trade" was a "natural right" of the American colonists "which no law of their own had taken away or abridged."[72] Wilson and Jefferson's use of the word "state" to describe the American colonies was significant. In eighteenth-century parlance, the words states and nations were interchangeable. They were their own political entities and were possessed of full powers of sovereignty. What Wilson and Jefferson were noting, then, was that, for all intents and purposes, the colonies were independent nations on par with England. They remained connected to England through their allegiance to the king and the role he

played in their governments, which was the exact role he played in relation to Parliament.

No American author wrote with more force on this topic than John
Adams in his 1774 "Novanglus" essays. Written as a response to Daniel
Leonard's "Masscahusettsnis," Adams' essays established the new emphasis on colonial sovereignty in the colonial arguments. Like Dickinson's essays seven years before, Adams noted how Parliament regulated
the external trade of the empire. Yet, Adams amended Dickinson's argument by linking Parliament's external authority to the idea of King-in-
Colonial-Assembly; Parliament was merely the convenient instrument to
carry out the desires of the king and colonies. He noted in his seventh
essay that the colonies, "have, by our own express consent, contracted to
observe the Navigation Act, and by our implied consent, by long usage
and united acquiescence, have submitted to other acts of trade."[73] Adams
implied that if the colonies removed this consent and were to determine
for themselves how to regulate their own trade, they could. As part of the
British Empire, Americans remained loyal to the British king but this
loyalty was "to the person of his majesty, King George III;" allegiance
was "to his natural, not his political capacity." In no way did this allegiance provide the king with any special authority over the colonies.[74]
Rather, it established the bonds that connected the colonies to England.

Adams stripped Parliament of any sovereign authority over the colonies. As he asked in another section of the seventh essay, "Will it follow
that parliament, as now constituted, has right to assume this supreme
jurisdiction?" His answer was curt: "by no means." The colonies were
happy "to continue subject to the authority of parliament, in the regulation of our trade, as long as she shall leave us to govern our internal
policy," because such regulation appeared to be in the best interest of the
colonies, which is why the colonies consented to these measures in the
first place. Advancing a nomocratic vision of the empire, Adams asserted
that the colonial assemblies preserved "[a]ll the blessing of [the British]
constitution."[75] Should Parliament become the supreme legislature, Adams warned, the colonies would suffer complete oligarchy or aristocracy
resulting in the destruction of their liberty. England had hoised the first
chains of this yoke over colonial necks with the Quebec Act, the altering
of the Massachusetts charter, and the other Intolerable Acts. Adams
prophesied darkly that if England failed to regain the common sense "we
must have a representation in our supreme legislature here" as "kings,
ministers, our ancestors, and the whole nation" realized over a century
earlier with the initial colonial settlements, "Great Britain will lose her
colonies."[76]

In the end, Adams' prophecy came true: Great Britain lost its colonies.
The inability of Parliament to accept nothing but its "supreme, irresistible
absolute, uncontrolled authority" forced the colonies to secede from the
British Empire. In the process of their debates with Parliament, colonial

Americans articulated a systematic case against an empire from which all sovereign power flowed from the center. Drawing upon their own constitutional experiences, colonial Americans advocated for a federal empire in which the separate colonial governments, although bound together in their allegiance to the king, possessed sovereign authority. When the colonies declared themselves "free and separate states," they were formally acknowledging a constitutional position they believed already existed. Thus, in the decade of 1765 to 1775, Americans had laid the foundations for a decentralized constitutional order rooted in the sovereignty of the states. Yet, the pressing and daunting task of fighting the world's most powerful nation demonstrated to Americans "the absolute necessity of union to the vigor and success of those measures on which we are already entered."[77] Thirteen separate entities they may have been, but they were small and weak; only collective action could protect them against the re-subjugation of the British. The challenge the Americans had to address was how to establish a union around a state sovereignty constitutional order.

NOTES

1. The literature on this topic is vast. For the best examples of it see J. G. A. Pocock, *The Ancient Constitution and the Feudal Law: A Study of English Historical Thought in the Seventeenth-Century* (Cambridge: Cambridge University Press, 1957); Glenn Burgess, *The Politics of the Ancient Constitution: An Introduction to English Political Thought, 1603–1642* (University Park: Pennsylvania State University Press, 1992) and *Absolute Monarchy and the Stuart Constitution* (New Haven, CT: Yale University Press, 1996); J. P. Somerville, *Politics and Ideology in England, 1603–1640* (New York: Longman, 1986); J. W. Tubbs, *The Common Law Mind: Medieval and Early Modern Conceptions* (Baltimore: Johns Hopkins University Press, 2000); Janelle Greenberg, *The Radical Face of the Ancient Constitution: St Edward's 'Laws' in Early Modern Political Thought* (Cambridge: Cambridge University Press, 2006).

2. The quotes are from Sir John Fortesque, *On the Laws and Governance of England*, Shelley Lockwood, ed. (Cambridge: Cambridge University Press, 1997), 18.

3. Steven Sheppard, ed., *The Selected Writings of Sir Edward Coke*, 3 vols. (Indianapolis, IN: Liberty Fund, 2003), see especially volume 2. Also see Pocock, *The Ancient Constitution*, and Burgess, *The Politics of the Ancient Constitution*.

4. John Phillip Reid, *The Rule of Law: The Jurisprudence of Liberty in the Seventeenth and Eighteenth Centuries* (DeKalb: Northern Illinois Press, 2004) 1–10.

5. Ibid.

6. John Phillip Reid, *Constitutional History of the American Revolution*, abridged ed., (Madison: University of Wisconsin Press, 1996), ix-xx.

7. H. T. Dickinson, "The Eighteenth-Century Debates over the Sovereignty of Parliament," *Transactions of the Royal Historical Society* 26 (1976): 189–210; Bernard Bailyn, *Ideological Origins of the American Revolution* (Cambridge, MA: Harvard University Press, 1967; 1991), 198–202.

8. William Blackstone, *Commentaries on the Laws of England*, 4 vols., Stanley Kurtz, ed. (Oxford: The Clarendon Press, 1765; reprint, Chicago: University of Chicago Press, 1979), 1: 49.

9. Jean Bodin, *On Sovereignty: Four Chapters from "The Six Books of the Common-wealth*, ed. and trans., Julian H. Franklin (Cambridge: Cambridge University Press, 1992), 49–50.

10. Blackstone, *Commentaries*, 1: 156–57.

11. Reid, *Constitutional History of the American Revolution*, abgd., 58, and Jack P. Greene, *The Constitutional Origins of the American Revolution* (Cambridge: Cambridge University Press, 2010), 52–63.

12. The term "salutary neglect" came from Edmund Burke's "Speech on Conciliation with America," *The Works of the Right Honorable, Edmund Burke*, 2 vols., (London: Holdsworth and Ball, 1803) 2: 186.

13. Mary Sarah Bilder, *The Transatlantic Constitution: Colonial Legal Culture and Empire* (Cambridge, MA: Harvard University Press, 2008), 1–15.

14. Jack P. Greene, *Peripheries and Center: Constitutional Development in the Extended Polities of the British Empire and the United States, 1607–1788* (Athens, GA: University of Georgia Press, 1986), 13–14, 45–46.

15. O.M. Dickinson, *The Navigation Acts and the American Revolution* (Philadelphia: Pennsylvania University Press, 1951).

16. Greene, *Constitution History*, 10, and Michael Kammen, *Deputyes & Libertyes: The Origins of Representative Government in Colonial America* (New York: Knopf, 1969), 11–12.

17. Georgia, the last of the original thirteen colonies, established in 1732, had its own assembly by 1750.

18. Kammen, *Deputyes & Libertyes*, 6–7.

19. Greene, *Constitutional History*, 12.

20. Greene, *Periphery and Center*, 28–42.

21. Donald S. Lutz, *The Origins of American Constitutionalism* (Baton Rouge: Louisiana State University Press, 1988), 13–49.

22. On this point also see Ibid., 50–69, and Lawrence H. Leder, *Liberty and Authority: Early American Political Ideology* (Chicago: Quadrangle Books, 1968), 95–117.

23. Kammen, *Deputyes & Libertyes*, 3–51. Also see David Grayson Allen, *In English Ways: The Movement of Societies and the Transferal of English Local Law and Custom to Massachusetts Bay in the Seventeenth Century* (New York: W. W. Norton, 1983).

24. Kammen, *Deputyes & Libertyes*, 29.

25. Gordon Wood, "Federalism from the Bottom Up: A Review of Alison LaCriox, *Ideological Origins of American Federalism*," *The University of Chicago Law Review* 78 (2011): 716.

26. Lutz, *Origins of American Constitutionalism*, 42.

27. Fundamental Orders of Connecticut, 1639, in Donald S. Lutz, ed., *The Colonial Origins of the American Constitution: A Documentary History* (Indianapolis, IN: Liberty Fund, 1998), 192–95, quotes on 192–93.

28. Lutz, *Origins of American Constitutionalism*, 43.

29. For the various plans of union see Oline Carmical, Jr. "Plans of Union, 1643–1783: A Study and Reappraisal of Projects for Uniting the English Colonies in North America (PhD Dissertation: University of Kentucky, 1975).

30. Greene, *Constitutional History*, 46–47.

31. Robert Middlekauff, *The Glorious Cause: The American Revolution, 1763–1789* (New York: Oxford University Press, 1982; 2005), 61, 22–26.

32. Ibid., 74–97; 142–58.

33. The quote is from the Stamp Act, found in Bruce Frohnen, ed., *The American Republic: Primary Sources* (Indianapolis, IN: Liberty Fund, 2002), 110.

34. Magna Charta, Chapter 12.

35. Greene, *Constitutional History*, 68–70.

36. Thomas Whately, "The Regulations Lately Made Concerning the Colonies and the Taxes Imposed upon Them, Considered" (London: J. Wilke, 1765), 102.

37. Ibid.

38. Ibid., 104.

39. Ibid., 109.

40. Ibid., 109–10.

41. Ibid., 113.

42. Thomas Fitch, "Reasons Why the British Colonies in America, Should not be Charged with Internal Taxes (New Haven, CT: n.p., 1764), 1–2.

43. Ibid.

44. Maurcie Moore, "The Justice and Policy of Taxing the American Colonies in Great Britain, Considered," reprinted in William S. Price, ed., *Not a Conquered People: Two Carolinians View Parliamentary Taxation* (Raleigh: North Carolina Department of Archives and History, 1975), 44–46.

45. "Aequus" from *The Craftsman*, Boston, 1766, reprinted in Charles S. Hyneman and Donald S. Lutz, eds., *American Political Writings during the Founding Era, 1760–1805*, 2 vols. (Indianapolis, IN: Liberty Fund, 1983), 1: 62–66, quotes on 65.

46. Fitch, "Reasons Why," 16.

47. Edmund Morgan, "Colonial Ideas of Parliamentary Power, 1764–1766," *William and Mary Quarterly* 5 (July 1948): 311–41, quote on 326; Bailyn, *Ideological Origins*, 209–19.

48. Richard Bland, "An Inquiry into the Rights of the British Colonies" (Williamsburg, VA: n.p., 1766), 20.

49. Richard Bland, "The Colonel Dismounted: Or the Rector Vindicated" (Williamsburg, VA: Joseph Royle, 1764), 22.

50. Answer of the House of Representatives of Massachusetts to the Governor's Speech," October 23, 1764, and Samuel Adams to George Whitefield, both in Alonzo Cushing, ed., *The Writings of Samuel Adams*, 4 vols. (New York: G. P. Putnam, 1904–1908), 1: 16, 28–29.

51. Stephen Hopkins, "The Rights of the Colonies Examined," in Hyneman and Lutz, eds., *American Political Writings*, 1: 57–58.

52. William Hicks, "The Nature and Extent of Parliamentary Power Considered," (New York: n.p. 1765), 11, and Fitch "Reasons Why," 16.

53. Alexander Hamilton, "The Farmer Refuted," in Richard B. Vernier, ed., *The Revolutionary Writings of Alexander Hamilton* (Indianapolis, IN: Liberty Fund, 2008), 94.

54. John Dickinson, "Letters from a Farmer in Pennsylvania," Letter 2, in Forrest McDonald, ed., Letters from a Farmer in Pennsylvania (John Dickinson) and Letters from the Federal Farmer (Richard Henry Lee) (Indianapolis, IN: Liberty Fund, 1992), 17 [Hereafter Dickinson, Letters]; Bailyn, *Ideological Origins*, 215–17.

55. Ibid.

56. Ibid., 38.

57. Ibid.

58. Aaron N. Coleman, "Debating the Nature of State Sovereignty: Nationalists, State Sovereigntists, and the Treaty of Paris (1783), *Journal of the Historical Society* 12 (September 2012): 315.

59. Benjamin Franklin to Lord Kames, February 25, 1767, in Leonard Labree et al., eds., *The Papers of Benjamin Franklin*, 37 vols. to date (New Haven, CT: Yale University Press, 1953-),14:68–69.

60. Charles de Montesquieu, *The Spirit of the Laws*, Anne M. Cohler, Basia C. Miller, and Horld S. Stone, eds. (Cambridge: Cambridge University Press, 1989), 112–30.

61. Declaratory Act in Frohnen, ed., *The American Republic: Primary Sources*, 137.

62. The details of the Mutiny Act are covered in John Phillip Reid, *Constitutional History of the American Revolution: The Authority to Legislate* (Madison: University of Wisconsin Press, 1991), 274.

63. Response from the Massachusetts House of Representatives to Governor Bernard, July 15, 1769, in *Journal of the Honorable House of Representatives of His Majesty's Province of the Massachusetts Bay in New England* (Boston: Edes and Gill, 1769), 81–82.

64. Quote taken from Reid, 3: 275.

65. Speech by Charles Townshend to the House of Commons, May 13, 1767 as recorded in "Parliamentary Diaries of Nathaniel Ryder, 1764–1767" P. D. G. Thomas,

ed., *Camden Miscellany* vol. XXIII, 4th series vol. 7 (1969): 344; Reid, *Authority to Legislate*, 276.

66. Reid, *Authority to Legislate*, 277.

67. Dickinson, *Letters*, 5.

68. Resolves of the New York Colonial Assembly, December 31, 1768, in *Journals of the Votes and Proceedings of the General Assembly of New York* (New York: Gaine, 1769): 74.

69. Middlekauff, *The Glorious Cause*, 225–37; Reid, *Authority to Legislate*, 26–33; and David Ammerman, *In the Common Cause: The American Response to the Coercive Acts of 1774* (Charlottesville: University Press of Virginia, 1974), 53–63.

70. Thomas Mason, "The British American" No. 7, in Peter Force, ed., *The American Archives*, 6 series (Washington, DC: St. Clair Clarke and Peter Force, 1937), Series 4, volume 1: 541.

71. James Wilson, "The Considerations on the Nature and Extent of the Legislative Authority of the British Parliament," in Kermit Hall and Mark David Hall, eds., *Collected Works of James Wilson*, 2 vols. (Indianapolis, IN: Liberty Fund, 2008), 1: 30.

72. Thomas Jefferson, "Summary View of the Rights of British North American," in Julian P. Boyd, ed., *The Papers of Thomas Jefferson*, 38 vols. (Princeton, NJ: Princeton University Press, 1950–2011), 1: 123.

73. John Adams, "Novanglus No. 7," in C. Bradley Thompson, ed., *Revolutionary Writings of John Adams* (Indianapolis, IN: Liberty Fund, 2000), 196.

74. Ibid, 197. For more on the connection of allegiance and protection see Alison LaCroix, *Ideological Origins of American Federalism* (Cambridge, MA: Harvard University Press, 2010), 83; James Kettner, *Development of American Citizenship, 1608–1870* (Chapel Hill: University of North Carolina Press, 1978), 165–168; Douglas Bradburn, *The Citizenship Revolution: Politics and the Creation of the American Union, 1774–1804* (Charlottesville: University of Virginia Press, 2009), 1–19; and Coleman, "Debating the Nature of State Sovereignty," 314.

75. Ibid., 198.

76. Ibid., 200.

77. John Witherspoon, "Speech in Congress," July 30, 1776, in Paul H. Smith, ed., *Letters to Delegates to Congress 1774–1789*), 25 vols. (Washington, DC: Library of Congress, 1976–2000) 4: 584.

TWO

Establishing and Debating the Nature of State Sovereignty

Articles of Confederation and the Politics of Early 1780s

The crisis with Britain had forced Americans to articulate a constitutional vision where the colonies were sovereign political units for all their internal affairs, with the crown exercising sovereign power over external issues. By declaring independence, the crown's sovereign authority had reverted to the colonies, who, as "Free and Independent States," had the "full Power to levy War, conclude Peace, contract Alliances, establish Commerce, and to do all other Acts and Things which Independent States may of right do." Although secession from the British Empire meant the states were thirteen distinct sovereigns, most Americans realized their independence would be short lived if they did not corporate. That realization required Americans to solve the constitutional dilemma of how to create a union that would balance their need for corporation while preserving the state sovereignty they claimed had always existed.

The debate was not as easily resolved as it first seemed. Although Article II of the Articles of Confederation enshrined state sovereignty, a distinct group of Americans argued for a national government that both represented the people of America and possessed robust sovereign power, including the use of implied powers. Throughout the entire Revolution and in the immediate aftermath of peace, this group fought against the idea of state sovereignty, claiming that it hindered the American war effort and threatened lasting peace. Despite their efforts, by the end of the war Americans had embraced state sovereignty as the constitutional foundation of the Revolution. In the process of those debates, moreover,

Americans had explained how that state sovereignty was to operate in their constitutional system.

***

The need for a union more permanent and structured than that of the Continental Congress was so important to Americans that before declaring independence, they authorized a committee to draft articles of confederation. On July 12, 1776, while the War of Independence thundered on the battlefields of New York and New Jersey, the committee submitted their product. Known as the "Dickinson Plan," after the chair of the committee and its chief author, John Dickinson, the plan created a confederation in which a "firm League of Friendship" existed between the sister states. Under the plan, states would voluntarily surrender elements of their sovereignty, especially powers associated with the former monarchial authority to wage war, conduct diplomacy, and settle disputes between sister states.[1] These particular delegations of powers were uneventful and uncontroversial. It was the primary reason they believed a union of the states was necessary.

The committee's draft maintained the internal and external dichotomy that Dickinson and others first explained in the 1760s, but two provisions provoked intense debate: the one state, one vote for congressional representation and Article III, which stated that "Each Colony shall retain and enjoy as much of its present Laws, Rights and Customs, as it may think fit, and reserve to itself the sole and exclusive Regulation and Government of its internal police, in all matters that shall not interfere with the Articles of this Confederation." Each provision effected the function of state sovereignty.

Inside the chamber where the Continental Congress met, debates over the "momentous question" of allowing each state an equal vote in the Congress added to the already uncomfortable summer heat.[2] These debates exposed the first division over state sovereignty and the nature of the American union. A small, but vocal, group of congressional delegates caused the breach. Known latter as the Nationalists, this group emerged first in 1776 during the debates over the draft of the Articles rather than in 1780 as most scholars assert.[3] These early Nationalists, led by Pennsylvania delegates James Wilson and Benjamin Rush, argued that the Confederation Congress was a national government representing the individual people of the states and not the states themselves.[4] "The members of the congress it is true are appointed by States, but represent the people [and] no State hath a right to alienate the privilege of equal representation: it belongs solely [to] the people," Rush noted in a speech on the floor of Congress. Wilson contended that "as to those matters which are referred to Congress, we are not so many states, we are one large state. We lay aside our individuality, whenever we come here."[5] John Adams joined with Rush and Wilson to note that "the confederacy [was] to make use one individual only; it is to form us, like separate parcels of metal, into one common mass. We shall no longer retain our separate individuality, but become a single individual as to all questions submitted to the Confederacy."[6] In other words, because the external issues of war and peace transcended local, internal concerns, on this issue the confederation was a unified state. A population-based representation for the confederation, or "one people—a new nation" as Rush and Wilson proclaimed, suggested a teleocratic national government that surpassed those issues and drew the states together and could circumvent them and operate directly upon individuals.[7] In essence, they hinted strongly for a supremacy in those same areas that Americans had denied giving Parliament throughout the previous decade.

The argument against the one state, one vote was the minority view. As soon as Wilson and Rush stated their positions, congressional delegates countered by referring to what had been the accepted understanding of the Congress, that it represented the several states. Connecticut's Roger Sherman noted "we are representatives of the States not individuals" while John Witherspoon equated "every colony [as] a distinct person." Equal representation was necessary to preserve the equal stations of each state with the other. These arguments, rooted in how Americans understood the Continental Congress as representing the individual states, defeated the Nationalists' attempt at creating a national sovereignty.[8]

Although the Nationalists lost their debate to remove the one state, one vote provision, Article III of the proposal appeared to make the confederation a national government. In particular, the final clause of that article provided the interpretative framework from which Nationalists could construct their argument. After noting in the first section of Article III that the colonies would "retain and enjoy" as much of their present laws as they deemed necessary, and reserving for themselves the "sole and exclusive Regulation and Government of its internal police" (note the use of "internal"), the last section qualified this internal authority, noting that it "shall not interfere with the Articles of this Confederation." In all likelihood, the committee may have been trying to establish that the states retained all powers not given to the confederation, but Article III's language implied that while states could wield their traditional authority, when it conflicted in any way with the Articles, the state would cease exercising that power. Rather than reserving to the states those powers not granted to the confederation, the article could potentially weaken state sovereignty. Adding to the problem, the draft did not clarify or define what constituted an "interference with the Articles." Nor did it create or specify any mechanism to settling the inevitable disputes between Congress and states over the clause. The article's silence on this mechanism, when combined with its language, indicates—even if unintentionally—that when conflicts between the state and confederation government occurred the state had to yield to the confederation.

Little documentary evidence exists for the deliberations of the Dickinson committee. What little is known suggests a difficult task fraught with arguments. It remains unclear if Dickinson and his committee actually intended for this final section to be pregnant with nationalist aspirations. Given Dickinson's forceful defense of colonial sovereignty over internal affairs, it seems unlikely that he or the committee intended this provision to corrode state authority, even if they sought a powerful Confederation.[9] Nevertheless, the small Nationalist faction saw its potential and thought they understood what the broad language implied, a national sovereign government. In 1787, James Wilson recalled the passage noting how, "[i]n the beginning of our troubles, congress themselves were as one State . . . The original draft of confederation was drawn on the first ideas."[10] While Wilson's remembrance of the Congress as being "one State" contradicted the reality that Congress met as a collection of sovereign states. Although his remarks were more of a polemical ploy to argue for a stronger federal constitution, his reminiscences of how he and other Nationalists viewed the Dickinson draft was accurate.

Other elements of the Dickinson draft allowed Nationalists to insist upon the confederation as a national government. The draft of the Articles required the states to honor the liberty, privileges, and immunities of citizens from other states. It also forbade states from engaging in warfare, keeping the military forces larger than what they needed to maintain posts, granting letters of marque and reprisals, or entering into treaties with foreign powers. Under the proposed Articles, Congress was granted the "sole and exclusive Right and Power" of making war and peace; creating rules of capture and prizes; granting letters of marque and reprisals; creating courts for crimes committed on the high seas; sending and receiving ambassadors; entering into treaties and alliances; settling boundary disputes between colonies; coining and regulating the value of money; managing Indian relations; "disposing" any land acquired from England; establishing post offices; and borrowing on the credit of the "United Colonies." The list of extensive powers mixed with the limitations placed upon the states led Nationalists to suggest that sovereignty rested in the Confederation Congress. Obviously, the states would continue to exist— any contrary thought seems not yet to have entered the minds of even the most ardent Nationalists—but, they would be rendered little more than administrative units disposing of the Congress' orders as they best saw fit, but obeying nevertheless. If the states defied or worked in open conflict against Congress' wishes, the proposed Article III would make short work of the resistance.

The exigencies of war postponed serious debate upon the draft Articles and stalled the Nationalists' advancement in transforming the proposed "league of friendship" into a national government. The delay proved critical. When Congress finally began to reconsider the proposals in the winter of 1777, the circumstances of the debate were different. Any potential Nationalist victory collapsed as Thomas Burke, a newly arrived congressional delegate from North Carolina, took his seat. His contribution to the Revolution's constitutional settlement was of singular importance.

Burke, a devout republican, feared centralized power and affirmed that the states were sovereign entities. Arriving to Congress as the determined champion of state sovereignty, he was ready to do battle against the Nationalists' attempt to weaken the authority of the states at the hands of Congress. What he witnessed in the debates in Congress confirmed his worries. The first several weeks of his tenure, he reported, were consumed with debates "whose object on one side is to increase the Power of Congress, and on the other to restrain it."[11] Because of his republican and federal sensitivities, Burke did not hesitate to proclaim his ideas on state sovereignty. Soon after joining Congress he told his colleagues that they were "exceedingly mistaken if they deemed him a Man who would tamely suffer any invasion or encroachment on" state sovereignty, no matter the reason or cause. If Congress "proceeded to so arbitrary and Tyrannical" an exertion of "Power he would Consider it as no longer that which ought to be trusted with the Liberties of their Fellow Citizens." At one point, he threatened that "if any such Question should be put" that risked the sovereignty of the states, North Carolina, "with determined resolution" would "withdraw from Congress."[12]

Burke worried that too many of his colleagues oscillated on the question of congressional power. He complained to North Carolina governor Richard Caswell that:

> [t]he same persons who on one day endeavor to carry through some Resolutions, whose Tendancy [sic] is to increase the Power of Congress, are often on another day very strenuous advocates to restrain it. From this I infer that one has entertained a concerted design to increase the Power.[13]

Burke believed he could account for the equivocation on the question of congressional power. "The attempts to [increase congressional power] proceed from Ignorance of what such a Being ought to be, and from the Delusive Intoxication which power naturally imposes on the human Mind."[14] Although reflecting his republican beliefs, Burke also feared that if those inebriated with power rose to prominence in the Confederation Congress as proposed in the Dickinson draft, tyranny would follow. Burke's concern, therefore, became protecting the liberties of the people against these potential concentrations of power. To curtail any "delusive intoxications" meant chaining Congress to only those particulars granted in the proposed Articles of Confederation. Burke believed two methods could help achieve his goals. The first included insuring that "patriotism in America must always be particular to the particular states," because "Patriotism to the whole will never be cherished or regarded but as it may be conducive or necessary to the other." Given men's "zealous love for that grandeur and preeminence, & a capacity to promote it that will be what must best distinguish & recommend any individual in it."[15] The people of the states must demand the protection of their liberties.

Localism, however, could not guarantee the permanent limitation of congressional authority. Having "the power of Congress . . . accurately defined" so that "adequate checks . . . prevented any excess" was necessary. Burke had cause to believe that such an adequate description of these powers was vital to the preservation of both state power and individual liberties. Soon after entering Congress, that body agreed to a report permitting it to authorize local officials, such as constables or justices of the peace, to arrest deserters without first seeking the permission of the states to use those officials. Wilson had defended the action on nationalist and teleocratic grounds that "every object of Continental Concern was the subject of Continental Councils, that all Provisions made by the Continental Councils must be carried into execution by Continental authority." Burke rejected this argument outright. Having forced the records of the Congress to record his dissent to this measure, Burke launched into a fierce defense of the nomocratic relationship between limited power, federalism, and individual liberty. To quote Burke at length:

> Congress, was herein assuming a Power to give authority from themselves to persons within the States to seize and Imprison the persons of the States, and thereby to endanger the personal Liberty of every man in the America . . . [he] denied that the provisions made by the Continental Councils were to be enforced by Continental authority. That it would be giving Congress a Power to prostrate all the Laws and Constitutions of the States because they might create a Power within each that must act entirely Independent of them, and might act directly Contrary to them. That they might by virtue of this Power render Ineffectual all the Bariers [sic] Provided in the State for the Security of the Rights of the Citizens for if they gave a Power to act Coercively it must be against the Subjects of some State, and the subject of every state was entitled to the Protection of that state, and subject to the Law of that alone, because to them alone did he give . . . That the states alone had Power to act Coercively against their Citizens, and therefore were the only Power Competent to carry into execution any Provisions whether Continental or Municipal. That he was well satisfied no Power on earth would ever obtain Authority to act Coercively against any of the Citizens of the State he represented expect under their own Legislature . . . That if Congress has the Power to appoint any Person to decide this Question the Congress has power unlimited over the Lives and Liberties of all men in America and the Provision so anxiously made by the respects States to Secure them, at Once Vanish before this Tremendous

Authority . . . No power could be Competent to this but such as is created by the Legislature of each state, and if any Question related to the internal Polity of a state it certainly was this which involved all the Rights of the Citizens personal Freedom.[16]

In this long passage, Burke connected Congress' actions as violations of the sovereign authority of the state and the liberty the citizens of the states. He strongly implied that citizens of the states owed no actual allegiance to the confederation. During the imperial debates with England, Adams and others, including James Wilson, held that allegiance was a reciprocal relationship between subjects offering allegiance and receiving protection from the king. Americans owed allegiance to the crown because it protected them. With the declaring of independence, this reciprocal relationship reverted to the states and its citizens. Burke therefore condemned Congress' authorization of local officials catching deserters because the citizens of the states were obedient only to the laws of their respective state since it was "to them [the state] alone did he give his Consent." Hence, because the citizen agreed to the laws of their state, he was "entitled to the Protection of that particular state."[17] No such agreement existed between the citizen and the confederation.

This episode convinced Burke that structural mechanisms were necessary to limit potential violations of both state sovereignty and, in turn, protect individual liberty. The Articles needed a statement acknowledging the individual sovereignty of the states. Scouring the submitted "Dickinson Draft" of the Articles, however, he found such a mechanism wanting. When Congress resumed debates on the draft of the Articles, Burke seized the opportunity. The language of the proposed Article III was so vague and open to broad interpretation, he argued, that "it left it in the power of the future Congress or General Council to explain away every right belonging to the States, and to make their own power as unlimited as they please." To fix this problem, Burke proposed an amendment to be situated directly after Article I of the Articles that would enshrine the sovereignty of the states. The amendment stated that each state retained "its sovereignty, freedom, and independence, and every power, jurisdiction, and right, which is not by this confederation expressly delegated." After some debate—the details of which are unknown because they were not recorded—Congress approved the amendment, eleven states in favor, Virginia opposed, and New Hampshire divided. Congress approved the Burke Amendment as Article II of the Articles of Confederation.[18]

The Burke Amendment was a stinging rebuke of the Nationalists' argument. It suppressed their interpretation of the draft Articles and forced the Nationalists to work within the nomocratic framework of a state sovereignty-centered constitutional order. For that reason alone, it is more important than scholars have given it credit. The Burke Amendment also crystallized several critical constitutional arguments and developments. First, it constitutionalized the American argument, originally expounded in the resistance to British efforts to consolidate the empire, that the colonies—now states—were sovereign entities. Secondly, by guaranteeing state sovereignty in all areas save those "expressly delegated" to the Confederation Congress, it secured the internal and external dichotomy Dickinson and others laid out in the 1760s while upholding Adams' argument of 1774 that the external authority of the empire, now the Confederation Congress, existed through consent of the states and not as a self-contained idea. The powers of the Confederation Congress existed only because each state consented to them. Thirdly, the Burke Amendment rejected the Nationalist idea that the "effects of unequal representation, would be to point out the principal cause of the downfall of liberty in most of the free States of the world," and instead endorsed what had been the standard American equation of state sovereignty with the protection of individual liberty.[19] If a state believed an action of the Confederation Congress violated the liberty of its citizen, the sovereignty of the state allowed it to ignore Congress and actively interpose and protect that citizen from the unauthorized action of the Congress. In other words, the Burke Amendment pointedly rejected the proposed Article III implication of making Congress supreme with the states having to obey Congress. The amendment also spurned Rush's notion that "the Objects before us are the people's rights, not the rights of States. Every man in America stands related to two legislative bodies—he deposits his property, liberty & life with his own State, but his trade [and] Arms, the means of enriching & defending himself & his honor, he deposits with the congress. If entitled to equal representation in the first case, why not in the second?"[20] Each state would determine for itself if Congress exercised its power properly. Finally, Article II of the Articles of Confederation ensured a nomocratic constitutional order by codifying that one of the purposes of the American Revolution was the protection of state sovereignty, making state sovereignty a fundamental aspect of the American constitutional order.

***

The Articles of Confederation that Congress submitted to the states did not contain the language found in Article III of its draft. The Burke Amendment had effectively destroyed it. Although Congress sent the Articles to the states for their approval in late 1778, ratification did not occur until 1781. During this intervening period, Americans accepted the Articles in a de facto manner. In terms of the relationships between states and the confederation, this meant that the impact of the Burke Amendment was immediate. Whereas Burke complained about the back-and-forth of delegates on questions of congressional power, after the submission of the Articles to the states, congressmen became more conscious of the limitations "chaulked out" to the confederation. Some embraced the demarcation, asserting that any congressional action beyond the limitation of the Articles would turn into a "right to legislate for the whole whenever they see fit."[21] The Nationalists, who, by 1780, were a more organized and distinct group, viewed the strict limitations imposed by the Burke Amendment as a direct threat to the Revolution's success.

Beginning in 1780, Nationalists began a sustained campaign to increase the powers of the confederation. The darkening prospects for victory, which, by 1780, were at their lowest during the entire war, coupled with the increasing financial crisis that brought the confederation to near insolvency, drove the renewed Nationalist push. While it is undeniable that the exigencies of the war certainly shaped the Nationalists' political programs and response—nor should one question their sincerity in believing their programs could remedy the situation—the Nationalist political agenda of 1781–1783 reflected the core tenets of their constitutional thinking that first emerged in 1776. In fact, the convergence of their political policies with their constitutional ideas were so intertwined, it becomes difficult to see each element without the other. Undoubtedly, the Nationalists would have had a policy response to the growing problems of the early 1780s, but their underlining constitutionalism explains the obvious nationalist bent of those suggestions. Their policies could only work, they believed, with a national government possessing more sovereign power.[22]

The Nationalists' policy program was not complicated, but it was sweeping. It focused on increasing the Congress' authority in areas of economic and military control with derivatives being an increased power at the confederation level and the improved prestige and honor both domestically and internationally of the Confederation Congress. In 1781, Nationalists in Congress secured Robert Morris, a devout member of their group, as secretary of finance. Morris wanted Congress to service the wartime debt by devaluating older currency and issuing new currency, create a Bank of North America whose notes could act as currency, and for Congress to establish a source of revenue independent from state requisitions by instituting a five percent impost tax. Morris believed these measures would reverse the potential financial calamity by shoring up Congress' credit. In the area of the military, Nationalists sought a national, and permanent, standing army. This force, Nationalists argued, would defend the frontier from Indian attacks while also serving as a check against British power along the Canadian border. Not only that, but with a permanent army came the need for greater infrastructure to move and house troops, store munitions, and other military needs. All of which, of course, would be supported by the confederation.[23] Of these lofty goals, the only success Morris had was creating the Bank of North America.

Morris and the Nationalists realized that to achieve their political and constitutional objectives they would have to combat the Burke Amendment and notions of state sovereignty. At the same time, however, they were more than aware that state sovereignty was a fundamental characteristic of American constitutionalism and a full-out assault upon state sovereignty would be not only imprudent but also counterproductive. If they wanted to fix the immediate political problems while advancing their constitutional aims, Nationalists had to work within the understanding of state sovereignty while trying to persuade and demonstrate the flaws of the Articles and its protection of state sovereignty.

The groundwork for the Nationalist assault upon state sovereignty began in 1780–1781, when Alexander Hamilton, recently resigned as General Washington's aide de camp, penned a long, and probably semi-private, letter to friend James Duane and published a series of six essays titled the "Continentalist." Hamilton diagnosed the "fundamental defect" facing the confederation as "a want of power in Congress . . . it is neither fit for war, nor peace." The primary culprit behind Congress' impotency was "the idea of an uncontrollable [*sic*] sovereignty in each state, over its internal police" that overrode congressional power. This sovereignty made the confederation "feeble." The states were so jealous of "all power not in their hands" that they had bullied Congress until it left only "the shadow of power." So haughty were the states, Hamilton averred, they had assumed the power of "judging in the last resort the measured recommended by Congress," despite having "chearfully [*sic*] submitted" when Congress had exercised "many of the best acts of sovereignty." Instead of becoming the "standard for the whole conduct of Administration," the Congress has succumbed to the "ambition and local interest" that was "constantly undermining and usurping" Congress. Without immediate remedies to "ENLARGE THE POWERS OF CONGRESS," Hamilton warned, the confederation would meet a "SPEEDY and VIOLENT END."[24]

Hamilton did more than register the Nationalists' complaints against state sovereignty. He offered several broad suggestions that blended the policy programs with constitutional reform. Hamilton's clearest advice came in the fourth "Continentalist" essay. There, Hamilton laid out six proposals to "augment the power of the confederation." First, the confederation needed power to regulate trade, both domestic and foreign. Second and third, the establishment of a small land tax throughout the United States and a capitation tax on young men, both designed to generate a revenue stream independent from state acquisition. Fourth, the disposal (i.e., selling) of "all unlocated land." Fifth, a percentage of "products of all mines, discovered, or to be discovered" for perpetuity. Hamilton's final proposal gave to Congress the appointment of all military and naval officers.[25] In his private correspondence, Hamilton added a seventh recommendation, that Congress call a special convention that would meet to

amend the Articles of Confederation to "give Congress complete sovereignty in all that relates to war, peace, trade, finance, and to the management of foreign affairs."[26] In essence, Hamilton's proposals sought to
break the confederation from its reliance upon the states. Anything short
of complete sovereign authority in these areas would be worthless and
perpetuate the problem.

With this call for unshared authority over these areas, Hamilton,
nevertheless, acknowledged state sovereignty. Not only was it too much
a part of American constitutionalism, but any attempt to deny states
complete control over internal issues would have been impolitic and
would undoubtedly result in a pushback by the states that could kill any
attempt to give Congress the powers he was advocating. Hence, while
Congress would have their complete sovereignty, the states would retain
theirs in all areas "of internal police which related to the rights of property and life among individuals and to raising money by internal taxes."
There is some suggestion in Hamilton's writings, however, that he might
have been playing a cat-and-mouse game with this acknowledgment of
state sovereignty. In his letter to Duane and again in his 1784 "Phocion"
essays, Hamilton noted that many times congressional actions "necessary
for the general good, and which rise out of the powers given to Congress" conflicted with the "internal police" of the state, or times when the
states, by organizing its internal authority, conflicted with Congress. Although never stated explicitly, the underlying theme of his letters and
essays suggested that the state must to concede to Congress in those
instances. This argument was a complete reversal of the intent of the
Burke Amendment. Thus, following Hamilton's logic, the natural question was how could the states be true sovereigns over their internal police
if they had to yield to the "instances without number" where the congressional actions interfered with state authority? Hamilton accepted and
acknowledged state sovereignty, to be sure, but he suggested that it
could be maneuvered against to make it as weak and ineffective as possible.

Hamilton and many Nationalists in Congress employed the concept of
implied powers to strengthen congressional authority. Hamilton first
mentioned this by noting how Congress, without the Articles and before
the Burke Amendment, had wielded power with the states' consent,
thereby making Congress powerful. "Undefined powers," he noted, "are
discretionary power" and could only be employed for "the object for
which they were given." In other words, the means upon which implied
powers were used were justified by the ends they were to be applied.
Since Congress was fighting for no less than the "independence and freedom of America," it stood that it could wield enormous powers.[27] When
coupled with Hamilton's other instance that states had to yield to congressional authority when the two came into conflict, clearly, this use of
discretionary power would weaken state sovereignty.

By 1781, however, the degree to which the confederation could wield broad discretionary power to fulfil the teleological ends of the Congress was questionable. The political misfortunes of the war and the constitutional protection of state sovereignty guaranteed that any attempt to expand congressional power at the expense of state sovereignty would be a difficult task, and that was especially true if that power came from implication. Even with this limitation, Nationalists pushed an implied powers argument to advance its financial policies. In particular, Nationalists used it in support of Robert Morris' plan for creating the Bank of North America. When Congress incorporated the bank on May 26, 1781, its justification rested almost exclusively on the teleological grounds. Congress "will promote and support" the bank by "such ways and means, from time to time, as may appear necessary for the institution and consistent with the publick [sic] good."[28] The only constitutional justification Congress offered was that the bank was for the "publick good," a justification that Hamilton had argued clothed Congress with a great deal of authority. But the difficulty in having implied powers provide for the expansion of federal power at the expense of state sovereignty demonstrated itself in the same resolution. Congress also requested the states to enact legislation forbidding the creation of other banks and to make counterfeiting a crime without benefit of clergy.[29] Although they pushed the limits of congressional power by claiming an implied power to create the bank, they were not willing to claim the power of prohibiting states to create other banks or punishing counterfeiters. State sovereignty blunted the Nationalists' bold ambition for constitutional revolution.

Not all members of Congress accepted the idea of implied powers, however. Some rejected the idea outright, or placed very strict limitations upon its use.[30] Although they sought a stronger confederation, only amending the Articles of Confederation could accomplish the task. This is an important point. Amending the Articles respected the nature of the proscribed powers of the Articles, including the process of amending included in Article XIII, and the requirement for state consent. This maintained the idea that the states consented to any exercise of power over them. James Madison of Virginia represented the moderate wing in Congress. Two critical actions Madison performed as a new member of Congress in 1781 revealed how he sought limitations to the Hamiltonian use of implied powers.

The first occurred early in 1781 during the attempt to secure Morris' plan for an impost tax. In February, John Witherspoon, a delegate from New Jersey and Madison's teacher at Princeton, moved to have Congress assume unitary authority to regulate foreign trade and institute an impost tax. Although most members of Congress backed the idea of an impost, the lack of the explicit power in the Articles meant Congress had to establish it via implication of Congress' authority over external issues. Madison, however, convinced Congress to alter Witherspoon's motion.

He stripped the implied power from Congress and instead had that body "earnestly recommend to the States" that they enact legislation that would establish a five percent import tax to "support the public credit and the prosecution of the war." Rather than rely upon state obedience to a congressional mandate rooted in what, at best, was a dubious constitutional interpretation, Madison had Congress amend its proposal. The change included a request from the states that as part of this impost tax Congress could "collect & to appropriate" the funds to pay the interest on all current and future debt and have power to appoint its own officials.[31] Madison's amendment is quite telling. As historians Lance Banning and Adam Tate have both pointed out, Madison's action demonstrated his attachment to state sovereignty, even while seeking an incremental increase in congressional power. At the same time, Madison also rejected the idea of an implied power that required a tortured reading of the Articles of Confederation.[32] The amendment was also interesting for how it connected the expansion of congressional power to the consent of the states. By having the states approve of this measure via legislation meant they would give a formal blessing to this power. This notion fit well with the Revolutionary argument as well as the intent and purpose of the Burke Amendment. Since Article II of the Articles protected state sovereignty and gave Congress only those powers expressly delegated to it, any expansion of congressional power required the consent of the states. In terms of Madison's amendment, therefore, if the states blessed the idea of congressional impost and collection, they could eventually retract it in the same way the colonies retracted their consent over parliamentary trade measures. Recall that one of the American arguments against parliamentary claims that it could regulate the empire's trade was that the colonies had consented to that trade but could remove that consent and regulate it themselves because the colonies were separate sovereigns. Madison's motion, which Congress accepted, embraced this established idea.

Twelve states agreed to establish an impost tax. The lone objection came from Rhode Island. William Bradford, the speaker of Rhode Island's assembly, informed Congress that the state rejected the tax because it violated state sovereignty in three distinct ways. First, it placed an unequal burden upon the commercial states. Since Rhode Island drew most of its economy from commercial trade, the impost would threaten the state's economic viability. Second, the impost would violate the state's constitution by "introduc[ing] into this and the other states, officers unknown and unaccountable to them." Finally, the amendment would make the Congress "independent of their constituents," the states, thereby making the impost "repugnant to the liberty of the United States."[33]

Rhode Island's rejection stunned Congress. Given the near universal agreement for the necessity of the impost, its rejection by the smallest state angered congressional members. To Nationalists like Hamilton, it represented everything that was wrong with the Articles and its stringent defense of state sovereignty. Congress responded by sending a delegation to Rhode Island to persuade the state to change its mind. At the same time, a congressional committee, consisting of Hamilton, Madison, and Thomas FitzSimons, drew up a written response to Bradford's letter. Written by Hamilton, the report can rightfully be called his first mature state paper. As was typical of Hamilton's style, the report offered a strong defense of the confederation's powers.

Hamilton met each of Rhode Island's objections. The impost could not burden the citizens of the state since it was a tax paid by only the consumers of imports. Thus, the impost corresponded to the "comparative wealth of the respective classes . . . the rich and luxurious pay in proportion to their riches and luxuries, the poor and parsimonious in proportion to their poverty and parsimony." There was no way to obtain an "absolute equality" in the confederation, Hamilton stated, because it violated the "imperfect state of human affairs" and "would stagnate all the operations of government." Hamilton then argued that Rhode Island's contention that its constitution prohibited federal officers was little short of sophistry. Should their objection stand, it "would defeat all the provisions of the Confederation and all the purposes of the union. The truth is that no Foederal [sic] constitution can exist without power." No constitution worthy of the name could establish the exact number of officers allowed in its state. The state legislatures "must always have a discretionary power of appointing officers." At the same time, it placed an authorized limitation upon the ability of the "Foederal government" to appoint officers "in cases where the general welfare may require it." From Rhode Island's reasoning, "all officers in the post-office," a power explicitly given to Congress in the Articles, "was "illegal and unconstitutional." The state's third objection, that it would make the confederation independent from the states, Hamilton readily admitted but dismissed the objection as lacking any "analogy between the principle and the fact." Interestingly, and not without irony, Hamilton argued that since the impost stated the date of its own termination as well as the percentage it was allowed to collect, it was not Congress' intention to "perpetuate that debt" the impost was designed to sink.[34]

As he often did, Hamilton devoted significant thought to the underlying nature of American constitutionalism. Not surprisingly, he offered a strong defense of the confederation and harsh assessment of state sovereignty. Because Congress had an "absolute discretion in determining the" amount of revenue it needed, "nothing remains for the states separately but the mode of raising." In other words, when it came to funding the confederation, the states were the administrative agencies of the Congress. Hamilton attacked the implications that the Burke Amendment allowed the states to judge the constitutionality of congressional actions.

"Such a refusal," he noted, "would be an exertion of power not of right." Interestingly, and despite not having to do so because of Congress' request for the impost, Hamilton also defended the use of implied powers. The impost might not be "within the letter" of the confederation but it was "within the spirit." Since Congress could borrow money on behalf of the United States, "by implication," then, Congress had the "means necessary to accomplish the end." Thus, for the first time, Hamilton tied the idea of implied powers to the stated powers of the general government. Finally, Hamilton noted that "there is a happy mean between too much confidence and excessive jealousy in which the health and prosperity of a state consist." The actions of Rhode Island suggested such an extreme jealousy of its sovereignty that it actually disrupted the operation of sound government. Venting his frustration with the entire system, Hamilton lamented how "the conduct of the war [was] entrusted to Congress and the public expectation turned upon them without any competent means at their command to satisfy the important trust." The result was a Congress that could not support itself, fight and win the war, achieve lasting peace, nor calm the "dissatisfaction of the army" with Congress that was "growing more serious."[35]

Hamilton's report was his first official stance on the nature of the confederation and the importance of implied powers. Although he would develop those ideas even further over the next decade, the foundation of the New Yorker's thoughts were present in the report. Hamilton thought that in areas where the confederation had clear authority, such as calling for revenue, the states were the subordinate agencies who fulfilled Congress' wishes. Hamilton allowed for state sovereignty, but the report made it clear that he viewed it as more dangerous than useful to the overall objective of securing independence and establishing the United States' international credit and reputation. It was Hamilton's defense of implied powers, however, that was in its infancy. Having developed the idea over the past two years, Hamilton tied the use of implied powers to the enumeration of authority contained in the Articles. Thus, if Congress did not have the power to borrow money, his argument suggested that the implied power of an impost tax did not exist. As we will see, he would develop his thinking on this point and would make implied powers a robust element of national sovereign power.[36]

The talks with Rhode Island went nowhere, and the impost amendment was defeated. Hamilton's report, however, received Congress' approval with Rhode Island's delegation ironically voting in favor of it. What remains unknown is Madison's role in the committee report. Although he voted in favor of it, it was not clear if he accepted the implications of what Hamilton wrote. Like most members of Congress, he was shocked and disappointed by Rhode Island's objection. Despite worrying deeply what the rejection meant for the confederation's future, he nevertheless remained opposed to the use of the implied power.

Further evidence of Madison's rejection of implied powers came shortly after Congress approved the impost. Congress followed up its request for an impost tax by establishing a committee, of which Madison was also a member, to consider submitting to the states a formal amendment to the Articles to empower Congress to enforce its measures against recalcitrant states. Submitted before Rhode Island had rejected the impost, Madison and Congress seemed to have had Delaware and all of New England in mind when proposing the amendment. Those states had purposely refused requests for aid to counteract the British invasion of the South in 1779–80. The proposed Amendment noted that through Article XIII of the Articles of Confederation the states were to "abide by the determinations" of Congress "on all questions which by this Confederation are submitted to them." In practical application, this meant Congress possesses "a general and implied power" of enforcing "all the Articles of the said Confederation against any of the States which shall refuse or neglect . . . or shall otherwise violate" Congress' recommendations or the established provisions of the Articles of Confederation.[37] As such, the wording of the proposed coercive amendment appears to be everything the Nationalists had been seeking, a Confederation Congress that was the supreme law of the land.

No doubt this proposal sought the general goals of the broad Nationalist faction, but a closer examination reveals several aspects of the amendment better reflected the Madisonian approach, thereby making the proposal not quite the boon the Hamiltonian Nationalists might have expected.[38] First, and quite simply, though often overlooked, the amendment was a written proposal to change the Articles. As an amendment, it required the consent of all thirteen states (unlike Madison's alteration of Witherspoon's proposal which asked volunteering states to enact their own laws for Congress' benefit) once again reaffirming what was the clearly established understanding of the constitutional system. Therefore, if the states adopted the amendment—and that was a gigantic if—it had to have the consent of all the states. Second, and also overlooked, the proposed amendment would create a written, proscribed power of Congress. Had the Nationalists carried the day in 1776 and turned the Continental Congress into a national government with no Burke Amendment, the need for this amendment would have been unnecessary; implied powers would have been the normal constitutional practice from the moment of independence. But the Burke Amendment's protection of the Revolutionary constitutional position of colonial/state sovereignty made the Nationalists push for sovereignty over the states the outlying and radical constitutional position.[39] The Burke Amendment's protection of state sovereignty made this proposed written acknowledgment of coercive and implied power necessary for the Nationalists. Finally, the use of the phrase "all questions which by this Confederation are submitted to them" suggests an inherent limiting principle. Congress would not be able to force state compliance with any recommendation it made. The request had to tie directly into a stated power in the Articles of Confederation. In other words, the proposed amendment was not a transformation of the confederation into a national government but rather an attempt to ensure the powers Congress did possess by the consent of the states via the Articles were not turned into what Madison called a "vain phantom." Ultimately, and not too surprisingly, the proposed amendment failed to gain approval within Congress and they never submitted to it the states.

Nationalist frustrations with state sovereignty reached a crescendo in 1783. In that year, a proposed amendment to the confederation giving Congress authority to collect an impost tax failed when New York rejected the amendment. Given that Congress had approved the amendment, and ratification of most of the states came swiftly, these suggested that most states still believed Congress needed this power. The failure of the amendment shook the Nationalists' faith that the union would even succeed in the post-war future. As a result, Nationalists began open criticism of the constitutional structure of the confederation and the powers of Congress. They started to embrace what Hamilton had broached as early as 1780, a calling of a special convention designed to amend the Articles. In fact, in 1782 Hamilton, who had joined Congress that year, drew up such a proposal—although he shelved it soon thereafter—and convinced the New York legislature to advocate for such a convention.[40]

Nationalist disillusionment with the confederation reached its greatest peak, however, when the preliminary articles of the Treaty of Peace finally arrived in the fall of 1783. In Articles IV, V, and VI, the proposed treaty required all prewar American debts to British creditors be paid in pounds-sterling, Congress would "earnestly recommend" the states open their courts for Loyalists to attempt to reacquire land confiscated during the war, and the treaty indemnified British (and American) atrocities committed during the conflict. Not surprisingly, the Nationalists supported these provisions and argued that the states must abide by the treaty's clause. Initially, Nationalists held that refusing to honor the terms of the treaty would stain the reputation of newly independent states, making "this . . . not a Country to live in." They soon followed that position with the argument that the Articles of Confederation empowered Congress to make treaties, meaning that the states had to abide by any treaty agreed to by the Congress. Across the states, various Nationalists pressed their state legislatures to repeal anti-Loyalist legislation that contravened the treaty's provisions.[41] Thomas Jefferson, although holding a lifelong enmity towards centralized power, nonetheless believed the Articles gave clear authority to conduct the treaty, and as such, worried that it is "neither consistent with the faith of an honest individual nor favorable to the character of a nation."[42]

As with so much else regarding the Nationalist argument, it was Hamilton who made the most forceful and public push to see the Treaty of Peace followed. In his famous 1784 case of *Rutgers v. Waddington* as well as his two "Phocion" essays, Hamilton drew upon his earlier thoughts and argued that a dual sovereignty existed, one in Congress and the other in the separate states. The Congress had "complete sovereignty" over the implementation of the treaty, he argued, because "our Sovereignty and Independence began by Foederal Act," the Declaration of Independence. Since the Declaration was the "fundamental constitution of every state," and New York (and, by extension, the other states) could not "pretend to authenticate the act, but only to give their approbation to it," Congress had the "unquestionable right" to enforce the treaty. Because the Articles of Confederation granted Congress "among the first rights of sovereignty . . . the sole power of making treaties with foreign" powers, Hamilton argued that states had to obey its strictures. Hamilton then turned to the argument he first broached in 1780, that of implied powers. Since Congress had sovereign power to conduct treaties, it implied that the "power of making conditions" to see the treaty carried out was a congressional power. "The common interests of humanity, and the general tranquility of the world, require," Hamilton continued, "that the power of making peace, wherever lodged, should be construed and exercised liberally; and even in cases where its extent may be doubtful, it is the policy of all wise nations to give it latitude rather than confine it." In other words, Congress should have broadly defined power to make treaties; otherwise, "it would be extremely dangerous to prescribe narrow bounds to that power, by which it is to be restored." If those conditions contradicted state laws or actions, then the state had to surrender. States had to obey the treaty, Hamilton averred, because it was "impossible for Congress to do a single act which will not directly or indirectly affect the internal police of every state." More importantly, however, the sovereign power of Congress made the treaty. Since the states were not sovereign on external issues of war and peace, they could not violate the treaty as only "sovereign authority may violate Treaties."[43]

Hamilton insisted that the authority to make treaties was "of a legislative kind." Thus, when Congress declared the treaty ratified in early 1784, "their proclamation enjoining the observance" became "a law paramount to that of any particular state." The states had no "legal jurisdiction to alter them."[44] Edward Shippen, the head of the Philadelphia County court, would expand Hamilton's logic even further in the 1788 case of *Camp v. Lockwood*. In his opinion for the court, Shippen held that the "first body that exercised anything like a sovereign authority was the Congress of the then United Colonies." Although the states retained their sovereignty under the Articles of Confederation, the "general power" of sovereignty remained with Congress, even if it remained "undefined." Nor was Shippen concerned with the indeterminate nature of the confederation's sovereignty because the states, "though free and independent," were nonetheless "not to be such distinct sovereignties as have no relation to each other but by treaties and alliances, but are bound together by common interest, and are jointly represented and directed to national purposes." He believed congressional recommendations "had generally the force of laws" and the states had to obey.[45]

What angered Nationalists during the first half of the 1780s was their opponents' continual reliance upon state sovereignty to frustrate Morris' and the treaty's provisions. Even as the Nationalists ascended in Congress in first years of the decade, they were defeated at every turn by defenders of state sovereignty. Although these "State Sovereigntists" were even less organized than the Nationalists they were a consistent enough phalanx to thwart the Nationalists' plans. Nor were their arguments "the most innovative development in the constitutional thinking of the early 1780s" as one historian has claimed.[46] Rather, the State Sovereigntists reinforced and maintained arguments that had birthed the Revolution.

From 1780 to 1783, State Sovereigntists in Congress relied upon these traditional arguments in their battles against Nationalists. When Hamilton and Wilson argued for a general power of taxation as an addendum to the proposed impost amendment, Virginia delegate and firm State Sovereigntist Arthur Lee connected state sovereignty with the protection of liberty. He noted that the states would "never agree to those plans which tend to aggrandize Congress" because the history of liberty taught the "danger of surrendering the purse into the same hand which held the sword." David Howell, the Rhode Island congressional member who played a role in his state's defeat of the impost by leaking false information, sought the congressional defeat of the impost amendment on grounds strongly reminiscent of Burke's arguments of 1777.[47] The impost would not only hurt the interests of Rhode Island, it would adversely affect "the moral of the community at large" because it encouraged "idleness and Luxury" and provided Congress with a large degree of corruptible patronage. Most important, however, the impost was "but an entering wedge, others will follow" all of which "derogated from the Sovereignty and Independence of the States."[48]

State Sovereigntists made their biggest stand, however, over the Treaty of Peace. Their resistance to the treaty played a critical role in shaping how Americans understood the role state sovereignty played in both the constitutional system and politics. For the first time since declaring independence, Americans publically debated the meaning and nature of state sovereignty. Prior to these debates, congressmen and others invoked the idea of state sovereignty in resisting measures and in explaining the limitations upon the confederation's power. Even the Burke Amendment, for all its significance in protecting state sovereignty, did not explain the application of state sovereignty in real political situations. Resistance to the treaty also marked the first time Americans applied to a major political issue. In short, they moved state sovereignty from a constitutional idea to an actual working political phenomenon. By doing so, they not only reaffirmed their Revolutionary commitment to state sovereignty as a fundamental constitutional idea, but they empowered the concept to operate on a political level to defend their liberty.

When the terms of the treaty first appeared in American newspapers in the spring of 1783, Americans reacted with surprise and anger. Although elated over the unexpected expansion of their boundaries and the final recognition of their independence (which, it should be noted, acknowledged them by individual names and not as a unified nation), what shocked most Americans were Articles IV through VI and how they appeared to interfere with state sovereignty. At first, this surprise renewed extralegal violence against Loyalists; in fact, it was the first violent actions against them since the early years of the War. While this violence would continue sporadically over the next year, it eventually gave way to more reasoned and political responses.

Local communities, where the terms of the treaty would be felt most, issued instructions to their representatives requesting that the states ignore those particular articles of the treaty that violated the state sovereignty. A Dutchess County, New York, gathering noted that the treaty's provisions were "the worst of policy and greatest injustice to the interest of zealous supporters of our liberty." Also in New York, "Brutus" warned his fellow New Yorkers that Articles IV and V of the treaty contained "seeds of inexhaustive feuds and animosities" between Patriot and Tory. Since "these states are sovereign and independent," however, New York and other states could ignore those provisions. Lexington, Massachusetts' meeting resolved in even more explicit terms; "while we sincerely wish, that the Faith of the Nation might be realized . . . we also wish that the Freedom, Independence, and Sovereignty of these states, respectfully considered, might not be forgotten." The use of the phrase of the Burke Amendment is telling and is a clear demonstration that Americans considered Articles IV, V, and VI as contradicting state sovereignty. Perhaps the most forceful example of this argument came in Essex County, New Jersey. In May 1783, a town meeting stated that "we know not on which principles it can be expected that the recommendations made [regarding Article V] will be complied with by a single state in the Union." The petition noted that "altho' Congress must 'earnestly recommend'" that Loyalists be offered the chance to reclaim confiscated land, "the Legislatures are not obliged to comply."[49]

States responded to this popular pressure by engaging in a new round of anti-Loyalist legislation. New Jersey and Maryland enacted measures that banned former Loyalists from holding political office or practicing law. Both Virginia and North Carolina denied citizenship to former Loyalists attempting to establish residence. Massachusetts and South Carolina began a new round of selling off confiscated Loyalist property, even after they knew the terms of the provisional treaty. The New York legislature responded to the treaty's terms by passing the Trespass Act that empowered the citizens of New York to sue Loyalists for damages caused by the occupation of that city by British soldiers and refugees. Even after Congress ratified the treaty in January 1784, states continued to enact legislation that contradicted the treaty's terms. Massachusetts enacted legislation to continue the sale of confiscated Loyalist property and declared "[a]n Act for Asserting the Right of this Free and Sovereign Commonwealth to expel such Aliens as may be Dangerous," and also stated that Loyalists who fled the state between October 1774 and 1780 forfeited their citizenship. The state then declared that the loss of this citizenship meant a loss of their estates, which were turned over permanently to the state, a clear violation of Article V of the treaty. Pennsylvania violated this portion of the treaty when it empowered its Supreme Executive Council to sell the property of its most notorious Tory, Joseph Galloway. New Jersey and North Carolina followed suit by passing new measures to sell off remaining confiscated Tory land.[50]

It is easy to dismiss the petitions and instructions of local communities and the post-war anti-Loyalist legislation as little more than efforts to keep confiscated lands and not pay prewar debts. After all, that was the hope of the local committee and outcome and purpose of the various legislative measures. But, to reject them as polemical or cynical political ploys misses the underlying constitutional argument. By invoking the sovereignty of the states, sometimes using the exact language of Article II of the Articles of Confederation, these various instructions and the state laws were rejections of the idea that they would be the administrative agencies of Congress, existing to carry out the wishes of the Confederation Congress. Rather, the states, because they were sovereign, would determine for themselves what was both constitutional and an intrusion into their internal affairs as well as threats to the liberty of their citizens.[51] The states were thus giving working definition behind the constitutional principle of state sovereignty.

More important than even defining what state sovereignty meant in the American constitutional order, the local instructions and petitions and the actions of the state legislatures against the treaty also explained how most Americans believed state sovereignty was to operate as a political and constitutional reality. In short, they did so by advocating state interposition. The states, as sovereign entities, had to intercede and protect their citizens against actions considered unconstitutional and threats to liberty. To be sure, neither the arguments of the imperial crisis nor the Burke Amendment specified interpositions as a power of the states; those arguments, and even the Burke Amendment, were statements of a long held idea that the colonies/states were sovereign. Nor did these arguments ever detail the practice of state sovereignty in a practical political sense. It is important to note, however, that in the years immediately following the adoption of the Burke Amendment, the need to explain exactly how state sovereignty was to operate did not arise. The states had few outright constitutional conflicts with the confederation where the confederation took action without the states' consent and where the states could argue that Congress acted outside of its bounds of power. The treaty was the first real instance. "The Treaty," wrote "Mentor" in his reply to Hamilton's "Phocion" essay, did not "even upon so liberal construction, as I believe Phocion himself would give it, debar the state from making law that may be salutary to the government, and advantageous to the people."[52] In other words, the Burke Amendment embraced and protected the traditional notions of state sovereignty by breathing life into the power of interposition. If the state was to protect its sovereignty, independence, and freedom and the liberty of its citizens against measures it considered unconstitutional, the only recourse short of rebellion was for the state to interpose.

The most important defense of state interposition came from Meriwether Smith of Virginia. His 1783 pamphlet, "Observations on the Fourth and Fifth Articles of the Preliminaries for a Peace," while lacking the elegance and nuance of extended constitutional analysis that Madison and Jefferson would employ fifteen years later, or that of John C. Calhoun half a century more, was the first open defense and explanation of interposition in American history. That virtually all historians have ignored it should be surprising. Smith asked whether Article IV was "consistent with the sovereignty and right of legislation of an individual state is worthy of consideration." He argued that the Articles of Confederation were not intended to operate directly upon the citizens of the state. In this, Smith maintained the nomocratic position of Congress' powers since this is the very issue that compelled Thomas Burke to seek his amendment. Because the confederation lacked this authority, it could not compel any individual to perform any action. Yet, Article IV of the treaty was "subjecting the citizens within the states" to pay debts owed to British subjects. This violation was particularly odious to Smith since Virginia had enacted wartime legislation that allowed its residents to pay their debts to British subjects with the commonwealth's money. Article IV, however, attempted to strip Virginia citizens of "those rights derived from the Revolution and the position law of the state." The same held true for Article V which threatened to allow Loyalists to recover land Virginia had confiscated and its citizens had bought, thereby threatening their property rights. In summation, Congress' stipulation to those provisions threatened the liberty of Virginians.[53]

By agreeing to these provisions, Smith maintained that Congress "depriv[ed] the state of its sovereignty and independence reserved by the confederation" through the Burke Amendment. What the "ministers of Congress" were attempting, Smith argued, was no less than "subjecting the citizens with the state to their authority, and directing a repeal of such laws as they disapprove." Yet, since Congress "had no right to stipulate in the manner they have agreed as to the 4th article, and consequently that there is no authority to carry it into execution but that which arises from the consent of the legislature of the state of the individual interested therein."[54] Smith once again followed the traditional argument of state sovereignty that Adams and others had established a decade earlier that held that states had to consent to any measure that affected them. In this case, Smith was more than clear that Virginia would not consent, nor force its citizens to obey, the unconstitutional actions of Congress. To insure that these measures would not be forced upon Virginians (and citizen of other states), its citizens needed to rely upon the "wisdom and firmness" of the state governments to act as the "sure safeguard to the people" and exercise their sovereignty and intervene on the behalf of their people to block implementation of the treaty.[55]

State Sovereigntists, led by Smith's argument and the actions of the states in 1783 and 1784, established the firmament of state sovereignty by moving beyond theoretical statements and into actual political and constitutional argument. The thrust of their argument was plain enough, as sovereign entities the states would decide for themselves what was constitutional, and, if found to threaten the liberties of their citizens, they reserved the right to interpose and ignore the odious provisions. At the same time, this use of interposition was not a rejection of the Articles or of congressional authority over treaties; no one questioned that authority. Rather, what moved the states to action were the provisions that circumvented the states and acted directly upon individuals. This is an important distinction to make. Too often, scholars treat the idea of state sovereignty, and interposition, especially, as rejections of the entire constitutional structure. This is not what State Sovereigntists argued. No serious American in 1783 rejected the idea or necessity of union or of confederation possessing power. Rather, State Sovereigntists believed that if state sovereignty was to have any real meaning in the constitutional order they were forging, it had to possess the ability to provide protection against unwarranted and centralizing threats. Interposition, then, was state sovereignty put into practice. Although it operated in the manner as another measure passed under the authority of the states, it was to be used sparingly and only in the defense of liberty, and not simply because states had policy disagreements.

By 1783, state sovereignty had transformed from a constitutional idea to a working element of American constitutionalism and politics. Of singular importance in this transformation was the Burke Amendment. It constitutionalized the Americans' arguments on the sovereignty of the colonies (now states) made during the imperial crisis, and quickly became the standard upon which Americans judged the confederation's actions. At the same time, however, the Nationalists began asserting that the Confederation Congress needed greater degrees of sovereign power, and that state sovereignty actually hindered the success of the Revolution. These opposing views came to a head with the Treaty of Peace. In these debates, Americans asserted that the Burke Amendment's protection of state sovereignty meant that the states possessed the power of interposition. It was the only legitimate and peaceful method of protecting their citizens' liberty against threats from centralized power. Although State Sovereigntists won these initial clashes, the Nationalists would continue their calls for constitutional reform.

NOTES

1. Jerrilyn Greene Marsten, *The King and Congress: The Transfer of Political Legitimacy, 1774–1776* (Princeton, NJ: Princeton University Press, 1987) explores in rich detail the transfer of these monarchial powers to the Congress.

2. Paul H. Smith, ed. *Letters of Delegates to Congress, 1774–1789*, 24 vols. (Washington, DC: Library of Congress, 1976–2000), 4: 593.

3. David Hendrickson, *Peace Pact: The Lost World of the Founding* (Lawrence: University Press of Kansas, 2003), 145, asserts that no clear alignments of "Nationalists" and "federalist" emerged in 1776. It is true that no rival factions emerged in 1776 over different interpretations or political power; nevertheless, we do see the beginnings of the Nationalist thinking with the debate over congressional representation. Also see Merrill Jensen, *The Articles of Confederation: An Interpretation of the Social-Constitutional History of the American Revolution, 1774–1781* (Madison: University of Wisconsin Press, 1940; 1970),107–60.

4. E. James Ferguson, "The Nationalists of 1781–1783 and the Economic Interpretation of the Constitution," *Journal of American History* 56 (Sept. 1969): 241–61; Lance Banning, *The Sacred Fire of Liberty: James Madison and the Founding of the Federal Republic* (Ithaca, NY: Cornell University Press, 1995), 13–42; and Forrest McDonald, *E Pluribus Unum: The Formation of the American Republic, 1776–1790* (Boston: Houghton Mifflin, 1965), 22–29.

5. Wilson's remarks can be found in Charles Francis Adams, ed. *The Works of John Adams*, 10 vols. (Boston: Little, Brown, and Company, 1850), 2: 490–91; Benjamin Rush, "Notes for a Speech in Congress," August 1, 1776 in Smith, *Letter of Delegates*, 4: 599–600.

6. Adams' remarks can be in Thomas Jefferson, "Notes of Proceedings in the Continental Congress, 7 June–1 August 1776," in Julian P. Boyd, ed., *The Papers of Thomas Jefferson*, 38 vols. (Princeton, NJ: University of Princeton Press, 1950–2011), 1: 299–329.

7. Rush, in Smith, *Letters of Delegates*, 599–600.

8. Sherman, ibid., 592.

9. See Dickinson's July 2 speech against the Declaration of Independence and Josiah Bartlett to John Langdon, June 17, 1776 both in ibid., 357–58 and 255–57. Merrill Jensen agrees that the Dickinson committee's work must have been a contentious affair. Jensen, *Articles of Confederation*, 126–29 argues unequivocally that the draft made Congress "theoretically, in not practically the supreme authority." While congressional supremacy might have been the practical outcome had Dickinson's draft been accepted as written, it remains unclear if that was the theoretical point the committee was trying to reach.

10. James Wilson, June 8, 1787 as recorded by Robert Yates in Max Farrand, ed., *The Records of the Federal Convention*, 4 vols. (New Haven, CT: Yale University Press, 1911), 1: 170.

11. Thomas Burke to Richard Caswell, February 25, 1777 in Smith, ed., *Letters of Delegates*, 6: 357; Jensen, *Articles of Confederation*, 161–76.

12. Burke, "Notes on Debates," February 26, 1777 in ibid., 369.

13. Burke to Caswell, March 11, 1777 in ibid., 427.

14. Ibid., 429–30.
15. Burke to Caswell, March 11, 1777 in ibid., 427.
16. Burke, Notes on Debates, February 25, 1777 in ibid., 357–58.
17. Ibid.
18. Burke to Caswell, April 29, 1777 in ibid., 673–74.
19. Benjamin Rush, "Notes on Speech," August 1, 1776 in ibid., 599–600.
20. Ibid.
21. John Matthews to Thomas Bee, August 30, 1779, ibid., 10: 534–35; Jack P. Greene, *Peripheries and Center: Constitutional Development in the Extended Polities of the British Empire and the United States, 1607–1788* (Athens, GA: University of Georgia Press, 1986), 176.
22. For an opposite view, that problems of the early 1780s were more important in shaping Nationalist ideology, see Gordon Wood, *Creation of the American Republic, 1776–1787* (Chapel Hill: University of North Carolina Press, 1970), 361.
23. A detailed examination of those policies is not relevant for our purposes here, but for excellent accounts of programs see Jack Rakove, *Beginning of National Politics: An Interpretative History of the Continental Congress* (New York: Knopf, 1978), 297–324; Banning, *Scared Fire of Liberty*, 13–42; and Richard Kohn, *Eagle and the Sword: The Federalists and the Creation of the Military Establishment in America, 1783–1802* (New York: The Free Press, 1975), 1–54.
24. Alexander Hamilton to James Duane, September 3, 1780, and "The Continentalists Nos. 1–6" in Harold C. Syrett and Jacob E. Cooke, eds., *The Papers of Alexander Hamilton*, 26 vols. (New York: Columbia University Press, 1956–1981) 2: 400–18; 649–65, 669–74; and 3: 75–82, 99–106 [hereafter, Hamilton, *Papers*]. Emphasis in the original.
25. Hamilton, "Contientialist No. 4" in ibid., 669–74.
26. Ibid.
27. Hamilton to Duane, September 3, 1780 in ibid.
28. The resolution incorporating the bank is printed in James Wilson, "Considerations on the Bank of North America," in Kermit Hall and David Hall, eds., *The Collected Works of James Wilson*, 2 vols. (Indianapolis, IN: Liberty Fund, 2007) 1: 60–61. Wilson's pamphlet, published in 1785, is a Nationalist defense of the institution.
29. Ibid.
30. Banning, *The Sacred Fire of Liberty*, 21–22.
31. James Madison, "Motion on the Impost," February 3, 1781, in *The Papers of James Madison*, William T. Hutchinson and William M. E. Rachal, eds., 17 vols. (Chicago: University of Chicago Press, 1962), 2: 303–304.
32. Banning, *Sacred Fire of Liberty*, 20–21; Adam Tate, "James Madison and State Sovereignty, 1780–1781," *American Political Thought: A Journal of Ideas, Institutions, and Culture* 2 (Fall 2013): 174–97.
33. William Bradford to the Continental Congress, November 30, 1782 in Worthington C. Ford, ed., *Journals of the Continental Congress*, 34 vols. (Washington, DC: Government Printing Office, 1904–1937): 23: 788–789.
34. Alexander Hamilton, "Continental Congress Report on a Letter from the Speaker of Rhode Island Assembly," December 16, 1782, in Hamilton, *Papers*, 2: 213–223.
35. Ibid.
36. Ibid.
37. Madison, "Proposed Amendment of Articles of Confederation," Madison, *Papers*, 3: 17–20.
38. For a compelling argument that Madison viewed the amendment and the American union through the lens of Emer de Vattel's law of nations theory see Tate, "James Madison and State Sovereignty."
39. For the opposite argument, that state sovereignty was the innovation during the early 1780s, see Rakove, *Beginning of National Politics*, 327.
40. "Resolution of the New York Legislature Calling for a Convention of the States to Revise and Amend the Articles of Confederation" in Hamilton, *Papers*, 3: 110–13.

41. North Carolina House of Representatives, June 3, 1784, in Clark, *State Records of North Carolina*, 19:716; "Resolutions on Private Debts Owed to British Merchants," June 7–23, 1784, in Madison, *Papers*, 8:58–63.

42. James Iredell to Hannah Iredell, May 31, 1783, in Don Higginbotham, ed., *The Papers of James Iredell*, 2 vols. (Raleigh, NC: Division of Archives and History Department of Cultural Resources, 1976), 2: 415; Thomas Jefferson to Philip Turpin, July 29, 1783, in Julian P. Boyd, ed., *The Papers of Thomas Jefferson*, 38 vols. (Princeton, NJ: University of Princeton University Press, 1951–2011), 6: 324–333.

43. Brief no. 3, in Julius Goebel, ed., *The Law Practice of Alexander Hamilton: Documents and Commentary*, 3 vols. (New York: Columbia University Press, 1964), 1: 349–350, 356, 374; and "A Letter of Phocion to the Considerate Citizens of New York," January 1–27, in Hamilton, *Papers*, 3: 483–497.

44. Hamilton, Brief no. 3, in Goebel, ed., *Law Practice of Alexander Hamilton*, 378–379.

45. *Camp v. Lockwood* can be found in James Alexander Dallas, ed., *Reports of the Cases Ruled and Adjudged in the Courts of Pennsylvania before and since the Revolution*, 4 vols. (Philadelphia: T. Bradford, 1790), 1: 393–404, quote on 403.

46. Rakove, *Beginning of National Politics*, 327.

47. Congress would formally censure Howell for his actions. See Hamilton, *Papers*, 3: 224–25.

48. For Arthur Lee's remarks see Madison, "Note on Debates," Madison, *Papers*, 6: 141–49, 158–65, 270–74; David Howell to William Greene, July 30, 1782; and Theodore Foster, October 9, 1782; see Smith, *Letters of Delegates* 18: 681 and 19: 244–45.

49. Proceedings of the Freeholders and Inhabitants of Amenia precinct, in Dutchess County, in *The Pennsylvania Packet*, July 19, 1783; A Meeting of the Freeholders and other Inhabitants of the Town of Worcester (Massachusetts), May 22, 1783, in *The Pennsylvania Packet*, June 19, 1783. Also see the "Petition of Inhabitants and Freeholders of Amherst County, Virginia" and "Petition of the Inhabitants of Essex County, Virginia," June 6, 1783, in Virginia Legislative Assembly, Petitions, 1782–1789; "Brutus," "To the Friends of Freedom and Independence in the State of New York," April 12, 1783, in *The Independent Gazetteer; or The Chronicle of Freedom*, May 10, 1783; "At a Meeting of the Freeholders and other Inhabitants of the Town of Lexington, Legally Assembled," May 22, 1783, in *The Boston Gazette*, June 9, 1783; "To the Respectable inhabitants of the County of — —, in the State of New Jersey," May 19, 1783, in *The New Jersey Gazette*, June 4, 1783.

50. Massachusetts General Assembly, March 24, 1784; *A Collection of the Acts or Laws passed in the State of Massachusetts Bay, relative to the American Loyalists and Their Property*, n.e. (London: John Stockdale, 1785), 26–35. *Pennsylvania General Assembly*, February 4, 1784, and September 9, 15, 16, 22, 23, 1784, (Philadelphia: Hall and Sellers, 1784), 114, 164–65, 324–25, 334–36, 345, 349–50. Also see Robert L. Brunhouse, *The Counter-Revolution in Pennsylvania, 1776–1790* (Harrisburg: Pennsylvania Historical Commission, 1942), 15–16, 161–64. For the action against Galloway, see *Pennsylvania General Assembly*, September 15, 1784, 335. For New Jersey, see *New Jersey General Assembly* (Trenton, NJ: Isaac Collins, 1784), December 23, 1784, 96, and Henry Brockholst Livingston to William Livingston, June 22, 1784, in Carl E. Prince, ed., *Papers of William Livingston*, 5 vols. (Trenton, NJ: New Jersey Historical Commission, 1979–1987), 5: 143; Clark, *State Records of North Carolina*, 24: 661–64.

51. This is the one of the main arguments of Coleman, "Debating the Nature of State Sovereignty."

52. Isaac Ledyard, "Mentor's Reply to Phocion's Letter" (New York: Kollock, 1784), 13.

53. Meriwether Smith, "Observations on the Fourth and Fifth Articles of the Preliminaries for a Peace with Great Britain designed for the Information and Consideration of the People of Virginia" (Richmond, VA: Dixon and Holt, 1783), 1–28, quote on 4.

54. Ibid.

55. Ibid. Several years later, Luther Martin, the devout State Sovereigntist from Maryland, would make a similar argument in the case of *Dulany v. Wells*. In his defense of Wells, Martin asked the court if "the treaty operate to destroy the acts which were done before its existence; to take away the right of individuals acquired under our laws, and which vested in them during the continuance of the laws? Had congress such power? I think, if necessary, it might be questioned. How is the treaty to operate for this purpose? It is said, either in its own nature, or in consequence of the law of our state, declaring it to be the supreme law of the land, it operates as a repeal of the former act. Admit it to be so; the repeal of a law cannot destroy acts done and rights acquired under the law during its existence, and before its repeal; and though it is declared to be the supreme law, still, as far as that declaration goes, it is but a law; nor doth that declaration cause it to be the supreme law, or any law, before it existed as a treaty. The repeal of a law prevents rights being afterward acquired under the law repealed, but doth not annul those acquired previously. The contrary construction would be replete with iniquity and injustice. Congress had no rightful power to infringe or annul any law of any state in the union, or to interfere with the right of any individual acquired under these laws." Thomas Harris, Jr. and John McHenry, eds., *Maryland Reports being a Series of the Most Important Law Cases*, 4 vols. (New York and Annapolis, MD: Wiley, 1809–1818), 3: 20–84, quote on 65–66.

THREE

Altering the Settlement

The Critical Period and the Constitutional Convention

At the end of the Revolution, Americans had established state sovereignty as the foundation of its constitutionalism. The political events at the end of the war had breathed life and meaning into the Burke Amendment's protection of state sovereignty, moving it from the realm of theory to constitutional reality. Politicians used state sovereignty to protect their states from the Confederation Congress' appeals to implied constitutional powers that transcended the written text of the Articles. Many believed that a state could exercise its sovereign authority to interpose whenever it thought Congress had overreached its authority and threatened the liberty of the citizens. These developments, which were critical in securing state sovereignty as the constitutional foundation, frustrated the Nationalists who clamored for a stronger centralized government that possessed unquestioned sovereignty.

As post-war events unfolded at the state level, the Nationalists had all but abandoned any hope that the states could successfully conduct republican self-government. They became increasingly convinced that if republican government were to survive—if the Revolution itself were to succeed—the confederation needed more than just additional powers; it required more sovereignty. The Nationalists wanted nothing short of a transfer of sovereignty from the states to the confederation. So pervasive was this thought amongst the Nationalists, and so desperate were they to achieve it, that instead of advocating for reform solely at the congressional level, the Nationalists began to focus upon the supposed problems at the state level to make their push for constitutional reform. As historian Gordon Wood has noted, "it was not pressure from above, from the manifest debility of the Confederation, that provided the main impulse for reform," but rather "pressure from below . . . that eventually made constitutional reform" possible.[1]

The persistent calls to reform eventually worked. By 1787, many Americans, including ardent defenders of state sovereignty, had accepted that the states needed to transfer some of their power to the Articles of Confederation while retaining their sovereignty. By the time the federal convention met in 1787, the issue became whether the states would keep their sovereignty while surrendering only elements of their sovereign power. To the Nationalists, the Philadelphia Convention represented their last hope for a more central government possessing full sovereignty. Yet, at that gathering the Nationalists' miscalculated Americans' adherence to state sovereignty. Any reform that would occur had to keep state sovereignty as the foundation upon which American constitutionalism rested. Their miscalculation nearly cost the Nationalists everything. The Constitution that emerged unexpectedly from Philadelphia late in the summer of 1787 certainly altered elements of the Revolution's constitutional settlement, as the states did relinquish some of their power, but it was not a wholesale reconstruction. State sovereignty remained.

The economic condition throughout the states following the Revolution was bleak.[2] The demobilization of both the Continental Army and state militias ended the constant need for military supplies, and contracts to mechanics and artisans.[3] Then Great Britain applied its mercantile policies towards the newly independent states. This meant that American merchants no longer had access to the British colonial ports, a once critical element of colonial American trade.[4] Not only did England restrict American access to British colonial ports, but they also flooded American markets with cheap and well-made manufactured goods. The influx of British goods hurt American craftsmen and merchants who struggled to compete with British prices. American manufacturers and artisans, who saw a wartime boom, now began to suffer as demand for their goods and skills declined sharply in the immediate post-war years in favor of British goods. Additionally, the abundance of specie that existed during the war because of the wartime presence of both the British military and French loans was becoming increasingly hard to find. In order to pay their overseas debts, American merchants had sent large quantities of specie across the Atlantic. This forced Americans to rely increasingly upon the vast quantities of paper money, the bulk of which were legislated out of existence by 1783.[5] Finally, the states and confederation all suffered from large wartime debts that totaled forty million dollars, a massive sum in the eighteenth century.

Unaccustomed to such economic hardships, Americans turned to their state governments for solutions. Pennsylvania, Rhode Island, Massachusetts, and New Hampshire, in hope of assisting their domestic manufacturers and artisans and in response to the British mercantile policy, placed tariffs on most foreign goods, including goods shipped from other states if they were on foreign-owned ships. At the same, those same states placed high impost taxes on luxury items in hopes of keeping more specie in their states and for their citizens to purchase domestic goods. The southern states, while not as economically dependent upon artisans and mechanics, were slower to follow, but follow they did. By 1786, practically every state had measures in place that curbed British and foreign imports. While the rates may have varied from state to state those protections were "strikingly effective" in jumpstarting the sluggish economies.[6]

At the same time, the states faced a significant problem with finances. The states had to pay their debts. While impost taxes and tariff duties helped, the states still had to resort to taxes. Regressive in their approach, the rate of taxation increased throughout the 1780s. When combined with the ending of paper money and merchants sending specie across the Atlantic, the regressive taxation only made the situation worse. "[D]ebtors and taxpayers," most of whom were rural farmers, "were trapped."[7] Their situation worsened as speculators began to buy wartime bonds from rural bondholders at significantly lower rates. Most original holders sold their bonds in order to pay their taxes.[8] While taxation measures were burdensome, and would cause political problems throughout the decade, many of the states, mostly those in the South, paid significant portions of their wartime debt.[9]

Throughout the states, rural debtors begged state legislatures to enact legislation to fend off creditors. State legislatures obliged. In the course of the 1780s, the states enacted a multitude of debtor laws designed to placate rural debtors. These laws ranged from stay laws, which delayed any contractual payment of debts, to measures that eased the punishment for failing to pay debts. Several states also enacted laws that allowed taxpayers to pay only what they could. Perhaps the most important development in this area was the return of paper money. Despite the Articles of Confederation's explicit prohibition against states creating their own legal tender, by 1786, seven states had enacted legislation that created paper money and made it legal tender with which to pay both taxes and debts. Because debtors could use the paper to pay their debts, creditors, who relied upon the specie to pay their own debts, were outraged. While some states, such as Georgia, saw their paper money depreciate, for the most part its value remained stable. In fact, several states used their paper money to pay their debts as well as help fund the confederation's debt.[10]

Most scholars agree that Massachusetts was the one state where the economic situation was the messiest. Rather than retire their debt through devalued bonds, the commonwealth purchased bonds at their original value, which only increased the state's debt. Additionally, since most of the rural population had sold their bonds to speculators at devalued prices in order to pay the onerous taxation rates, the buying back of bonds at full value became another source of rural agitation since the benefits went only to the speculators. By the mid-1780s, Massachusetts farmers made multiple unsuccessful appeals to the legislature to revalue the debt or decrease taxation. The final break came as these rural farmers, unable to pay their taxes and mortgages, had their property seized by state courts as payment. In the fall of 1786, these farmers rose in rebellion. Led by Daniel Shays, the farmers closed the local courthouses and attempted to seize the federal arsenal at Springfield only to be stopped by the Massachusetts militia.[11] While it did not cause widespread violence or upheaval, Shays' Rebellion did force Massachusetts to adopt significantly less stringent taxes and debt reduction methods. As we will see, its long-term impact was profound.

While the states focused on rejuvenating their sluggish economies, the confederation became increasingly unimportant. Often, the Congress met only its minimum number for a quorum. Yet, this did not mean the states abandoned the confederation. As Keith Doughtery has revealed in his extensive review of congressional requisitions during the 1780s, an average of nine of the thirteen states met their yearly requisition request, with at least eight states paying every year. In fact, as the 1780s wore on, all but one state, Georgia, contributed to the confederation's treasury.[12] These payments were not always in the amount Congress requested, and states were often unpredictable as to when they would pay, but it does show an involvement and concern with the confederation that Nationalists and most historians claim was not present in the post-war period. It also calls into question the Nationalists' repeated accusations that the states, in a fit of jealous protection of their sovereignty, all but abandoned the confederation. Since most states sent funds to the confederation, but struggled to pay due to their own debts and economic issues, the Nationalists' charges of abandonment seem more of hyperbolic rhetoric than reality.

The confederation's foreign debts were deep into arrears. By 1785, Congress could not pay Dutch banks the interest on its 10,000,000 livre and the next year it defaulted completely on its French loan. The failure of the impost in 1781, 1783, and another failed attempt in 1784, had deprived the confederation of the independent source of revenue it could use to pay the interests of those debts.[13] If the confederation could not find a continual source of independent income, the future of the confederacy was in doubt.

The inability to pay its foreign debts was illustrative of the foreign policy problems that plagued the confederation throughout the 1780s.[14] In many ways, the confederation lacked real foreign policy in the traditional sense. Its primary focus was on securing trade agreements with Europe's powers while avoiding the quagmire of its balance-of-power politics.[15] American ministers John Adams and Thomas Jefferson struggled to defend the viability of the confederation in foreign courts. Be-

The most important of these amendments was third on the list. It stated that when a state failed to send Congress its requisition after a majority of the other states had, the Congress shall have full power and authority to levy, assess, and collect all sums and duties with which any such state so neglecting to comply with the requisition."[29] Should a state fail to assign someone to collect the federal tax, Congress would then make the appointment. In other words, Congress was requesting the power to tax directly the members of recalcitrant states. Previous experience taught that "very man who wishes to strengthen the federal Government, and confirm the Union, is represented as unfriendly to the liberties of the People," Congress made this power applicable only to states failing to comply and would impinge upon the sovereignty of the state only if a state refused to pay.[30]

Although Monroe's committee drafted the amendments with careful attention to balancing the need for congressional revenue with the necessity of maintaining state sovereignty, Congress never considered the committee's recommendation. Immediately following the committee's report, Congress became embroiled over a potential commercial treaty with Spain. In his negotiations with Spanish minister, Don Diego de Gardoqui, John Jay had requested that Congress relinquish the United States' navigation rights to the Mississippi River for twenty-five years in exchange for favorable commercial terms with the European power. Southern states viewed the request as a surrender to northern economic interests and a betrayal of the common good. As such, southern states worked as a sectional bloc to defeat the treaty.[31]

The controversy over the Jay-Gardoqui treaty ended any hopes that Congress would submit the proposed amendments. Since the amendments provided Congress with power over international commerce as well as a power to tax citizens, this ensured that southern states, already distrustful of Congress because of the context of events surrounding the treaty, would not approve the measures. The failure worried members of Congress, both Nationalists and those, like Monroe himself, who were sensitive to state sovereignty. They viewed the amendments as a final attempt to empower a confederation that was "deficient in powers of Commerce; in raising Troops, and in the means of Executing those powers that were given." The failure to secure "[s]uch powers as was necessary to enable them [i.e., Congress] to administer the Federal Government]" meant the Confederation "[m]ust fall."[32]

The amendments were the final failed attempt to secure more authority for the confederation. Since the end of the Revolution, however, Nationalists had attempted to persuade the public that the Articles needed reforming to preserve the union. Many attempted to provide blueprints on exactly how this reform of the constitutional system should occur. Among the first public calls for reform came from Pelatiah Webster and his 1783 pamphlet, "A Dissertation on the Political Union and Constitution of the Thirteen United States."[33] In his essay, Webster called for a wholesale restructuring of the confederation, with most sovereign power resting with what he repeatedly called the "Supreme Authority." While he maintained that the states needed to keep their sovereignty in order to keep internal order, he nevertheless suggested that the states "necessarily and unavoidably" needed to "part with and transfer . . . so much of their own sovereignty" to a "supreme power." This supreme power, despite needing to be "limited and checked," would exercise a broad range of powers to "secure and make effectual the ends of it."[34] Many of the powers Webster believed needed to be vested in the supreme power—the powers of war and peace, the appointing both civil and military officials, making contracts, borrowing and coining money, establishing post-offices, and regulating trade—reflected the traditional powers the Articles either already had or Nationalists wished they had. These were just the start of the supreme authority's powers, however. To be effectual, it needed all the sovereign authority that did not "come within the jurisdiction of the state" or that "any particular state is not competent" to exercise. Webster did not explain what constituted a power the state was not competent to exercise, or fell exclusively within its realm, but clearly, he defined it narrowly.

In two areas, however, Webster's ideas moved past those of other Nationalists. First, he argued for restructuring of the government of the supreme power, starting with a bicameral legislature. The states should still appoint the members of these houses but only according to popular election, as that was the only way to ensure the "real substantial representatives" of the people. Popular election, Webster continued, would "cloth[e]" the supreme authority "with that vast authority which is necessary" for the common good because it would ensure men of talent and quality.[35] From there, Webster suggested the establishment of several executive departments, including Finances, Foreign Affairs, War, and State, the final of which would oversee the internal issues of the nation. These departments would not only oversee the business of the supreme authority, but would serve as non-voting advisers to the Congress. The supreme authority would also need its own judiciary to enforce its laws. Finally, Webster also called for a national Chamber of Commerce composed of the states' leading merchants. Because "trade is of such essential importance to our interests" and merchants possessed "full and extensive intelligence" of foreign and domestic affairs and of the general wealth of the country, they could advise Congress on all trade and commercial legislation.[36]

Webster turned his final thoughts on how this supreme authority was to enforce its power. In particular, he was concerned with preventing the states' interference with national authority. Here, he clearly displayed his belief in the near absolute sovereignty of the supreme authority. Every state, he argued, was "under the highest obligation to obey the supreme of Union; and to call forth the force of the Union ag[ain]st any member" refusing to "fulfill its duty." [61] In this one resolution, Madison—via Randolph—had cast aside the Articles as they stood in 1787 and proposed a sweepingly new and teleological system.

Although Madison did not record the immediate reactions of delegates after Randolph completed his series of resolutions, it is not difficult to imagine their shock. The states did not send their delegates to Philadelphia to establish a new constitutional order, but rather to discuss potential grants of powers to the existing confederation. [62] Still, the Nationalists pressed their initiative and over the next six weeks launched barrages upon state sovereignty. At its feet, they laid all the fault and problems plaguing the confederation and the internal affairs of the states. Madison, reiterating the points he made privately before the convention, told his colleagues that it was the states' abuses of "republican liberty," by failing to protect individual liberty and exercising arbitrary justice, that were the "evils" making the convention necessary. [63] Gouverneur Morris, a Nationalist ideologue, argued how a "Union of the States merely federal" was not sufficient to preserve the common defense, the general welfare, and liberty and what was needed was a "national Government" that had a "supreme Legislative, Executive, & Judiciary." [64] Delaware delegate George Read argued that the confederation was "founded on temporary principles," which led to too much attachment to the state governments. "We must look beyond their continence. A national govt must soon of necessity swallow them up." [65]

Despite these determined attacks on state sovereignty, the battle lines between State Sovereigntists and Nationalists were not as clear in Philadelphia as those in the 1777 or the early 1780s. Those factions existed, but few members of the convention were decided ideologues of either camp. By sending delegates, the states acknowledged they were willing to surrender some of the authority they enjoyed under the unamended Articles. Much of the Philadelphia Convention's early debates, therefore, centered on how much sovereignty the states would surrender. If state sovereignty is kept at the center of American constitutionalism rather than the Nationalist critique of it, as is more often the case, a different, and more accurate, view of the Constitutional Convention's debates emerges. Rather than being the traditional story of a heroic group of Nationalists fighting to secure the critical and necessary concessions needed to save the Revolution from itself, the story should be flipped. A careful examination that moves past the preeminent Nationalists reveals that the story of the Constitutional Convention must include how defenders of the American constitutional settlement sought to correct the confederation's real problems while stopping, or at least curbing, a constitutional movement they considered a threat to the Revolution. [66]

This threat to state sovereignty and the Revolution explains why the sweeping proposals offered by Virginia, and the overt calls for a national sovereignty that Morris and others advocated, troubled so many delegates, including those who were sympathetic to considerable change. Most delegates believed state sovereignty had to remain a central element of the American constitutional order, even if taken down from its somewhat lofty perch. Keeping this view in mind, the battle over representation in the legislature, the one issue that nearly destroyed the convention, becomes not just a battle between small states versus large states, but principally a clash over competing visions of where sovereignty should resided.[67] In essence, and without exaggeration, the convention's arguments over representation were an Americanized version of the arguments between the colonies and England that created the imperial crisis. At stake then, as in 1765–1774, was nothing short of how Americans were going to be governed. Madison's proposal to have both houses of the legislature based upon population signaled to the convention that some members, like Robert Morris, James Wilson, Gouverneur Morris, and Alexander Hamilton, were "for raising the federal pyramid to a considerable altitude" above the states and perhaps even destroying them.[68]

Defenders of state sovereignty, however, refused to stay quiet. The first serious defense of state sovereignty came on the first day of real debate, May 30, when Charles Pinckney of South Carolina asked Gouverneur Morris if his desire for a supreme national government was "meant to abolish the state govern[ments] all together."[69] From there, the defense of state sovereignty never ceased. Critics charged Madison's plan, and the aggressive stance made by many of its supporters, with "taking so many powers out of the hands of the States as was proposed, tend[ing] to destroy all that balance and security of interest among the States which it was necessary to preserve."[70] Even those who sought a stronger government believed the proposals far too centralizing and threatening to liberty. As John Dickinson, a supporter of a stronger confederation, noted, "he had no idea of abolishing the State Governments as some gentleman seemed inclined to do. The happiness of this Country in his opinion required considerable powers to be left in the hands of the States."[71] New York's John Lansing believed the Virginia Plan, "in short[,] absorbs all power except what may be exercised in the little local matters of the States which are not objects worthy of the supreme cognizance."[72]

To be sure, ideologues of state sovereignty were present too. None more so than Luther Martin of Maryland. On June 27 and 28, he delivered perhaps the most impassioned defense of state sovereignty at the convention. In a learned, if windy and at times vehement, discussion, Martin expressed the State Sovereigntists' position. The general government, he noted, was meant "merely to preserve the states: not to govern individuals." As such, those powers should be "narrow." If the convention erred by not giving enough powers, more could added at a future date. If too much power was given, however, "it could never be resumed." Continuing, Martin worried that a "resort to the Citizens at large for their sanction" of the new government placed individuals by into a state of nature resulting in the "dissolution" of the states. The convention, furthermore, did not have the right to allow the people to dissolve the states; only the people of each state had the power to alter their states. The "federal idea" of state equality was "founded in justice and freedom, not merely in policy." It made the states, as free and independent sovereigns, in a state of nature in regards to each other. To surrender their equality in favor of popular representation would be the end of their liberty and would establish a "system of slavery" for the ten smallest states. Martin concluded that the real problem with the confederation was not state sovereignty; it was the "want of power."[73]

The influence of Martin's lengthy address is difficult to gauge. Most delegates shared his basic argument, but differed from the prickly Marylander by accepting—where Martin could not—at least some degree of direct action upon the people by the general government. What the Virginia Plan, and the aggressiveness of the Nationalist phalanx, had shown most delegates was that if the convention was to succeed, some compromise on the issue of state sovereignty was necessary. At the same time, however, the states had to remain critical actors on the national scene, lest the new government swallow them and liberty. The only way to combat the Nationalists' push for a bicameral legislature rooted in popular representation that could potentially destroy the states was to demand the "preservation of the States in a certain degree of agency [as] necessary." The states, Dickinson noted, "were the planets, and ought to be left to move freely in their proper orbit. If the State Governments were excluded from all agency in the national one, and all ownership drawn from the people at large, the consequence would be that the national government would . . . run into all the same mischiefs."[74] Dickinson's remarks once again reflected the traditional arguments he and others first espoused during the imperial crisis and that had developed during the Revolution and post-war years, that state sovereignty was a check upon consolidated power and thus an aegis of liberty.

This desire to force Nationalists into accepting some element of state sovereignty was the essence and purpose of the counter-proposal offered by New Jersey's Paterson in June.[75] What Paterson proposed contrasted sharply with the Nationalists' vision of reform. Rather than a new plan, it was a series of proposed amendments to the Articles of Confederation. It maintained that "if the sovereignty of the States [was] to be maintained," the states must have equal representation under the Articles.[76] While it proposed separate branches of government, the other critical element of the plan was how it made:

> all Acts of the U. States in Congs made by virtue & in pursuance of the powers hereby & by the articles of Confederation vested in them, and

all Treaties made & ratified under the authority of the U. States shall be
the supreme law of the respective States so far forth as those Acts or
Treaties shall relate to the said States or their Citizens, and that the
Judiciary of the several States shall be bound thereby in their decisions,
any thing in the respective laws of the Individual States to the contrary
notwithstanding; and that if any State, or any body of men in any State
shall oppose or prevent ye carrying into execution such acts or treaties,
the federal Executive shall be authorized to call forth ye power of the
Confederated States, or so much thereof as may be necessary to enforce
and compel an obedience to such Acts, or an observance of such Treaties.[77]

In essence, while the New Jersey Plan sought to protect state sovereignty
it was also a testament to how far the Nationalists had moved the argument for reform during the mid-1780s. In many ways, it reiterated Nationalists' proposals from earlier in the decade. Not only would the treaties and other acts be supreme by explicitly acknowledging it, but the
confederation would possess the coercive power needed to enforce its
actions. Yet, by keeping state sovereignty central, the New Jersey Plan
made greater sense and was much more in keeping with American constitutionalism than what the more ideological Nationalists sought. State
sovereignty as protected by Article II of the Articles remained intact, even
if curbed. Keeping state equality in the Congress in the capacity reflected
by the Articles insured that any action taken by the new government
would have the consent of the states, a critical element of state sovereignty expressed first in the writings of the colonial arguments against Parliament's taxation measures. At the same time, however, and in the context
of the convention's debates of mid-June, the New Jersey Plan seemed
more a political counter against the Nationalists than a serious attempt at
reforming the Articles. In other words, given the degree to which delegates had accepted some element of republicanism at the national level,
the New Jersey Plan forced the more stalwart Nationalists to accept some
element of state equality. What Paterson made clear, refusing to have a
branch of the legislature represent one of core constitutional elements of
the revolution, would have assured defeat of the plan both in the convention and in its ratification.

At first, the Nationalists were not in a compromising mood. Wilson
"could not persuade himself that the State Govts. [and] sovereignties
were so much the idols of the people, nor a Natl. Govt. so obnoxious to
them."[78] Randolph believed the New Jersey Plan would force the confederation to wield "impracticable and expensive" coercive powers that
would be "cruel to individuals."[79] Hamilton responded by delivering his
famous speech of June 18th, where he argued that the idea that "leaving
the States in possession of their sovereignty could possibly answer" the
crisis at hand was nonsense. The only solution, he told the delegates, was
a "complete sovereignty in the general Govermt" where an elected execu-

tive and one house of the legislature held life tenures, and the legislative branch could pass "all laws whatsoever." Madison attacked Paterson's plan claiming that it did not address the vices of the confederation. The plan offered no curbs to the states' ability to interfere with treaties and the law of nations. Nor did it account for "encroachments on the federal authority;" "trespasses of the States on each other;" It also did not "secure the internal tranquility of the states . . . a good internal legislation and administration to the particular states . . . [or] the Union agst. the influence of foreign powers over its members." By leaving too much of the confederacy intact, "their pertinacious adherence" to the New Jersey Plan would destroy the Union.[80]

The unwillingness to compromise on the issue of state representation, when most had made known their willingness to do so, caused rising tension and nearly destroyed the convention. For several weeks in June, the convention deadlocked over the issue. The Nationalists, as Dickinson pointed out to Madison, were "see[ing] the consequence of pushing things too far."[81] If compromise on the issue of state representation in the new plan of government could not be obtained, "our meeting would not only be in vain but worse than in vain" worried Connecticut's Oliver Ellsworth.[82] Only when cooler heads, in the form of Roger Sherman, intervened was the convention saved. Sherman's compromise gave one house of Congress to the Nationalists and one to state representation, thereby creating what Oliver Ellsworth called a "partly national and partly federal" plan.[83] Scholars note that Sherman's plan saved the convention. It did just that, but it saved much more. By forcing the Nationalists to accept state representation and equality in the one house of the new government, the compromise effectively secured state sovereignty's position in the constitutional order. Not only would state representation provide "State Legislatures . . . some means of defending themselves against encroachments of the Natl. Govt.," but it gave the one element that proponents of state sovereignty had claimed essential since the imperial crisis, consent.[84] All actions the new government would take would have the consent of the states.

Defenders of state sovereignty won another battle on July 17, when Madison's cherished proposal for a federal veto of state laws was defeated seven states to three.[85] Although Madison considered the federal veto a defensive measure to resist state encroachment, and would forever consider the absence of this power a fundamental flaw in the Constitution, many of his colleagues viewed this potential new power as more threatening to state sovereignty than any other provision. Even his June 8 speech, in which he defended the veto by using Dickinson's solar system analogy, failed to persuade. The federal veto, he argued, was the "great pervading principle that must control the centrifugal tendency of the proper orbits and destroy the order and harmony of the Political system." Most, however, viewed it as "giving a power that might restrain the

States from regulating their internal police." Elbridge Gerry said such a power "may enslave the States" and had "never been suggested or conceived among the people." Gerry also contended that the federal veto would allow the general government to "depress a part for the benefit of another part" and restrict the state's authority to "establish a military Force" leading "finally [to] a despotism."[86] Madison attempted to persuade his colleagues that "laws of urgent necessity must be provided for by some emanation of the power from the national government." His idea of a "temporary assent," he said, reflected "the practice in Royal Colonies before the Revolution."[87] Having a federal veto of any law the states enacted was "striking at the existence of the smaller states" since the largest three states would have the largest representation in at least one house of Congress. Even Gouverneur Morris argued that "this power is as likely to be terrible to the States."[88] Not only that but the entire notion seemed to Martin "improper and inadmissible" and seemed to make "so strange and obscure" the "once familiar and understood . . . language of the States being sovereign and independent." With such strong attacks upon the federal negative, and fears of its leading to consolidation and tyranny, it is not surprising that it failed to pass.[89]

Interestingly enough, as soon as Madison's proposal for the federal veto failed, Martin motioned for the convention to add to the proposed government "that the Legislative acts of the U.S. made by virtue and in pursuance of the articles of Union, and all Treaties made and ratified . . . shall be the supreme law of the respective states." His motion included for "the Judiciaries of the several States" to be bound by it "laws of the individual States to the contrary notwithstanding. The convention accepted his proposal without debate.[90] In its polished form, what Martin proposed was the supremacy clause. Although the clause has been the source of tremendous constitutional controversies, the fact that such a proposal came from the one State Sovereigntist ideologue at the convention seems shocking. Yet, Martin's proposal, following directly the defeat of the veto, was a simple restatement of the nomocratic idea that the convention had already accepted in theory, that the general government would be sovereign only in those strict areas it had authority. More importantly, and because it did come on the heels of the veto's defeat, Martin may have thought that such a provision was more of a guarantee of state sovereignty than Madison's veto. It reflected State Sovereigntists' acceptance of a divided sovereignty between the federal and state governments. The emerging government would wield specific and defined powers, he well knew, and by declaring outright that it would be supreme in those areas where it had defined authority would hopefully prevent the state encroachments that led to the convention and the near-death of state sovereignty. At the same time, the language he used, which would remain in the more polished form of the supremacy clause of Article VI of the Constitution, suggests that the any action taken by the general government that went outside its proscriptive powers would be a violation of the constitution, state sovereignty, and liberty, or a combination of three.[91]

Most of the first half of the convention was spent on trying to preserve an element of state sovereignty's presence in the new system that the delegates were crafting. Defenders of state sovereignty succeeded in this regard, as the Senate would represent the states in their sovereign capacity. State sovereignty received other protections, some more obvious than others. The supremacy clause, as has been noted, seemed a protection of both the general and state sovereignties. Defenders of state sovereignty considered the enumerations of congressional powers in Article I, Section 8 as necessary to preserving, at least to some degree, the traditional constitutional arrangements. By literally listing the powers of the proposed government it limited—but could not eliminate—the temptation to resort to the idea of implied powers and thus destroy state authority. Nevertheless, the general government remained nomocratic in nature by being limited to certain powers within specific areas, most of which were confined to broader national issues. Even the amending process of the constitution protected the states. All amendments, whether adopted by the Congress or submitted by a convention of the states, required the approval of state legislatures and not popular referendum. Thus, the states remained theoretically protected from attempts to amend them out of existence, although it remained to be seen if they would be swallowed by the new government's power.

This does not mean that State Sovereigntists achieved total victory, either. The proposal that emerged from the convention was an unmistakable reordering of the constitutional settlement of the Revolution. Nationalists achieved many of their goals. The powers of the proposed government were great, even if limited. Not only did the new government retain all of the powers the Confederation Congress possessed (a fact rarely acknowledged), but it gave the general government control of the state militias when necessary, the power to regulate international and interstate trade, to collect duties on imposts, and to tax all Americans. All of these were powers Nationalists had sought since 1780. At the same time, this government was the undisputed sovereign in those areas as Martin's supremacy clause made clear. The new government even retained the possibility of relying upon implied powers, albeit in more limited sense than what Nationalists had asserted in the early 1780s, through the "necessary and proper" clause. The states could not print money, enter into interstate compacts with each other without congressional approval, nor could they suspend habeas corpus, enact ex post facto laws or bills of attainder, or impair obligations of contracts. All of these limitations were frustrations Nationalists had voiced throughout the decade. Finally, the Wilsonian argument of 1776 won a major concession by having one branch of the legislature elected by popular vote thus making the government represent the American people as well as the states. This embodiment of popular sovereignty—the other mainstay of the Revolutionary constitutional settlement—was elevated to the national stage by requiring ratification of the document by the people of the states rather than by state legislatures.

***

While the convention debated and proposed a new government in the summer of 1787, at Harvard University, a young John Quincy Adams delivered his graduation address. America, the young Adams argued in his valedictory, was in a "critical period." The years after independence were ones where the entire confederacy was "groaning under the intolerable burden of . . . accumulated evils." Adams' address, unique in coining the phrase "critical period" to describe the decade of the 1780s, was little more than a restatement of the Nationalists' growing frustration with state sovereignty and the confederation.[92] Throughout the 1780s, they had advocated for reform of American constitutionalism, each attempt meeting with failure. By 1787, they universally accepted the idea that the confederation was on the brink of dissolution, all thanks to an overattachment to state sovereignty. If the Revolution were to survive, they argued, a fundamental reordering of America's constitutional settlement had to occur. A complete reordering was what the Nationalists attempted at the Philadelphia Convention.

Were the 1780s truly a "critical period" as Nationalists then, and scholars since, have maintained? Much of the actions the states undertook during the 1780s, especially in the realm of their economic policies, were within their sovereign power. The states sometimes made ill-conceived decisions that often caused more problems than they solved, but those policy decisions were theirs to make. Yet, by 1786, most Americans, wherever they fell on the Nationalist or State Sovereigntist spectrum, agreed that the confederation was weakening. The states, in their attempt to address their own fiscal issues, struggled to supply the confederation with the funds it needed to address its domestic and foreign affairs. With civil unrest gripping many states, Americans had come to accept the need for some reform of the confederation. When the Nationalists sought to take advantage of this agreement by tearing down the state sovereignty-centered settlement and replacing it with a centralized national government, defenders of state sovereignty reacted. They forced the Nationalists to accept that the sovereignty of the states had to remain the foundation upon which any reordering were to occur. It was state sovereignty's defenders, then, that achieved the "miracle at Philadelphia," and not the Nationalists. Nor was the defense of state sovereignty as the bedrock of American constitutionalism ended at Philadelphia. The states had surrendered some of their power, but their sovereignty remained. Yet, because the Constitution failed to use the word sovereignty anywhere in the document, before Americans accepted the new Constitution, they would demand explicit protections for state sovereignty. That is the topic of the next chapter.

NOTES

1. Gordon Wood, *Creation of the American Republic, 1776–1787* (Chapel Hill: University of North Carolina Press, 1969), 465.

2. Although specific works focused on the particular issue will be mentioned, the following section relies upon Merrill Jensen, *The New Nation: A History of the United States during the Confederation* (New York: Vintage Books, 1950). Despite its age and its progressive proclivities, Jensen's book is a much more balanced treatment than that found in the extremely nationalistic Richard B. Morris, *Forging the Union: 1781–1787* (New York: Harper Collins, 1988).

3. E. Wayne Carp, *To Starve the Army at Pleasure: Continental Army Administration and American Political Culture, 1775–1783* (Chapel Hill: University of North Carolina Press, 1984), especially 169–218.

4. Michael Schwarz, "The Origins of Jeffersonian Nationalism: Thomas Jefferson, James Madison, and the Sovereignty Question in the Anglo-American Commercial Dispute of the 1780s," *Journal of Southern History* 79 (August 2013): 569–79.

5. Jensen, *A New Nation*, 313–26.

6. Ibid., 295–301; quote on 300. The exception to the slower response of the southern states was Maryland. It was the first state to respond to the British order that stopped American shipping to its colonies.

7. Ibid., 303.

8. Woody Holton, *Unruly Americans and the Origins of the American Constitution* (New York: Hill and Wang, 2008), 21–46.

9. Jensen, *New Nation*, 306–307.

10. Ibid., 302–20, 326.

11. For the background and development of Shays' Rebellion see Leonard L. Richards, *Shays's Rebellion: The American Revolution's Final Battle* (Philadelphia: University of Pennsylvania Press, 2003).

12. Keith L. Dougherty, *Collective Action Under the Articles of Confederation* (Cambridge: Cambridge University Press, 2001), 44–45.

13. Ibid., 77–82.

14. Peter and Nicholas Onuf, *Federal Union, Modern World: The Law of Nations in an Age of Revolution, 1776–1814* (New York: Madison House, 1993), 117–23.

15. David Hendrickson, *Peace Pact: The Lost World of the American Founding* (Lawrence: University Press of Kansas, 2003), 201–202.

16. Schwarz, "The Origins of Jeffersonian Nationalism," 581–85.

17. Peter Onuf, *The Origins of the Federal Republic: Jurisdictional Controversies in the United States, 1775–1787* (Philadelphia: University of Pennsylvania Press, 1983), 31–21, 103–26.

18. Morris, *Forging of the Union*, 251.

19. John Jay, "Report on State Laws Contrary to the Treaty of Peace" in Mary A. Giunta, ed., *The Emerging Nation: A Documentary History of the Foreign Relations of the United States under the Articles of Confederation, 1780–1789*, 3 vols. (Washington, DC: Government Printing Office, 1996), 3: 333–49, quote on 346.

20. Wood, *Creation*, 403; Alexander Hamilton, "Second Letter From Phocion," April 1784, in Harold Syrett, ed., *The Papers of Alexander Hamilton*, 27 vols. (New York: Columbia University Press, 1961–1987), 3: 549–50.

21. Jonathan Parsons, "A Consideration of Some Unconstitutional Measures, Adopted and Practices in this State," (Newburyport, MA: John Mycall, 1784), 10.

22. Quote found in Wood, *Creation of the American Republic*, 463.

23. For those reforms, see ibid., 430–63.

24. Henry Knox to George Washington, October 23, 1786, in W. W. Abbot et al., eds., *The Papers of George Washington: Confederation Series*, 5 vols. (Charlottesville: University Press of Virginia, 1992–1997), 4: 299–302.

25. Dougherty, *Collective Action*, 104–107.

26. Morris, *Forging of the Union*, 265.

27. Quote taken from ibid.

28. The report can be found in Worthington C. Ford, ed., *Journals of the Continental Congress,* 34 vols. (Washington, DC: Government Printing Office, 1904–1937) 31: 494–98.

29. Ibid.

30. Rufus King to Elbridge Gerry, June 18, 1786, in Paul L. Smith, ed., *Letters of Delegates to Congress*, 25 vols. (Washington, DC: Library of Congress, 1976–2000), 23: 364.

31. For the Jay-Gardoqui fiasco see Morris, *The Forging of the Union*, 235–43; Hendrickson, *Peace Pact*, 204–206.

32. Thomas Rodney, diary entry for May 3, 1786, in Smith, ed., *Letters*, 23: 364.

33. Pelatiah Webster, "A Dissertation on the Political Union and Constitution of the Thirteen United States (Philadelphia: Bradford, 1783).

34. Ibid., 3–4.

35. Ibid., 18–21.

36. Ibid., 27–28.

37. Ibid., 38–47.

38. Roger Sherman, "Remarks on a Pamphlet, Entitled, 'A Dissertation on the Political Union'" (New Haven, CT: n.p., 1784).

39. Ibid., iii.

40. Ibid., vi, x.

41. Ibid., 24.

42. Ibid., 33.

43. Ibid., 36.

44. Ibid., 39.

45. Noah Webster, "Sketches of American Policy" (Hartford, CT: Hudson and Goodwin, 1785), 31.

46. Ibid., 32.

47. Ibid., 35.

48. Ibid., 44.

49. Ibid., 48.

50. Morris, *The Forging of the Union*, 250–52.

51. Alexander Hamilton, "Address of the Annapolis Convention," in Hamilton, *Papers*, 3: 686–87.

52. Morris, *The Forging of the Union*, 252.

53. Benjamin Rush, "Address to the People of the United States," in *American Museum* 1787.

54. For examples of other ideas for reform, see John Jay to George Washington, January 7, 1787, and Henry Knox to George Washington, January 14, 1787, in Washington, *Papers: Confederation Series* 4: 502–504 and 521–22.

55. James Madison to Edmund Randolph, April 6, 1787, in Robert A. Rutland and William M. E. Rachal, eds., *The Papers of James Madison*, 17 vols. (Chicago: University of Chicago Press, 1962–1991), 9: 368–71.

56. Madison, "Vices of the Political System," in ibid., 345–58.

57. Hendrickson, *Peace Pact*, 216.

58. Madison to Randolph, April 6, 1787, in Madison, *Papers,* 9: 345–48.

59. Madison to Thomas Jefferson, March 19, 1787, ibid., 317–22.

60. Madison to Randolph, April 6, 1787, ibid., 345–48.

61. James Madison, *Notes of the Debates in the Federal Convention of 1787*, Adrienne Koch, ed., (Columbus: Ohio University Press, 1966; reprint, New York: W. W. Norton, 1987), 31 [hereafter, Madison, *Notes*].

62. For those instructions, see *Documentary History of the Ratification of the Constitution*, Merrill Jensen, John P. Kaminski, Gaspare J. Saladino, Richard Leffler, Charles H. Schoenleber, and Margaret A. Hogan, eds., 26 vols. to date (Madison: University of Wisconsin Press, 1976 –), 1: passim.

63. Madison, June 6, 1787, in Madison, *Notes*, 75–76.

64. Gouverneur Morris, May 30, 1787, in ibid., Madison, *Notes*, 34.

65. George Read, June 6, 1787, in ibid., 78.

66. This idea is hinted at, and explored through the character of John Dickinson, in Forrest McDonald, *Novus Ordo Seclorum: Intellectual Origins of the Constitution* (Lawrence: University Press of Kansas, 1987), 225–60, and Forrest McDonald and Ellen Shapiro McDonald, *Requiem: Variations on Eighteenth-Century Themes* (Lawrence: University Press of Kansas, 1988), 1–30. Also see M. E. Bradford, *Original Intentions: On the Making and Ratification of the United States Constitution* (Athens: University of Georgia Press, 1993).

67. For an opposing view see Jack N. Rakove, "On Understanding the Constitution: A Historian's Reflections (and Dissent)," in Robert L. Utley, Jr. and Patricia B. Gray, eds., *Principles of the Constitutional Order: The Ratification Debates* (Lanham, MD: University Press of America, 1989), 33–49, especially, 39–41.

68. The quote is that of James Wilson, May 31, 1787, in ibid., 40.

69. Charles Pinckney, May 30, 1787, in ibid., 34.

70. Pierce Butler, May 31, 1787, in ibid., 41–42.

71. John Dickinson, June 2, 1787, in ibid., 55.

72. John Lansing, June 16, 1787, in ibid., 121.

73. Luther Martin, June 27–28, 1787, in ibid., 201–204.

74. Dickinson, June 7, 1787, in ibid., 84–85.

75. In "On Understanding the Constitution," 39–40, Rakove contends that it "becomes more difficult to gauge the sincerity" of the supporters of the New Jersey Plan. He asserts that the plan defended the "fictive notion" of state sovereignty out of political necessity, as the only means to "press for their claims of representation." This claim can only be true if state sovereignty was the "mystical conception" Rakove claims it was. Since it was a constitutional reality from the start of the Revolutionary period, however, the clarity of the New Jersey Plan's protection of state sovereignty becomes clearer and more understandable.

76. William Paterson, June 16, 1787, in ibid., 123.

77. Patterson, June 15, 1787, in ibid., 120–21.

78. Wilson, June 16, 1787, in ibid., 125.

79. Randolph, June 16, 1787, in ibid., 127–28.

80. Hamilton, June 18, 1787, in ibid., 129–39.

81. Dickinson to Madison, June 15, 1787, in ibid., 118.

82. Oliver Ellsworth, June 29, 1787, in ibid., 218–19.

83. Ibid. For the committee report that brokered the compromise on representation see Ibid., 232–38.

84. George Mason, June 7, 1787, in ibid., 87.

85. Debates of July 17, 1787, in ibid., 305.

86. Madison, Hugh Henry Williamson, and Elbridge Gerry, all June 8, 1787, in ibid. 88–90.

87. Madison, ibid., 92.

88. Peterson, June, 9 and Morris, July 17, 1787, in ibid., 96, 304.

89. Martin, July 17, and June 29, 1787, in ibid., 304 and 217.

90. Debates, July 17, 1787, in ibid., 305–306.

91. On this point, see Alison LaCroix, *The Ideological Origins of American Federalism*, (Cambridge, MA: Harvard University Press, 2010), 165–72.

92. Quote taken from Wood, *Creation of the American Republic*, 393.

FOUR

Ratification of the Constitution and Continuation of the Settlement

"As I enter the building I stumble at the threshold," wrote Samuel Adams after reviewing the Constitution, "I meet with a National Government instead of a federal Union of Sovereign States."[1] Adams' shock reflected the sentiment many Americans felt towards the Constitution. The product produced by the Philadelphia Convention was not a series of amendments to the confederation at all, but rather an entirely new government. Although only the members of the convention realized the degree to which state sovereignty was forced to remain the foundation of the constitutional system, to those out-of-doors, the Constitution represented little more than centralized tyranny in the name of the people. "The question turns," said Patrick Henry, "on that poor little thing—the expression, We, the *people*, instead of the *states* of America."[2] What disturbed the Constitution's critics was the lack of explicit statement acknowledging state sovereignty. Without a Burke Amendment-type of statement, nothing could stop this proposed government from wielding Blackstonian sovereignty for unspecified purposes and destroying the states. Since Americans connected state sovereignty to a defense of liberty, the consequence for people's liberty was clear to the Constitution's critics.

Although the ratification debates operated on a multitude of levels and issues, and engaged a degree of popular participation of all levels of society unseen since the early months of the Revolution, a constant theme emerged from the critics' analysis, namely that the Constitution was a direct threat to state sovereignty.[3] As the debates wore on, the Constitution's opponents, both in published essays and during the ratification conventions, asserted that without an explicit protection of state sovereignty and individual liberties, they would not accept the new government. Thus, the Constitution's supporters had the dual responsibility to explain the benefits arising from the new government as well as to demonstrate how the proposed government did not destroy state sovereignty. This effort was not easy since many of the Constitution's defenders agreed with Madison's private assessment that the Constitution "neither effectually answer[ed] its national object or prevent[ed] the local mischiefs."[4] Nevertheless, it is a testament to how devoted Americans were to a nomocratic order with state sovereignty as the foundation of that constitutional order that they forced the Constitution's supporters to defend what many thought privately was the real problem. In the end, the Constitution's proponents realized that to secure the Constitution's ratification, they would have to accept amendments that not only protected individual liberties, but also one that acknowledged state sovereignty. Their defense of state sovereignty and the promise to protect it via amendment would have long-term consequences neither they nor their opponents realized.

Most critics of the Constitution accepted that problems existed throughout the confederation and that an increase in Congress' powers would help remedy it.[5] Yet, the plan that emerged from Philadelphia would only make matters worse. Rather than solving the few issues that plagued the states, the Constitution would eventually consolidate the states into one universal sovereign and destroy liberty. In fact, this notion that the Constitution would destroy the federal nature of the American constitutional system and replace it with a consolidated nation was the most consistent critique opponents leveled. Elbridge Gerry, one of three non-signers of the Constitution, explained his reasons for not signing that "the Constitution proposed has few, if any federal features, but is rather a system of national government," meaning that it was a consolidated government.[6] "I have never heard of two supreme co-ordinate powers in one and the same country before," noted William Grayson.[7] Robert Yates and John Lansing informed New York governor George Clinton that they abandoned the convention in the middle of summer because that body was creating a "system of consolidated government" bent on "depriv[ing] the State Governments of [their] most essential rights of sovereignty."[8] At the Pennsylvania ratification convention, Robert Whitehill invoked the traditional republican fear that power always sought to aggrandize itself. Eventually, he "anticipate[d] the annihilation of the several state governments, an event never expected by the people, and which would . . . destroy the civil liberties of America."[9] Another Pennsylvanian Anti-Federalist noted that because the Constitution would affect the everyday lives of people the result would be the destruction of the "sovereignty of the different states . . . in its most essential parts."[10] Such a fear would lead to either the states being "swallowed up" or civil war. Luther Martin, in his letter to the Maryland legislature explaining why he left the convention early, claimed the that the government the convention was "forming was not in reality a federal, but a national, government, not founded on the principles of the preservation, but the abolition or consolidation, of all state governments."[11]

These arguments against a consolidated nation echoed those offered against Britain by Dickinson and others two decades earlier. The Anti-Federalist writer "Centinel" even referenced Dickinson's ninth "Pennsylvania Farmer" essay to prove his point on the consolidationist aspects of the plan. "I beg lead to adduce the Farmer's Letters, see particular letter 9th, in which Mr. Dickinson has clearly proved, that if the British Parliament assumed the power of taxing the colonies, *internally*, as well as *externally*, and it should be submitted to, the several colony legislature would soon become contemptible, and before long fall into disuse."[12] To govern such a large, extended republic not only flew in the face of received wisdom of political philosophy from Aristotle to Montesquieu, but it was certain to lead to tyranny since the thirteen states were too geographically and economically diverse for such a consolidation to work. Thus, critics who expressed intense skepticism regarding the new government's ability to govern such vast territory and maintain its supposed republican character often did so by relying on the continent's great diversity and local needs. No one tied these local and diverse interests to questions of state sovereignty and consolidation better than Richard Henry Lee. Lee noted that to govern a territory that size would force a consolidation. "The people would govern themselves more easily," he noted in one letter, since the "laws of each state [are] adapted to its own genius and circumstance." In a continental wide republic, however, such diversity would succumb to a gross uniformity of consolidation that could not address the various local interests, needs, or desires.[13]

The two particular provisions of the Constitution that occasioned the fears of Anti-Federalists and proved to them the consolidationist character of the document were the necessary and proper clause of Article I, section eight, clause eighteen, and the supremacy clause of Article VI. The enumeration of congressional power meant very little because of the necessary and proper clause, opponents declared, because it granted Congress the dreaded use of implied powers. "Implication is dangerous," warned Henry at the Old Dominion's ratification convention, "because it is unbounded: If it be admitted at all, and no limits prescribed, it admits the utmost extension."[14] Although State Sovereigntists had fought off such powers in the Articles of Confederation earlier in the decade, such a provision seemed to find its way into the Constitution. The writer "Brutus," perhaps the most articulate Anti-Federalist essayist, warned that the clause "implies that the Constitution is not to receive an explanation strictly, according to its letter; but more power is implied than is expressed. And this clause, if it is to be considered, as explanatory of the extent of the powers given, rather than giving a new power, the spirit, intent and design of the clause, should be attended to, as well as the words in their common acceptation."[15] "A Federal Republican" in Pennsylvania cautioned that the clause "proves clearly that the whole country is to be comprised into one system of lordly government" since the "mode of expression be construed into a tyrannical grant to enforce tyranny itself." "An Impartial Examiner" echoed these sentiments, holding that the necessary and proper clause allowed Congress to interfere with the "legislatures of every state" and "invest[ed] [Congress] with supreme powers of legislation . . . annihilating the separate independency of each; and, in short swallows up and involves in the plentititude of its jurisdiction of all other powers whatsoever." [16] "An Old Whig" agreed. "The Congress," he wrote, "[could] judge of what is necessary and proper in all these cases and in all other cases; in short, in all cases whatsoever." The connection to parliamentary power alluded to by "An Old Whig" was not lost on the provision's critics. "An Old Whig" continued, noting how even "The British act of Parliament declaring the power of Parliament to make laws to bind America in all cases whatsoever, was not more extensive." With this provision, therefore, Congress becomes the equivalent of Parliament, wielding the Blackstonian sovereignty. "An Old Whig" asked his readers to answer who, under the Constitution, "shall set themselves above the sovereign?" [17] The "Federal Farmer," one of the leading Anti-Federalist authors, acknowledged the importance of having the states yield when their laws and constitutions conflicted with national treaties or the "laws of congress made in pursuance of the Constitution." Those laws however "should extend to only a few national objects." The necessary and proper clause, however, violated that maxim. It permitted the Congress to interfere with the "internal as well as external." Since it was impossible to determine how many laws "which may be deemed necessary," the clause was a Trojan Horse designed for stealing the sovereignty of the states and threatening the states and individuals' liberty. [18]

Anti-Federalists feared that the necessary and proper clause would aid federal judges in destroying state sovereignty and liberty. The clause "will undoubtedly be an excellent auxiliary to assist the courts to discover the spirits and reason of the Constitution, and when applied to any and every of the other clauses granting power, will operate powerfully in extracting the spirit from them," wrote "Brutus". Having already noted the dangers to liberty and state sovereignty already posed by the "sweeping clause," he prophesied that if rights were not better secured in the Constitution, the moment an individual sought a redress from a court, the government will plead before the court that the encroachment was "necessary and proper." [19] The Massachusetts Anti-Federalist "Agrippa" connected the clause to the judiciary and the loss of liberty more explicitly than any other essayist. Since the federal courts could hear controversies between citizens of different states, when coupled with congressional power under the necessary and proper clause:

There is then a complete consolidation of the legislative powers in all cases respecting property. This power extends to all cases between state and citizens of another state. Hence, a citizen, possessed of the notes of another state, may bring his action, and there is no limitation that the execution shall be levied on the public property of the state but the property of individual is liable. This is a foundation for endless confusion and discord. This, right to try causes between a state and citizens of another state, involves in it all criminal causes; and a man who has accidentally transgressed the laws of another state, must be transported, with all his witnesses, to a third state, to be tried. He must be ruined to prove his innocence. These are necessary parts of the new system . . . They effectually prove a consolidation of the states, and we have before shewn the ruinous tendency of such a measure.[20]

What made the necessary and proper clause ever the more frightening was not only that this new government's power would touch upon the everyday lives, liberties, and property, of all people, but also "the Constitution or laws of any state," could not "in any way prevent or impede the full and complete execution of every power given" to the new government.[21] Timothy Bloodworth, speaking at the first North Carolina ratification convention, worried that the supremacy clause allowed for the government to "trample on the rights of the people of North Carolina" since no "sufficient guards and checks" existed to limit the clause. Even the word "pursuance" could mean "bad as well as good measures," since the supremacy clause failed to distinguish. Hence, even tyrannical laws trumped state laws.[22] This one provision, "Brutus" noted, in an unreferenced nod to Blackstone, placed in possession of the proposed government an "absolute and uncontrollable power." The moment that a state attempted to exercise what little sovereignty it still possessed to protect itself or the liberties of its citizens—interposition, in other words—the new government would view this act as a "clog upon the wheels" of its power and enact legislation via the necessary and proper clause and destroy the last vestiges of state sovereignty.[23]

Federalists had to assuage fears that the adoption of the Constitution would not lead to a consolidated government. Accomplishing the task would not be easy, however. The first push of these self-styled "Federalists" was to acknowledge state sovereignty's position as a viable and foundational element of American constitutionalism—the states would lose some powers, but their sovereignty would remain. That stalwarts for a national sovereignty were forced by popular sentiment to defend the idea was a testimony to just how deeply Americans accepted state sovereignty as absolutely necessary to their order and liberty. It should also be noted that these defenses of state sovereignty are also representative of the political acumen of many of the more aggressive Nationalists who had to swallow their pride, and at least listen to popular sentiments in order to see the adoption of a system more preferable than the Articles.

This is especially true in states such as Massachusetts, New York, Virginia, and South Carolina where Federalists were evenly matched or were a noticeable minority.[24]

Yet, the state sovereignty that Federalists defended, however, was a qualified and much less robust version of that asserted by their opponents. As James Wilson observed in his "State House Speech" of October 6, 1787, the most widely reprinted Federalist defense of the Constitution during the entire ratification contest, when forming their state constitutions the people vested the state governments with "every right and authority which they did not in explicit terms reserve." This vesting of such authority made the state governments capable to address a wide range of issues. "But in delegating federal powers," he continued, the people gave a "positive grant expressed in the instrument of the union. Hence, it is evident, that in the former case everything which is not reserved is given; but in the latter the reserve of the proposition prevails, and everything which is not given is reserved." This positive grant of power negated the need for a Bill of Rights because the projected Constitution did not grant any authority that touched upon fundamental liberties such as trial by jury or freedom of the press. Any threat posed to state sovereignty under the Constitution was a phantom, Wilson insisted, because "upon their existence depends the existence of the Federal plan." Since the president (via the Electoral College) and the Senate depended directly upon the state legislatures for their selection, the states had to remain separate entities. Had it been the plan of the convention to annihilate the states, why did it "bound their connection with such indissoluble ties?"[25] Wilson's analysis reflected his lifelong belief, first revealed in the 1776 debates over the Articles of Confederation, in the existence of a national popular sovereignty derived from an aggregate American people. This adherence to preexisting national popular sovereignty is what allowed Wilson to describe so easily the differences between state and federal authority. The people, in Wilson's thinking, distributed their sovereignty authority in any way they best saw fit for the preservation of their liberty and happiness. The State House address also revealed the qualifications Federalists placed upon state sovereignty throughout the ratification ordeal. State Sovereignty would remain, to be sure, but it was much more confined to the internal actions of the states. What degree the federal government recognized it was limited strictly to those few instances he mentioned and as the residual of authority not granted to the new government.

While Wilson's speech served as the blueprint for the Federalists' defenses of the Constitution, most Federalists retreated from his stance on a preexisting national popular sovereignty, knowing that such an argument was not rooted in American history or constitutional tradition. Madison, for example, made repeated notions that the only popular sovereignty that existed was that of the people of the states, and not a supposed American popular sovereignty.[26] Despite this hesitation to embrace Wilson's theories on popular sovereignty, most Federalists did support his arguments regarding the proscribed limitations placed upon the federal government. Alexander Hamilton, writing as "Publius," pushed Wilson's case further.[27] A Bill of Rights, he noted, "in the sense and in the extent in which they are contended for, are not only unnecessary in the proposed Constitution, but would even be dangerous. They would contain various exceptions to powers which are not granted; and on this very account, would afford a colourable pretext to claim more than were granted. For why declare that things shall not be done which there is no power to do?"[28] Hamilton implied, of course, that providing a list of certain inviolable rights equated to an endorsement that the Constitution granted the same implied power that its supporters were trying to demonstrate did not exist. Since it was an inevitable that list would not cover all rights, the acknowledgment of the right to implied powers actually threatened more rights than a bill of rights could protect. Although he did not extend the argument to how it touched the issue of state sovereignty, Hamilton's argument moved easily to the relationship between the federal and state government. In admitting the government had powers that extended beyond the strict limitations confined in the document people acknowledged that the proposed government could interfere with state sovereignty when it did not have the right to do so.

While some Federalists addressed the connection between the states and the general government, not all were as conciliatory as Wilson and others. Benjamin Rush, in one of the truly Nationalist ideological writings of the entire ratification debates, argued that the states did not have sovereignty and thus had little room with which to be concerned about consolidation. Real sovereignty had always rested with the Confederation Congress since it exercised powers of war and peace. Nor were the states ever truly independent, no matter what the Articles may say to the contrary. They were independent only "in a union with her sister states in Congress." Finally, Rush noted sovereignty was not "sealed in the people," but "derived" from them. They exercised it "only the days of their elections," after that it is the "property" of their rulers.[29] William Dauer, writing as "Philo-Publius," scoffed that the real reason many were worried about the new plan resulted from knowing that a "diminution of state authority, is, of course, a diminution of the POWER of those invested with administration of that authority." He advised his readers to ignore those Cassandras since the "people of each state have already delegated these powers for their own protection and security," the real question before them was how to redistribute the sovereign powers for to better protect their security and happiness.[30]

Yet, Rush and Dauer were more the outliers than the norms when it came to Federalist explanations of how the proposed government would affect the states. Most borrowed Wilson's dual argument of a modified form of state sovereignty on the national level while maintaining the necessity of states for the new plan. "A Federalist" told readers that "the existence of every branch of the federal government depends upon the state legislatures, and both must stand or fall together." Many Federalists placed a special emphasis on the Senate, claiming as Fisher Ames, Rufus King, and Francis Dana did at the Massachusetts ratification convention, that it prevented consolidation because it "kept alive their individuality and Sov[ereign]ty."[31] Tench Coxe and John Dickinson, among the more important Federalist writings on this topic, both tied the Senate to the sovereignty of the states and, subsequently, to the prevention of consolidation. Coxe, a former Loyalist turned patriot and supporter of the Constitution, noted in his "A Freeman" and "An Examination of the Constitution" essays that even with the explicit protection of state sovereignty in the Articles of Confederation, that plan of union still contained "observable" elements of consolidation but that upon close inspection were merely an "appearance" of consolidation. Backing away from Wilson's national popular sovereignty claim, Coxe noted that had the delegates of the convention sought—or believed in—a real consolidated nation, they would have abandoned any notion of union within the document. Since the term union, he noted, meant an inherent compact among several states, the opening words of the preamble would have read "We the people of America" rather than "We the people of the United States" if consolidation was the real goal of the convention. Furthermore, by having the Senate selected by the "legislatures of a free, sovereign, and independent" states demonstrated the lack of consolidation since the attachment to their state ensured they would work to keep the federal government in line with its proscribed powers. Coxe's unattributed use of the Burke Amendment was certainly intentional, his readers would have noticed its use immediately, and he meant to reassure his readers that the sovereignty of the states would remain a vital force within the new system.[32]

Writing under the pseudonym "Fabius," Dickinson, who had defended state sovereignty at the convention, used his essay to explain to his more skeptical readers how the Constitution would not destroy state sovereignty. The very combination of national popular sovereignty with state sovereignty "forms an adequate security against every danger that has been apprehended," he noted. More importantly, however, in the third "Fabius" essay Dickinson met head-on the fear that the Constitution meant the doom of the states. The notion that "this superintending sovereign" would "destroy the subordinate sovereignties of the several states" infers that "a manifest and great usefulness must necessarily end in abuse." Such an assumption was an absurdity. "In short," he wrote, "the government of each state is, and is to be, sovereign and supreme in all matters that relate to each state only." While Dickinson embraced the idea of a qualified sovereignty for the states at the federal level, he argued that even in issues of a more national character, the states' representation in the Senate meant they were "subordinate barely." Dickinson, more than most Federalists, placed a strong emphasis on connection of the Senate to state sovereignty. Because the states retained a clear sovereignty in most areas, and had the Senate for itself in the projected plan, if the "federal sovereignty" interfered with state authority "it will be [the states'] *own faults*" and would establish a "dangerous precedent as to all." It was the duty of the senators "as the trustees or servants of the several states" to not "violate the independent sovereignty of their respective states, that justly darling object of American affections."[33]

Even "Publius" contributed to the states-as-necessary argument. In *Federalist 39* Madison noted that "in strictness," the convention's plan was "neither a national nor a federal Constitution, but a composition of both . . . it is neither wholly federal nor wholly national."[34] While the thirty-ninth essay is well known (although overshadowed by others such as the tenth essay), in essay forty-six, Madison connected the proposed Constitution to the necessary survival of the states. He did so by reiterating much of what other Federalist writers and speakers had said. "It has been already proved, that the members of the federal will be more dependent on the members of the state government, than the latter will be on the former," he wrote. Someday, Madison prophesied, the people could become more affectionate towards the general government than their state governments. Even then, however, the states had little to fear in the way of consolidation because "it is only within a certain sphere, that the federal power can, in the nature of things, be advantageously administered."[35] Further in the essay, however, Madison made an original, and startling, contribution to the argument. He admitted:

> [s]hould an unwarrantable measure of the federal government be unpopular in particular States, which would seldom fail to be the case, or even a warrantable measure be so, which may sometimes be the case, the means of opposition to it are powerful and at hand. The disquietude of the people; their repugnance and, perhaps, refusal to co-operate with the officers of the Union; the frowns of the executive magistracy of the State; the embarrassments created by legislative devices, which would often be added on such occasions, would oppose, in any State, difficulties not to be despised; would form, in a large State, very serious impediments; and where the sentiments of several adjoining States happened to be in unison, would present obstructions which the federal government would hardly be willing to encounter.[36]

In this remarkable—and oft overlooked—passage, Madison acknowledged that should the federal government take actions outside of the confines of its constitutionally proscribed authority, or what he called "unwarrantable measures," the states remained as a necessary check upon the federal government. Not only could popular opposition to the law obstruct it in a manner similar to American resistance to the Stamp and Tea Acts of 1765 and 1773, but also "embarrassments created by legislative devices." Although Madison did not use the word interposition, it is difficult to imagine what other sort of legislative embarrassment he was thinking.[37]

Nor was *Federalist 46* the only expression of interposition hinted at by "Publius", although it was its strongest appearance in those essays. Earlier, in essay twenty-six, Hamilton, who was no friend of state sovereignty, noted that:

> the state legislatures, who will always be not only vigilant but suspicious and jealous guardians of the rights of the citizens against the encroachment from the federal government, will constantly have their attention awake to the conduct of national rules, and will be ready enough, if any thing improper appears, to sound the alarm to the people, *and not only to be the voice, but if necessary the ARM of their discontent.*[38]

As with Madison's remarks, it is difficult to interpret Hamilton's comments as meaning anything but state interposition in defense of liberty. The real question was whether Hamilton meant what he said.

Madison, and especially Hamilton, may have engaged rhetorical strategies meant only to secure support for the Constitution, and scholars should not discount the use of such devices in a political battle with the political stakes as high as ratification, but it is difficult to dismiss these passages as just polemics. Given the contextual background that both essayists and, more importantly, their readers were familiar with, namely that practice of state sovereignty in a political context meant state interposition to defend against unconstitutional actions, these passage confirmed several critical developments. First, that before the Constitution many Americans, although not the Nationalists, accepted state interposition in defense of liberty as a power associated with state sovereignty. Second, while the adoption of the Constitution certainly led to increased power of the general government, and upon Madison and Hamilton's assurances, nothing altered the states from continuing to wield interposition when compelled to do so. Thirdly, that this exercise of interposition was not connected in any way to the acknowledgment of the state sovereignty in the Senate, the one area where most Federalists attempted to mollify the Constitution's critics. Finally, the remarks—even if accepted only as polemical—demonstrate how the constitutional reality of state sovereignty forced Federalists to reaffirm the centrality of state sovereignty in their proposed government. While some of the more aggressive Nationalists such as Hamilton may have never liked the idea of states being anything more than administrative units for the national government, such a desire was little more than wishful thinking, even in 1788; state sovereignty was a constitutional reality that had to be accepted and accommodated, albeit begrudgingly. Other supporters, such as Madison, who, by 1788, was already distancing himself from his brief flirtation with nationalism that characterized his thinking in 1786 and 1787, learned from the convention and ratification struggle not just the reality and attachment most Americans placed upon state sovereignty, but had grown to accept, and even appreciate, it as another potential check upon tyranny.[39] In other words, the Nationalists' attempts at establishing a new constitutional settlement would be, at best, only a partial victory.

Despite assurances that state sovereignty would remain intact after the adoption of the Constitution, critics refused to accept those arguments. The idea that the Senate served as the repository of state sovereignty struck many as disingenuous. Richard Henry Lee, for example, brushed the idea off by noting that the Roman Senate had given Caesar power, and with it, chimed the death knell of the Roman republic.[40] "Cincinnatus" challenged what he called Wilson's "egregious pedantry." If state sovereignty meant only selecting senators and Electoral College members, that was not sovereignty at all; it was administrative activity. The "attributes of sovereignty" were all removed from the states and placed at the federal level, leading the author to ask "is it not a mockery of common sense to tell us, the state sovereignties are not annihilated?"[41] One of the ways to ensure the federal government did not absorb state sovereignty would be to make the Senate an actual repository of state sovereignty. At the New York ratification convention, John Lansing recommended an amendment to the Constitution to allow states to recall and replace senators, a power the states possessed under the Articles. Having the power of recall would give the states "a Constitutional and peaceable mode of checking mal-administration" and allow for an easier redress of grievances and would give the states a clear role at the federal level.[42]

The most important way to protect state sovereignty, however, was for the Constitution to have an explicit stipulation acknowledging the sovereignty of the states. Without a Burke Amendment-like provision protecting state sovereignty, the federal government eventually would prevent any attempt by the states to object to the exercise of unbounded and implied authority via the twin threats of the supremacy and necessary and proper clauses. This dystopian future of consolidated tyranny, a real concern to many Americans however chimerical it appears to us now, provided all "the greater reason . . . to take the necessary precaution for securing a due administration and guarding against unwarrantable abuse" by amending the Constitution to acknowledge the reality of state sovereignty.[43] As the second essay of "Centinel" argued, the Burke Amendment was "thought proper" enough for the Articles of Confederation because a "positive grant was not then thought sufficiently descriptive and restraining upon Congress." That is to say, the Articles of Confederation also enumerated the powers of the Continental Congress just as the proposed Constitution did but as the Burke Amendment suggested that listing was not protection enough for the states and individual liberty. In language that could have been copied straight from Thomas Burke, "Centinel" noted that because the proposed Constitution had an even larger sweep of power, and "the lust of power is so universal, that a speculative unascertained rule of construction would be a poor security for the abuses of power," the proposed constitution required a state sovereignty stipulation.[44] Such a provision would counter the prediction John Smilie made at the Pennsylvania ratification convention, where he noted the new government, by draining the states of their authority to "promote their [citizens'] welfare and interest," will turn the state into a "shadow . . . suffered to dwindle and decay . . . by its own insignificance."[45]

These continual fears of consolidation and the loss of state sovereignty and personal liberty, then, led to persistent calls throughout the ratification debates, and especially at the various state ratification conventions, for amendments to the Constitution. Because the Federalists wanted an all-or-nothing vote on the Constitution, many called for a second convention to correct the perceived problems with the document.[46] Others, however, were willing to offer suggestions for amendments that should be included once the new government began operation. Others, still, made amendments to the Constitution a condition of that state's acceptance of the Constitution. In most cases, those making the calls for amendments to the Constitution often divided these amendments into two general categories, a bill of rights to protect specific individual civil liberties and structural amendments intended to correct what they perceived to be the major design flaws of the Constitution. Scholars have devoted enormous attention to the calls made to protect the civil liberties, but few have paid any real attention to the structural proposals. What they miss is how, in each of these cases, the call for the protection of state sovereignty was a leading proposal.

The first and most important calls emanating from the actual ratification conventions—rather than just the essay and pamphlet battles—came from the Pennsylvania convention. When that state voted 46–23 to approve the Constitution, the minority attempted to have the convention adopt into its minutes a report spelling out their particular grievances against the Constitution. Although the Pennsylvania Federalists—who, by all accounts, acted badly towards their opponents through the entire ratification period—refused to adopt the report, newspapers throughout the country reprinted it.[47] Adding to the dissent by the minority of the Pennsylvania convention was the gathering of these Anti-Federalists in Harrisburg in the fall of 1788. That gathering, "being convinced that a confederacy of republican states, and no other, can secure political liberty, happiness, and safety, throughout a territory so extended as the united States of America," recommended that a new convention meet to remedy the Constitution's flaw to destroying state sovereignty. The first item on their list of suggestions stated:

> That Congress shall not exercise any powers whatever, but such as are expressly given to that body by the Constitution of the United States; nor shall any authority, power, or jurisdiction, be assumed or exercised by the executive or judiciary departments of the Union, under color or pretence of construction or fiction; but all the rights of sovereignty, which are not by the said Constitution expressly and plainly vested in the Congress, shall be deemed to remain with, and shall be exercised by, the several states in the Union, according to their respective Constitutions; and that every reserve of the rights of individuals, made by the several Constitutions of the states in the Union, to the citizens and inhabitants of each state respectively, shall remain inviolate, except so far as they are expressly and manifestly yielded or narrowed by the national Constitution.[48]

The report used Wilson's own argument that the Constitution was a document of proscribed, limited powers, but lacked his faith that the federal government would never transgress those boundaries. Thus they sought, as their primary change, an explicit protection of state sovereignty. This defense was for more than just keeping the states sovereign, however. Following the traditional connection between state sovereignty and personal liberty, Pennsylvania Anti-Federalists wished to ensure that the Constitution would not sweep away the liberties the states protected via their own declaration of rights.[49]

The Pennsylvania minority knew their report would have no effect upon their state's acceptance of the Constitution, but they were hopeful that other conventions would use their call for amendments. Their hopes were realized as seven other states adopted suggestions or demands requiring some stated acknowledgment of state sovereignty in the Constitution. So important were the calls that of the seven other states who proposed a state sovereignty amendment only one, New Hampshire, did not make it an explicit condition of their adopting the Constitution, and even that state made it their first suggestion in their list of amendments. Even after the Constitution's ratification and implementation, North Carolina and Rhode Island, the two states that had rejected the Constitution at first, entered the union with stipulations that, as North Carolina's convention stated in its first requirement, "each State in the Union shall, respectively, retain every power, jurisdiction, and right, which by this Constitution delegated" to the new government. Rhode Island was even more explicit giving as their first suggested amendment a verbatim use of the Burke Amendment.[50]

The three most important state ratifications were those of Massachusetts, Virginia, and New York. Not only were they the three of the four biggest states (Pennsylvania was bigger than New York in 1787), but they were also the political leaders of the union. Their actions often informed and influenced the smaller states. Thus, how they ratified the Constitution and their stance towards the Constitution carried significant weight. Adding to the intensity, in each of these states the opponents of the Constitution were a noticeable majority. If Federalists were going to win ratification in each state, they were going to have to concede major points. They would concede on the issue of state sovereignty.

In Massachusetts, the first of the big three states to consider the Constitution, the Federalists waged an effective defense of the Constitution, winning over the considerable opposition.[51] Even in the last week, victory still seemed so uncertain that Federalists were more than willing to compromise and bargain with Anti-Federalists. On January 31, 1788, John Hancock, the president of the convention, who had been absent for the entirety of the convention due to the death of his son and a severe illness, rose and delivered an address. Suspected of having anti-federal leanings, Hancock had kept his sentiments to himself. Only after wheeling and dealing with the Federalists, where he secured personal promises of support in the upcoming gubernatorial election as well as promises to amend the Constitution, did he finally speak.[52] The Constitution, he opened, should be adopted by the Bay State. Yet, the Constitution should not be left untouched after its adoption. The debates had demonstrated real flaws in the plan, he said. Only with protections that "more effectively guard against the undue administration of the federal government" would the people of his state believe the Constitution truly sound. Hancock then proceeded to recommend the convention adopt, and urge the new Congress to adopt, nine separate amendments. Most of these amendments addressed the concern most Americans had over the consolidationist tendencies within the Constitution. Leading the list of Hancock's suggestions was a basic restatement of Article II of the Articles of Confederation.[53]

The convention sent Hancock's proposals to a select committee of twenty-five. After polishing and tweaking the proposal's language, they submitted their report to the convention. After several days of debate, on February 6, the Massachusetts ratification convention agreed 187 to 168 to adopt the Constitution. Yet, Massachusetts' instrument of ratification repeated Hancock's suggestions by signifying that the state expected amendments to the Constitution as soon as possible. The first suggested amendment stated "that it be explicitly declared that all powers not expressly delegated by the aforesaid Constitution are reserved to the several states, to be by them exercised."[54] Thus, the Federalists had carried the day in Massachusetts but not before first conceding that the Constitution needed amending in order to preserve state sovereignty.

The same held true in the Old Dominion. There, Massachusetts' strategy of ratification with the firm expectation that the first Congress would amend the Constitution would be deeply influential. That influence, however, did not come easily. Initially, Anti-Federalist sentiment was so strong that it appeared it would carry the day.[55] Many Virginians agreed with Richard Henry Lee when he explained to Patrick Henry that the idea of subsequent amendments after ratification rather than hosting a new convention "was little better than putting oneself to death first in expectation that the doctor, who wished our destruction, worked afterward and restored us to life." Since "the most essential danger from the present system arises . . . from its tendency to a consolidated government," it was necessary to kill it before it came alive. In case the Constitution were adopted, however, Lee maintained that it would fall to "the friends of liberty to guard with perfect vigilance every right that belongs to the states, and to protest against every invasion of them, taking care always to procure as many protesting states as possible." This vigilance would "create caution, and establish a mode of conduct as well as create a system of precedent that will prevents a consolidating effect from taking place by slow but sure degrees."[56]

On the surface, Lee's defense of state sovereignty and its connection to personal liberty is difficult to distinguish from that offered by Madison and Hamilton in the Federalist Papers. All three drew this traditional connection and advocated for a vigorous exercise of state sovereignty. A closer look, however, reveals the difference. "Publius" was attempting to calm fears of a consolidation under the Constitution by demonstrating the states retained enough sovereign power to thwart unconstitutional and potentially tyrannical actions. Lee, however, sought to kill the Constitution before its launching. As he argued, any real alteration to state sovereignty weakened the entire structure and, over time, a power-hungry federal government would chip away and circumvent the states' authority. Yet, Lee's remarks should not be interpreted to mean that he and others disapproved of Massachusetts' suggested amendments. Quite the opposite, in fact. Lee told Edmund Pendleton on the eve of the Old Dominion's convention that "it is a question deserving intense consideration, whether the state sovereignty ought to be supported in a manner similar to Massachusetts proposed Amendments." Lee also informed Samuel Adams that his calls to protect state sovereignty at the Massachusetts Convention gave him hope that "others, in stations similar to yours, might take frequent opportunities" to express the same sentiments.[57] At that convention Adams referred to a Burke Amendment-like statement as a:

> summary of a bill of rights, which gentlemen are anxious to obtain. It removes a doubt which many have entertained respecting the matter, and gives assurance that, if any law made by the federal government shall be extended beyond the power granted by the proposed Constitution, and inconsistent with the constitution of this state, it will be an error, and adjudged by the courts of law to be void. It is consonant with the second article in the present Confederation, that each state retains its sovereignty, freedom, and independence, and every power, jurisdic-

tion, and right, which is not, by this Confederation, expressly delegated to the United States in Congress assembled.[58]

When the Virginia ratification convention met in June of 1788, Virginia's position as a sovereign state was the underlying theme. Federalist defenders of the Constitution obviously argued that the fears of consolidation were polemical exaggerations. Led by Madison, Edmund Randolph, and John Marshall, they maintained what had become the standard Federalist response to accusations of consolidation, that the Constitution was one of delegated and proscribed powers. This system, they assured skeptics and critics, preserved personal liberty and state sovereignty. Opponents, led by Henry, George Mason, and William Grayson noted the seemingly aristocratic nature of the Senate, and other provisions such as the necessary and proper clause, the taxing provisions, and the noticeable lack of a Bill of Rights, would destroy both Virginia's sovereignty and Virginian's liberties.[59]

After several weeks of heated debates, it remained unclear if Virginia would adopt the Constitution. Towards the end of the month, Federalists, looking to Massachusetts' example, mentioned that it was possible that "the stile of the ratification" would remove the "mischief" of an ambiguously and potentially arbitrary government.[60] Edmund Randolph, one of the three delegates at the Constitutional Convention who refused to sign but who had become a strong defender of the Constitution, proposed that "if in the ratification we put words to this purpose, — that all authority not given is retained by the people, and may be resumed when perverted to their oppression; and that no right can be canceled, abridged, or restrained by the Congress, or any office of the United States." An instrument of ratification with this language, Randolph argued, expressed "the principles on which Virginia adopted it" and the state "would be at liberty to consider as a violation of the Constitution, every exercise of a power not expressly delegated therein."[61] In other words, the Old Dominion would adopt the Constitution only on the condition that state sovereignty, and individual liberties, remained protected.

Although Randolph's speech did not stop the debates, it certainly signaled the beginning of the end. The convention appointed George Wythe, the great Virginian lawyer, jurist, and legal mentor to Thomas Jefferson, to head a committee to propose amendments necessary to secure Virginia's ratification.[62] Henry, speaking at some length, made an impassioned argument against a conditional ratification, holding that it was useless to do so. Since the Constitution was a compact between two parties, if Virginia proposes conditional amendments, they are entering the compact before the other member (i.e., the states) had the chance to agree or reject the proposal. "Do you enter into a compact of Government first, and afterwards settle the terms of the Government?" he asked. Furthermore, Congress would not care about which provisions Virginia deemed important enough to include in a list of amendments. "They will not reason with you about the effect of this Constitution. They will not take the opinion of this Committee concerning its operation. They will construe it as they please" because the Constitution removed Virginia's sovereignty. To ask Virginians to surrender their sovereignty to the national government was akin to asking them "to apostatize from their native religion." Henry then proposed a series of his own bill of rights and amendments for the other states to consider prior to entering the compact.[63] Although the exact copy of Henry's proposals have been lost, they were probably the resolutions the convention defeated by a vote of eighty-eight to eighty on June 25.[64]

Admittedly, Randolph and Henry's suggestions did not specify the sovereignty of the states, yet, the idea underpins their remarks. At the same time, their debate on the nature of when to amend the Constitution is of great importance in American constitutional history. Despite arguing opposing positions, both offer the first traces of what would be called the Compact Theory of the Union, that the Constitution is a compact among the several states rather than an agreement amongst fictional American national popular sovereignty. Although made famous by the Kentucky and Virginia Resolutions of 1798 and John C. Calhoun's theories of the 1830s, their first real intellectual thrust came from Randolph and Henry at the Virginia Convention.[65] Popular sovereignty remained, to be sure; it would be a rejection of the American Revolution to assert otherwise, but this popular sovereignty remained connected to, and entwined with, state sovereignty. Thus, whether Virginia entered into the reformulated union with conditional amendments (Randolph's idea) or with a new convention to consider amendments (Henry's), either way the people of the Commonwealth of Virginia were entering into a compact with the citizens of the other several states. What is more, in the other states the overwhelming majority subscribed to the compact theory, no matter how supportive of the Constitution they might have been, and, with the exception of James Wilson and a few other notable Nationalist ideologues, the idea of an aggregate American people never seemed to be entertained seriously by anyone. Randolph and Henry were merely giving the first voices to an idea in which most already subscribed.

Two days after the defeat of Henry's proposals, the Wythe committee reported its suggestions for amendments. Following the established pattern of separating a bill of rights from structural amendments, the committee used its bill of rights in a fashion similar to that of their own 1776 Declaration of Rights. It concentrated more on the principles of government than actual liberties that needed protection, although it did acknowledge a few specific liberties such as no cruel or unusual punishment, and the protection of the trial by jury. On the structural amendment side, the Wythe committee suggested twenty-one alterations all of which were issues that dominated the debates at the convention. The first suggestion on the list regarded the explicit protection of state sovereignty. It stated that "each State in the Union shall respectively retain every power, jurisdiction and right, which is not by this Constitution delegated to the Congress of the United States, or to the departments of the Federal Government."[66] When these suggestions passed, the Virginia convention attached the conditions to its instrument of ratification, thereby making amending the Constitution an expectation of Virginia's ratification. At the same time, Virginia's resolution adopting the Constitution was the first formal instrument that invoked the idea of "that which is not given is reserved" as part of their reasoning for adopting the Constitution. It openly embraced the compact theory by stating how the "people of the United States" granted all the powers given to the Constitution. If the new government "perverted to their injury or oppression and that every power not granted thereby remains with them and at their will" then the people of each state reserve the right to reassume those powers.[67]

While Virginia was the first state to make both amendments an expectation of ratification and acknowledge the compact theory, it was not the only state to do so. New York, the last major state to ratify, also endorsed both forms. Like Massachusetts and Virginia, New York leaned heavily against ratifying the Constitution.[68] Also similar to those states, they had very talented and able Federalists willing to defend the Constitution. Although parts of New York's convention witnessed animosities sometimes overtaking reasoned debate, after several weeks the state still seemed unwilling to embrace the new plan of government. Most Anti-Federalists, such as the very capable Melancton Smith, the rumored author of several major Anti-Federalist tracts, remained committed to their belief that the Constitution, and its siphoning of state powers, equated the loss of liberty and throughout the convention offered numerous proposals to amend the document. Even after word of New Hampshire's ratification—the ninth state to do so, which signified the Constitution's formal adoption—and Virginia's conditional ratification they remained determined to see amendments proposed.[69]

Therein lay the problem with New York's ratification convention. By early July, the New York convention had suggested a multitude of amendments, but it was not clear which amendments the Anti-Federalists considered the most important. This problem was complicated on July 7 when Anti-Federalist John Lansing proposed a bill of rights that he demanded be "prefixed" to the Constitution and made their acceptance conditional for New York's ratification.[70] By that point, however, ten states had ratificed the Constitution. Thus, Federalists asked what purpose would forcing a conditional ratification serve? Adding to the question, John Jay, a strong Federalist, co-author of several "Publius" epistles, and author of his own influential essay, mentioned that any proposed bill of rights could "incorporated in the Ratification" in a manner similar to

Virginia's.[71] A committee appointed to sort out all the various amendments added to the confusion when it categorized some proposals as "recommendations" while noting others as merely explanatory of the convention's sentiments.[72] The committee also reported that New York would ratify the Constitution on the "firm Reliance and on the express Condition that the Rights" contained in their list would not be "lost[,] abridged[,] or violated" by the Constitution.[73]

Once again, Jay argued that this form advocated a conditional ratification and such a condition was impermissible. Jay then sought a compromise. He requested the convention strike out any explicit reference of conditional ratification but added that suggestions for amendments that might clarify aspects of the Constitution or that the state deemed necessary "ought to be recommended." Although Jay did not specify which amendments should be included, and he probably did so on purpose, he hoped his gambit would pay off as it had for Virginia.[74]

At first, however, Jay's efforts seems doomed for failure. Melancton Smith tried to reconcile the call for conditional ratification with the Constitution's amending procedure of Article V by altering Jay's proposal by stipulating that Congress could not exercise several powers until a "Convention shall be called and convened for proposing amendments."[75] At this juncture, Hamilton restated Jay's position that the state ratify the Constitution but include an actual list of amendments it would like to see included in the charter. Hamilton hoped that having a concrete list of amendments might appease members who would be willing to ratify on the expectation that the first Congress would meet their desire for amendments. The convention took over a day debating Hamilton's motion, resulting in what one recent commentator aptly described as a "mind-boggling" number of motions, including a motion by Hamilton to adjourn the convention in fear of losing the vote for ratification.[76]

Hamilton's attempt to have the convention accept an amended version of Jay's motion failed, but it was not a total failure. Soon after the dizzying motions began to work themselves through the convention, the convention began consideration of Melancton Smith's earlier proposal to accept ratification "on express condition" of having the Constitution amended. By this point, however, the New York convention was well aware of Virginia's instrument of ratification, as New York delegates used it in their discussions of various proposed amendments.[77] Virginia's conditional ratification, however, gave the Federalists the edge they needed. Once again, after a complicated debate and the creation of a committee to draw up an instrument of ratification, which included a host of the amendments proposed during the convention, New York ratified the Constitution by a vote of thirty to twenty-seven on July 26, 1788. Yet, along with approving the Constitution the New York convention unanimously endorsed a circular letter they sent to other states calling for a new convention to propose amendments to the Constitution.[78]

New York's resolution adopting the Constitution is the longest of the thirteen states, but in many ways it is very similar to Virginia's, although its list of individual liberties it requests to be protected via amendment was much longer. New York, like Pennsylvania and Virginia, embraced Wilson's non-delegation idea as well as the compact theory by asserting that the "Powers of Government may be reassumed by the People, whensoever it shall become necessary to their Happiness" and that "every Power, Jurisdiction and right, which is not by the said Constitution clearly delegated . . . remains to the People of the several States, or to their respective State Governments."[79] The convention went further than the other states by declaring that it would not tolerate Congress relying upon implied powers to aggrandize itself. Simply because the Constitution denied the government specific powers in Article I, Section 9, did "not imply that Congress is entitled to any Powers not given by the said Constitution; but such Clauses are to be construed either as exceptions to certain specified Powers, or as inserted merely for great Caution."[80]

Concern for preserving state sovereignty played an integral role in the ratification of Constitution in these three states. Not only was the lack of a statement protecting it one of the primary points opponents could point to as a failure of the Constitution, but it was proof that the new system would lead to tyranny. Thus, for Anti-Federalists to accept the Constitution they needed assurances that this reordering protected the constitutional settlement of the Revolution. Although Federalists maintained that the Constitution was not a threat to the state sovereignty, they nevertheless had to assure their colleagues in a manner more forceful and tangible than just argumentation and wishful thinking. They had to agree that the Constitution would reflect the importance of state sovereignty in the new government. Thus, they agreed to—and in some cases like Virginia—suggested that the instruments of ratification expressed those beliefs. Doing so saved the Constitution from failure.

At the same time, historians often overlook how these instruments offered the first "original meaning" of the Constitution.[81] As Massachusetts, and especially Virginia and New York's adoption made clear, the Congress was not to construct interpretations of the Constitution that would lead to the granting of powers not contained in the charter. To do so would violate the terms of the contract that the states were entering into with one another. In other words, these ratification instruments were trying to kill any tendency to use implied powers before the temptation presented itself.

***

The Constitution's ratification seemed all but over when New Hampshire became the ninth state to ratify, followed quickly by Virginia and New

York. With the Federalists' promises of protecting both the sovereignty of the states and individual liberties hammered out during the battles between Federalists and Anti-Federalists, the Articles of Confederation were replaced. At the same time, however, two states, Rhode Island and North Carolina, both initially refused to adopt the Constitution. Although scholars normally gloss over this important fact, noting that both states accepted the Constitution by 1791, understanding their rejection reveals both the various purposes to which state sovereignty could serve, and, more importantly, the length to which the idea was to remain a critical element of American constitutionalism.

Divided by internal politics born out of economic hardship, Rhode Island's rejection of the Constitution shocked no one.[82] Since the formation of the confederation, the state had asserted its sovereignty in numerous instances and usually with a cantankerous attitude. Their assertions, moreover, often came at the expense of the unified actions of the other twelve states, with the most important being the 1781 impost amendment debacle. Rhode Island's refusal to consent to the amendment led to its failure, destroying the Nationalists' plans and angering many who considered the state as little more than being "with ease be to Satan's resign'd."[83] At the same time, and not without some irony, their rejection in 1781 started the chain of events that led to the Constitutional Convention. Not that that seemed to matter or bother the state since it was the only one who refused to send a delegation to the Philadelphia Convention.

Rhode Island's rejection of the Constitution can be explained by the internal political strife within the state and its near conspiratorial belief any strengthening of federal power would destroy its own economic interest. After rejecting the 1781 impost on grounds that it would strengthen Congress and weaken the export trade, the years following the War for Independence were ones of severe economic depression for the state. The decline was particularly harmful to farmers; the collapse of produce prices left many with crushing debt and calls for relief. The downturn also led to intense political divisions within the state. One faction, called the "Mercantile" party, because its political base was the port towns of Providence and Newport, controlled the state legislature. Ironically, they sought relief by calling for a strengthening of the confederation, hoping that it would rejuvenate the economy. The other faction, calling themselves the "Country" party, sought to alleviate the farmers' struggles with relief laws and paper money. As the economic hardship of the farmers worsened, the state legislature rejected their clamors for paper money, debtor relief laws, and reduced taxation. Frustration boiled over in 1786, when the Country party swept the elections and seized control of the state government. Upon coming to power, they enacted a radical legislative scheme, canceled tax collection, passed debtor relief laws, and issued paper money that creditors were forced take as legal tender or face the forfeiting of their bonds. The Country party even discouraged farmers from selling their crops in Providence and Newport, the centers of opposition to the Country party's policies. Although the intensity of the political strife continued unabated, by 1787, the Country party, through either repudiation or depreciated debt, was on the path of fiscal stability.[84]

This background explains why the state resisted the Constitution. Dominated as it was by the Country party, any attempt to ban paper money—as the Constitution did—as well as grant Congress more authority over foreign and domestic commerce, made this resistance unsurprising. Were the Constitution adopted, it could reverse the Country party's policies and restore the Mercantile party to power. Thus, if Rhode Island were to be fiscally stable, the Country party argued, the Constitution would have to be rejected. The Country party, worried by the possible strength of the Mercantile faction in any potential ratification convention, maneuvered to marginalize their rivals. Rather than hosting a ratification convention as all other states did, the state legislature determined to base the decision upon a popular referendum. On March 24, 1788, in a vote of 2,711 to 239, Rhode Island overwhelmingly rejected the Constitution. Although the state legislature noted that its citizens had rejected the Constitution "upon pure Republican Principles," the reality was not quite idyllic.[85] There is no doubt that most residents of the states believed the Constitution could threaten Rhode Island's sovereignty; nevertheless, this appeal to their sovereignty was not based upon the fear that liberty itself was threatened. Rather, they feared the Constitution would repeal popular policies of the Country party. In essence, economic self-interest rather than "pure republican principles" drove Rhode Island's rejection.

North Carolina's refusal to ratify, however, derived from their traditional defense of self-government and belief fettered authority best secured liberty.[86] This principled, and distinctly nomocratic, stance both complicates scholars' understanding of North Carolina's rejection and, ultimately, makes its rejection all the more important. At the same time, because the state decided to hold its ratification convention in July 1788, with full knowledge that ten states (New York's ratification had not reached North Carolina by the time its convention met) had accepted the Constitution, many outside observers assumed the state would ratify quickly rather than risk being outside the union. The convention, however, refused "to be thus intimidated into a measure of which we may disapprove" and risked standing alone.[87]

That Anti-Federalist sentiment ran very high in the Tarheel state was not surprising. Its citizens, skeptical of centralized power, had jealously protected their rights, as evidenced during the Regulator Rebellion of 1765–1774 and the Revolution. During the Revolution, the state applied its traditional resistance to central authority by adopting a lengthy declaration of rights. More than just a mere statement of fundamental principles, the declaration restricted the state's power with explicit protections of civil liberties such as protecting trial by jury, prohibiting cruel and unusual punishment, and forbidding blanket search warrants. In essence, the declaration enumerated the limitations of government power and indirectly stated that when government was limited in purpose and confined to known powers, liberty remained secured.[88]

This principled belief that government required strict limits not only manifested itself in the state's declaration of rights, but also in North Carolina's actions as part of the Continental Congress. Recall that it was Thomas Burke, the state's representative in the Congress, who fought for a provision in the Articles of Confederation protecting the sovereignty of the states. Although the details and overall importance of the amendment have been discussed earlier, it bears repeating here that Burke's amendment sought to contain the Articles to only those strict purposes for which was created. In turn, this limitation provided further protection of North Carolinians' liberty.

North Carolina's traditional belief that government required strict limitations explains much of its large-scale resistance to the Constitution. It also makes the Tarheels' rejection of the Constitution less surprising than it might seem at first glance. At the same time, leading opponents in the state such as Willie Jones, Samuel Spencer, and Timothy Bloodworth, realizing the size of their majority, maneuvered to guarantee the defeat of the Federalists.[89] In many ways, then, the Federalist defeat at the Hillsborough convention was all but assured; only the debates remained. Yet, the convention's debates were analogous to those of the other states, with its central theme being the impact of the Constitution upon liberty and the states.

North Carolina Federalists and Anti-Federalists united in defense of state sovereignty at the convention. Few Federalists in the other ratification conventions were as bold as James Iredell, the Federalist leader of the convention, who "heartily agree[d] . . . that, if any thing in this Constitution tended to the annihilation of the state government, instead of exciting the admiration of any man, it ought to excite the resentment and execration. No such wicked intention ought to be suffered."[90] Instead, he argued, states "must be left to the operation of its own principles." Federalists in other states avoided such definitive statements on the convention floor, offering, instead, weak assurances. Iredell's comments, however, were typical of Federalists in North Carolina. They reflected the general concern that state sovereignty remain the foundation of the constitutional settlement of the Revolution. In other words, Federalists insisted that the union remained a "government for confederated states; that, consequently, it can never intermeddle where no power is given."[91]

North Carolina Anti-Federalists did wax hyperbolically about the potential dangers of the Constitution, but most agreed with many of the Constitution's provisions. Yet, they opposed the document on grounds that it lacked any real limitation upon federal power. Rather, by draining too many of the states' sovereign powers, it repudiated the Revolution by "apparently look[ing] forward to a consolidation of the government of the United States, when the state legislatures may entirely decay away."[92] The Constitution's power was so uncontrollable, it would "sweep off all the Constitutions of the states . . . [and] repeal of every act and Constitution of the states" and destroy the people's liberty.[93] Making this potential for tyranny all the worse, the Constitution named itself the superior when the inevitable "clashing and animosities" between state and federal law occurred, even if state law that might be better suited to protect the people and the state.[94] Nor could states or the people obtain a redress from federal action as the Constitution provided no recourse. Even the judiciary, the primary place to obtain justice, was sworn to uphold the supremacy of the Constitution.[95]

To the Anti-Federalists, then, the proposed Constitution threatened the very foundations of what North Carolina considered necessary for liberty. Were the Constitution adopted as written, the state would be impotent and unable to protect the liberty of its people. Ultimately, there-fore, they insisted the people of North Carolina resist surrendering more authority and reject the Constitution lest the "iron glove of tyranny" be forever placed around their necks. Otherwise, to adopt it "in its present mode, must end the subversion of our liberties."[96]

To prevent this tyranny, Judge Spencer, believing "the rights of indi-viduals ought to be properly secured," argued for "such a clause in the Constitution as there was in the Confederation, expressly declaring, that every power, jurisdiction, and right, which are not given up by it, remain in the states." Protecting state sovereignty "would render a bill of rights unnecessary" and "constitute this security" because it limited the Consti-tution to only its delegated powers.[97] Should the Constitution fail to in-clude such an amendment, Spencer and the Anti-Federalists, like other conventions, submitted a list of amendments—many of which they bor-rowed from the Virginia Convention's suggestions—to protect individual liberties. In the end, the convention demanded twenty-six alterations to the Constitution, the first being an amendment declaring "[t]hat each state in the Union shall respectively retain every power, jurisdiction, and right, which is not by this Constitution delegated to the Congress of the United States, or to the departments of the federal government." Until the Constitution reflected these changes and North Carolinians were satis-fied that federal power was limited and more specifically proscribed, the state would not join the union.[98]

Federalists criticized making amendments a precursor to adopting the Constitution. Despite agreeing that state sovereignty and liberty required protecting, the demand of the Anti-Federalist majority, they demurred, smacked of dictating to the other states. It meant being out of the union, and the possibility of dire consequences for the state. It was better to follow the other states and accept the Constitution and Federalists' promise that the first Congress would protect state sovereignty.[99] The Anti-Federalist majority, however, pugnaciously refused to acquiesce in their demand. They lacked "apprehension that the other states would refuse to admit them into the Union, when they thought proper to come in."[100] The position was clear: either change the Constitution to protect liberty and state sovereignty or North Carolina would remain out of the union.

The North Carolina convention did not reject the Constitution wholesale. They argued that they would adopt the document only if Congress amended the Constitution to protect state sovereignty and personal liberties. This is an important distinction. Although other states suggested alterations, they based their ratifications upon Federalists' promises that the first Congress would amend the Constitution. North Carolina took the bold step of actually making these conditions prerequisites for adoption. Promises could be broken, but actions could not. In a subtle way, then, they transformed the ratification process from an adopt or reject situation into one where, if the union was to be made more perfect, the sovereignty of the states would be protected.

The ratification of the Constitution came with conditions.[101] Americans were too devoted, too attached, to state sovereignty and its role in protecting their liberty to agree to a new government that did not protect what the Revolution established. Thus, the Federalists made promises that the new government would not only remain contained to those powers it had, but would include a provision acknowledging state sovereignty. Critics of the Constitution, ever weary of centralizing tendencies of the document, would watch to see if the Federalists kept their promises. As the next section will demonstrate, the Federalists would initially honor that pledge but would break the pledges they made to secure ratification shortly thereafter. Thus, the political conflict of the 1790s focused around the continual struggle to maintain state sovereignty's role as the foundation of American constitutionalism.

NOTES

1. Adams to Lee December 3, 1787, in Alonzo Cushing, ed., *The Writings of Samuel Adams* 4 volumes (New York: G. P. Putnam, 1904–1908), 4: 324–25.
2. Patrick Henry to the Virginia Ratifying Convention, June 4, 1788, in Herbert Storing, ed., *The Complete Anti-Federalists*, 7 vols. (Chicago: University of Chicago Press, 1979), 5: 212.
3. Pauline Maier, *Ratification: The People Debate the Constitution, 1787–1788* (New York: Knopf, 2010); Jurgen Heideking, *The Constitution before the Judgement Seat: the Prehistory and Ratification of the American Constitution*, John P. Kaminiski and Richard Leffler, eds. (Charlottesville: University of Virginia Press, 2012).
4. James Madison to Thomas Jefferson, September 6, 1787, in Robert A. Rutland and William M. E. Rachal, eds., *The Papers of James Madison*, 17 vols. (Chicago: University of Chicago Press, 1962–1991), 10: 163–65.
5. Among the leading Anti-Federalist essays, only "Agrippa" called for maintaining the Articles with only slight modifications.

6. Elbridge Gerry, "Objections to Signing the National Constitution," October 18, 1787, in Storing, ed., *The Complete Anti-Federalists*, 2: 6–7.

7. William Grayson, Speech at the Virginia Ratification Convention, June 12, 1788, in John Kaminiski et al., eds., *The Documentary History of the Ratification of the Constitution*, 29 vols. to date (Madison: University of Wisconsin Press, 1976–), 10: 1185.

8. Robert Yates and John Lansing to George Clinton, January 1, 1788, in Bernard Bailyn, *Debates on the Constitution*, 2 vols. (New York: Library of America, 1993), 2: 4.

9. Robert Whitehill, Speech at the Pennsylvania Ratification Convention, November 28, 1787, in Kaminski et al., eds., *Documentary History of the Ratification of the Constitution*, 2: 398.

10. William Findley, "Letter by an Officer of the Late Continental Army," in Storing, ed., *The Complete Anti-Federalists*, 3: 92.

11. Luther Martin, "The Genuine Information Delivered to the Maryland State Legislature," in ibid., 2: 45.

12. "Centinel," Essay 2, in ibid., 147.

13. Richard Henry Lee to Edmund Pendleton, May 22, 1788, in James Ballagh, ed., *The Letters of Richard Henry Lee*, 2 vols. (New York: Macmillan, 1914): 2: 470–72.

14. Henry, Speech to the Virginia Ratifying Convention, June 7, 1788, in Kaminiski et al., eds., *Documentary History of the Ratification*, 9: 1046.

15. "Brutus," Essay 11, in Storing, ed., *Complete Anti-Federalists*, 2: 420.

16. "Impartial Examiner," February 20, 1788, in Murray Dry, ed., *The Anti-Federalist: An Abridgment of the Complete Anti-Federalists* (Chicago: University of Chicago Press, 1985), 282.

17. "An Old Whig," in Storing, ed., *Complete Anti-Federalists*, 3: 24–25.

18. "The Federal Farmer," Essay 4 in ibid., 2: 247.

19. "Brutus," Essay 12 in ibid., 426.

20. "Aggrippa," January 14, 1788, in ibid., 4: 96–97; quote on 97.

21. "Brutus," Essay 1, in ibid., 2: 366.

22. North Carolina Ratification Convention in Philip Kurland and Ralph Learner, *The Founders Constitution*, 5 vols. (Indianapolis, in: Liberty Fund, 2000), 4: 604.

23. "Brutus," Essay 1 in Storing, ed., *Complete Anti-Federalists*, 2: 367.

24. For the "Anti-Federalist" majority in those states see Maier, *Ratification*, passim.

25. James Wilson, "Speech in the State House Yard," October 6, 1787, in Kaminiski et al., eds., *The Documentary History of the Ratification of the Constitution*, 2: 167–72.

26. *Federalist* 39 in George W. Carey and James McClellan, eds., *The Federalist: The Gideon Edition* (Indianapolis: Liberty Fund, 2001), 193–99.

27. Joshua Miller, "The Ghostly Body Politic: The Federalist Papers and Popular Sovereignty," *Political Theory* 16 (1988): 99–119. The classic work on popular sovereignty remains Edmund S. Morgan, *Inventing the People: The Rise of Popular Sovereignty in England and America* (New York: W. W. Norton, 1988).

28. *Federalist* 84 in Carey and McClellan, eds., *The Federalist*, 442–51.

29. Benjamin Rush, "Address to the People of the United States," January 1787, in Colleen Sheehan and Gary L. McDowell, eds., *Friends of the Constitutions: The Writings of the "Other" Federalist*. (Indianapolis, in: Liberty Fund, 1998), 3.

30. William Dauer, "Philo-Publius," in ibid., 110.

31. Fisher Ames, Speech to the Massachusetts Ratification Convention, January 19, 1788, in Kaminiski et al., eds., *Documentary History of the Ratification of the Constitution*, 6: 1255–56. Maier, *Ratification*, 177. Also see ibid., 516n71 that suggests that Ames and other Massachusetts Federalists might not have been as sincere about the Senate's role in protecting state sovereignty as they seem to suggest at the ratification convention.

32. Tench Coxe, "A Freeman" and "An Examination of the Constitution," both in Sheehan and McDowell, eds., *Friends of the Constitution*, 91, 475.

33. John Dickinson, "Fabius" essays 2 and 3 in Sheehan and McDowell, eds., *Friends of the Constitution*, 69.

34. *Federalist* 39 in Carey and McClellan, eds., *The Federalist*, 199.

35. *Federalist* 46 in ibid., 244.

36. Ibid.

37. Ibid.

38. *Federalist* 26 in ibid., 130.

39. Lance Banning, *The Sacred Fire of Liberty: James Madison and the Founding of the Federal Republic* (Ithaca, NY: Cornell University Press, 1995), 195–264.

40. Lee to Edmund Pendleton, May 22, 1788, in Ballagh, ed., *The Letters of Richard Henry Lee*, 2: 470–72.

41. "Cincinnatus," Essay 5, in Bailyn, 1: 118–20, quote on 119.

42. John Lansing, Speech at the New York Ratification Convention, June 24, 1788, in Kaminski et al., eds., *Documentary History of the Ratification of the Constitution*, 22: 1871, 1858–59

43. "Impartial Examiner," February 20, 1788, in Dry, ed., *The Anti-Federalist*, abridged., 282. Also see Mercy Otis Warren's "Columbian Patriot" essay for further fears that the Constitution equated slavery.

44. "Centinel," Essay 2, October 24, 1787, in Storing, ed., *Complete Anti-Federalists*, 2: 146–47.

45. John Smilie, Pennsylvania Ratification Convention, November 28, 1787, in Bailyn 1: 263.

46. Maier, *Ratification*, passim.

47. For the actions of the Pennsylvania Federalists, see ibid., 59–64.

48. Pennsylvania Minority Report in Kaminski et al., eds., *Documentary History of the Ratification of the Constitution*, 2: Storing, *Complete Anti-Federalists*, 617–40. For the Harrisburg gathering see John Bach McMaster and Frederick D. Stone, eds., *Pennsylvania and the Federal Constitution, 1787–1788* (Indianapolis: Liberty Fund, 2011), 561–64, quotes on 561 and 562.

49. Ibid.

50. The amendments are compiled in, Helen E. Veit, Kenneth R. Bowling, and Charlene Bangs Bickford, eds., *Creating the Bill of Rights: The Documentary Record from the First Federal Congress* (Baltimore: The Johns Hopkins University Press, 1991), 14–28.

51. For the Massachusetts ratification debates see Maier, *Ratification*, 155–213.

52. Ibid.

53. Hancock's speech of January 31, 1788 and list of amendments can be found in Kaminiski et al., eds. *Documentary History of the Ratification of the Constitution*, VI: 1379–85.

54. Massachusetts Instrument of Ratification, February 6, 1788, in ibid., 1469–1471.

55. Maier, *Ratification*, 255–319.

56. Lee to Patrick Henry, September 14, 1789, in Ballagh, ed., *Letters of Richard Henry Lee*, 2: 502.

57. Lee to Edmund Pendleton, May 22, 1788, and Lee to Samuel Adams, August 8, 1789, in ibid., 471 and 495.

58. Samuel Adams, Speech of February 1, 1788, at the Massachusetts ratification convention in Kaminiski, et al., eds., *Documentary History of the Ratification of the Constitution*, 6: 1395.

59. For those debates see Maier, *Ratification*, and volumes 8–10 of *Documentary History of the Ratification of the Constitution*.

60. Edmund Randolph, Speech of June 21, 1788, in Kaminski et al., *Documentary History of the Ratification of the Constitution*, 10: 1455.

61. Ibid., 1455–56.

62. Ibid., 1513–14.

63. Henry, Speech to the Virginia Ratification Convention, June, 24, 1788, in ibid., 1474–81.

64. Ibid., 1508n7.

65. Kevin Gutzman, "Edmund Randolph and Virginia Constitutionalism," *The Review of Politics* 66 (Summer 2004), 469–97. I agree with Gutzman's take but would also add Henry's remarks of June 24. I also believe, as I argue throughout, that the idea of

state interposition emerges earlier in the decade during the struggle over the Treaty of Peace.

66. Wythe Committee Report, June 27, 1788, in Kaminski et al., eds., *Documentary History of the Ratification of the Constitution*, 10: 1551–58.

67. Virginia Instrument of Ratification, June 26, 1788, in ibid., 1546.

68. Maier, *Ratification*, 345–400; Linda Grant De Pauw, *The Eleventh Pillar: New York State and the Federal Constitution* (Ithaca, NY: Cornell University Press, 1966); John Kaminski, "New York: The Reluctant Pillar," in Stephen L. Schechter, ed., *The Reluctant Pillar: New York and the Adoption of the Federal Constitution* (Lanham, MD: Rowman & Littlefield, 1985); Robin Brooks, "Alexander Hamilton, Melancton Smith, and the Ratification of the Constitution in New York," *William and Mary Quarterly* 24 (1967): 339–58.

69. For discussion of Smith's possible authorship of several leading Anti-Federalist tracks see Michael Zuckert and Derek Webb, eds., *The Anti-Federalist Writings of the Melancton Smith Circle* (Indianapolis, IN: Liberty Fund, 2009), 397–420;

70. John Lansing, Motion made on July 7, 1788, in Kaminski et al., eds., *Documentary History of the Ratification of the Constitution*, 22: 2110; Maier, *Ratification*, 372.

71. John Jay to George Washington, July 4 and 8, 1788, in ibid., 2115.

72. George Clinton, Speech to the New York Ratification Convention, July, 7, 1788, in ibid., 2112.

73. John Lansing, Draft of Conditional Amendments," July 10, 1788, in ibid., 2126.

74. John Jay, Resolution," July 11, 1788, in ibid., 2130–33.

75. Melcanton Smith, Speech to the New York Ratification Convention," July 17, 1788, in ibid., 23: 2177–78.

76. Maier, *Ratification,* 388.

77. Ibid., 389–93.

78. Ibid.

79. New York Instrument of Ratification and Proposed Amendments in Kaminski et al., eds., *Documentary History of the Ratification of the Constitution*, 23: 2326–34.

80. Ibid., 2326–27. Compare the language quoted here in the New York Instrument with that of Virginia's in ibid., 10: 1551–1556.

81. The exception is Gutzman, *Virginia's American Revolution*, 115–17 and *James Madison and the Making of America*, 233–37.

82. The following paragraphs are taken from John Kaminski, "Rhode Island: Protecting State Interest," in Michael Allen Gillespie and Michael Lienesch, eds., *Ratifying the Constitution* (Lawrence: University Press of Kansas, 1989), 368–90.

83. "A Fair Bargain," *American Museum: Or Repository of Ancient and Modern Fugitive Pieces Prose and Poetical*, vol. 4 (Philadelphia: Mathew Carey, 1787), 189–90.

84. Kaminski, "Protecting State Interest," 370–75.

85. Ibid., 379–80.

86. For North Carolina's convention see Michael Lienesch, "North Carolina: Preserving Rights," in ibid., 343–67; Alan D. Watson, *States' Rights and Agrarianism Ascendant*, in Patrick Conley and John P. Kaminski, eds., *The Constitution and the States: The Role of the Originial Thirteen in the Framing and Adoption of the Federal Constitution* (Madison, WI: Madison House, 1988), 251–68; Louise Irby Trenholme, *The Ratification of the Federal Constitution in North Carolina* (New York: AMS Press, 1967).

87. Griffith Rutherford, Speech at the North Carolina Ratification Convention, in Jonathan Elliot, ed., *The Debates in the Several Conventions on the Adoption of the Constitution* 5 volumes (Washington, DC: n.p. 1836), 4: 15.

88. Lienesch, "Preserving Rights," 343–44.

89. Ibid., 347–50.

90. James Iredell, Speech of July 25, 1788, in Elliot, *Debates in the Several Conventions*, 4: 53.

91. Ibid.; Archibald MacClaine, Speech of July 24, 1788, in ibid., 34.

92. Samuel Spencer, Speech of July 25, 1788, in ibid., 51.

93. Timothy Bloodworth, Speech of July 29, 1788, in ibid., 179.

94. Spencer, Speech of July 28, 1788, in ibid., 136.
95. Ibid., 137.
96. William Goudy, Speech of July 24, 1788, in ibid., 10.
97. Spencer, Speech of July 29, 1788, in ibid., 163.
98. North Carolina Proposed Amendments in ibid., 249.
99. William Davie and Willie Jones, Speeches of August 1, in ibid., 242 and 247.
100. Jones, in ibid., 240.
101. Jack Rakove, *Original Meanings: Politics and Ideas in the Making of the Constitution* (New York: Knopf, 1996), argues throughout that Federalists secured an unconditional ratification of the Constitution. The evidence presented in this chapter flatly contradicts this. Also see Gutzman, *Virginia's American Revolution*, 86.

II

Defending the Revolutionary Settlement

FIVE

Preserving State Sovereignty

The Judiciary Act and the Tenth Amendment

The traditional narrative of American constitutional development in the first decade after the Constitution's adoption stresses change. New Hampshire's ratification of the Constitution in June 1789 completed the secession from the Articles of Confederation and established the *novus ordo seclorum*. Gone was the "league of friendship" that characterized the Articles, replaced by the clarion call for a "more perfect union." Power shifted permanently, if slowly, to the national government, while state sovereignty shrank in importance; so much so, that by 1798, most states seemingly rejected any role for it in constitutional affairs. In essence, the "miracle at Philadelphia" corrected the Revolution's mistaken adherence to state sovereignty. This change, sweeping and total, even if it materialized slowly, created the strong central government necessary for the United States to reach its national greatness.

Like many stories, this traditional one possesses elements of truth, yet oversimplifies by omitting details that might clarify events, and, more importantly, challenge its accepted wisdom. Thus, the story of the Constitution's first decade requires a retelling that is faithful to the sources and the broader context. Rather than being a new "Age of Federalism," ushering in fundamental and necessary changes needed to fulfill a teleological purpose, the years 1789–1800 continued the ideas, concerns, and debates that established constitutional settlement of the Revolution. Although no one could deny that the Constitution had altered some elements of that settlement, during ratification, the Federalists had insisted repeatedly that the Constitution was not a fundamental dismantling of that order nor did it establish a teleological government. Moreover, they promised that the Constitution was a nomocratic government of delegated powers and nothing more, with the enumeration of powers guaranteeing the persistence of liberty and state sovereignty. Throughout the 1790s, the Federalists broke those promises and advanced constitutional arguments that contradicted their positions as articulated during ratification. As the next two chapters demonstrate, the Federalists' arguments of the 1790s orginated with the Nationalists a decade earlier, although the Federalists developed them more fully. In other words, just how the Federalists abandoned their promises, and how Americans responded to Federalist arguments, characterizes much of the history of the Constitution's first decade. The rise of the Federalist and Republican parties, the most important political development of the period, was rooted in the constitutional struggle between Federalists and their nationalist arguments and the Republicans who fought to maintain the Revolution's constitutional order.

***

At first, it seemed the Federalists would keep their promises. Having a firm control of the House of Representatives and a majority in the Senate, they demonstrated sensitivity to questions of state sovereignty in the two major issues that involved federalism during the first session of Congress, the Bill of Rights, and the Judiciary Act. These measures would also be the last times the Federalists demonstrated significant consciousness to state sovereignty. Examining the debates over both issues reveals, even as Federalists exhibited an appreciation of state sovereignty, that the first hints of their duplicity were already present. By the time Secretary of the Treasury Alexander Hamilton offered his suggestions on establishing public credit and a Bank of the United States—the subject of the next chapter—the Federalists were ready to abandon their promises and promote a nationalistic vision radically different from what they had offered during ratification.

Amending the Constitution was the most important issue carried over from the ratification debates. Recall that during the state conventions a statement acknowledging state sovereignty was among the most important recommendations, with some delegates even suggesting that it alone would be enough security against federal power. The significance of a state-sovereignty amendment revealed itself further when Rhode Island and North Carolina refused the Constitution on the explicit grounds that it lacked a protection of state sovereignty. Federalists responded to these calls for amendments by promising to address the issues in the first Congress. In his inaugural address, President Washington made fulfilling this promise his only policy recommendation to Congress.[1] Thus, when the first Congress met, the question was supposed to be not if, but when, and what form these amendments would take. Despite some disappointment in the most fervent Anti-Federalists, when Congress sent a recommended set of amendments to the states for ratification, the last of twelve amendments provided a titular acknowledgment of state sovereignty. As the events of the 1790s proved, a statement recognizing state sovereignty would become an essential weapon in the constitutional battles that lay in the future. At the same time, the fact that the Constitution would actually contain amendments, including a state sovereignty provision, owes itself almost exclusively to James Madison.

If one were to have mentioned in 1788 that Madison would deserve credit for being the "Father of the Bill of Rights," few would have believed it. During the ratification debates, Madison held the Federalist position that a bill of rights was unnecessary since the Constitution was a document of limited and enumerated powers with the states retaining all other sovereign powers.[2] Yet, the strength of Anti-Federalist opposition throughout the country—especially in his home state of Virginia—the arguments from his close friend, Thomas Jefferson, and, what is more debatable, a conversion to the actual importance of amendments, convinced Madison of the necessity of amendments if the Constitution was to be ratified.[3] Despite doubts about the utility of amendments, Madison assumed the role of promise-keeper. During the winter of 1788, Madison reviewed the states' various suggestions for amendments. By 1789, Madison's proposals were ready.

On May 4, 1789, just as the Senate began discussing the Judiciary Act and the House worked on the issue of financing the new government, Madison informed the House that on the twenty-fifth of the month he would submit amendments for consideration. His notification was timely. The next day, fellow Virginia Representative William Bland submitted to the House Virginia's request for Congress to call a second constitutional convention to draft and submit amendments to the Constitution. Although Bland's action stirred some frustration as well as concerns over how to handle the issue, Congress was able to fend off the request by appealing to Madison's previous notification. When Madison's appointed day arrived, the House, in the midst of pressing issues, received Madison's blessing to postpone the issue for two more weeks.

Then, on June 8, Madison asked that the House begin consideration of amendments. His suggestion met intense resistance from some of the Constitution's strongest supporters. Some of the objections were reasonable. James Jackson, who entered Congress as a marginal Federalist from Georgia, believed it was too early in the government's existence to propose changes. Experience would best guide future Congresses to necessary constitutional amendments.[4] Others stressed that considering amendments so soon would delay consideration of more pressing business. Roger Sherman feared that a consideration of amendments at such an early juncture would "alarm more persons than would have their apprehensions quieted thereby."[5] Several suggested sending the idea to committee to "get rid of the subject."[6]

Congress' most devout Federalists, however, lacked their colleague's largesse. They objected to the very purpose for amendments and even questioned Madison's motivations. Fisher Ames, the intellectual leader of the nationalist-minded House members and soon to be Madison's most serious antagonist in the House, suggested privately that Madison was only trying to secure "some popularity—which he wishes." Ames actually applauded the Virginian's natural brilliance and the research conducted to suggest amendments, but mocked the amendments as little more than "hasty-pudding" designed only to "stimulate the stomach" and for "quieting men who attend to sounds only."[7] Another delegate warned that Madison's push for amendments "unhinges the public mind, gives an opening to the artful, unprincipled, and disaffected."[8] Theodore Sedgewick reported to a friend that Madison was a brilliant and true friend to the people, but was "constantly haunted by the ghost [sic] of Patrick Henry." His amendments offered nothing other than "water gruel business" that would do little to "complete the natural arrangement of the national union."[9] The most famous denunciation of the amendments came from Philadelphia Federalist George Clymer. The amendments, he suggested in Congress, were "merely a tub to the whale," a reference to the eighteenth-century practice, made famous by Jonathan Swift's story, "A Tale of a Tub," where whalers would throw tubs overboard in hopes of distracting whales from damaging ships.[10]

These calls for delays, and the outright mocking of the amendments and their sponsor, were the first hints of the Federalist retraction of the promises made during ratification. They may have pledged to add amendments in order to secure ratification, but once the Constitution was adopted, they apparently no longer saw a need to follow through on those guarantees. The scorn the more ardent Federalists heaped upon the proposal is revealing for two other reasons. First, during ratification, Federalists such as Hamilton, James Wilson, Ames, and even Madison, all argued that the limited and enumerated powers of the Constitution rendered a bill of rights unnecessary but agreed to them in order to secure adoption. Yet, when Madison attempted to follow through on those promises, the Federalists did not fall back to those original arguments. Instead, they claimed it was too soon for the amendments as more important business needed addressing first, or that Madison was seeking political gain. In other words, the Federalists sought to delay any consideration of amendments for as long as possible, and with strong implications that they hoped the longer they waited, the less of an issue it would remain. Second, Federalist scorn and delay seemed to be further rooted in the fear that accepting Madison's amendments would be tantamount to accepting the constitutional interpretation of the Anti-Federalists. Madison, however, was doing no such thing. Instead, and as he would later point out, he was simply trying to put into writing the Federalists' understanding of the Constitution at the time of ratification, namely that the document was one of limited and enumerated powers.[11]

Madison seemed to sense the real meaning behind the obstruction when he rejected the pleas for delay. Of course Jackson sought delay, Madison noted, because he was a known opponent of a bill of rights. Madison could have applied his retort to nearly all the Federalists in Congress. He was bound, he said, to his duty to "myself and my constituents" to no longer "let the subject pass in silence." Although he was not seeking a detailed debate at that moment and later agreed to send his proposal to committee for consideration, he nevertheless believed that initiating the subject then, rather than at some unknown date, would demonstrate to the public that Congress planned to honor the promises of the Constitution's supporters. There were simply too "great a number of our constituents . . . among whom are many respectful for their talents, their patriotism, and respectable for the jealous[y] of their liberty" who remain "dissatisfied" with the Constitution. Additionally, if the "two states who have not thought fit to throw themselves into the bosom of the confederacy" could see these amendments, they could enter into "re-union." Therefore, by considering amendments now, "we have in this way something to gain, and, if we proceed with caution, nothing to lose."[12]

Perhaps not too surprisingly, Madison received reinforcements from the few Anti-Federalists in the House. His fellow Virginian John Page warned that "unless you take early notice of this subject you do not have the power to deliberate" because "the people will clamor for a new convention."[13] Page's warnings were echoed by Thomas Sumter of South Carolina who warned that failure to consider amendments would "give fresh cause for jealousy; it will rouse the alarm which is now suspended, and the people will become clamorous for amendment" and might resort to another convention.[14] Elbridge Gerry, who had refused to sign the Constitution, also supported Madison. He reminded his colleagues to "consider the situation of the states." Several states had ratified the Constitution "with a perfect reliance on congress for its improvement." Should those states' recommendations be "totally neglected" it could create "no small occasion for disgust." Gerry furthered his argument by reminding Congress that the Massachusetts ratification instrument had instructed its federal delegation to "press the amendments recommended by the convention at all times, until they had been maturely considered by congress."[15]

Nor were these warnings idle threats. Should the Federalist postpone—or permanently delay—the promised amendments, including an acknowledgment of state sovereignty, the states were more than ready to seek these changes themselves. The Virginia proposal to call for a new convention, which Bland submitted the day after Madison gave his notice, was not the first time a state had threatened a new convention. As soon as it had ratified the Constitution, Virginia Anti-Federalists had made calls for a new convention, as had those in New York and Pennsylvania. Several states, including those just mentioned, had instructed their congressional delegation to make a push for amendments until Congress acted.[16] Although Federalists considered this a nightmare scenario, nevertheless if they refused to follow through on their promises, the states were ready to act. Historians dismiss too quickly the Anti-Federalists' calls for a second convention. To do so ignores not only the sincerity of Anti-Federalists' desires to see changes made to the Constitution, but also the degree to which they were ready to hold Federalists accountable for their promises, or, if that failed, to make the changes themselves.

With this small, but vocal, support, Madison read aloud his suggested amendments. Two of his suggestions are of particular importance for our purposes. First, Madison proposed an amendment denying the federal government and the states the power to "violate the equal rights of conscience, or the freedom of press, or the trial by jury in criminal cases."[17] Although the proposal's application might seem odd and a violation of state sovereignty, Madison explained that most Americans considered these particular liberties as the most important, and thus his suggestion was commensurate with those thoughts. The Constitution already denied the states certain powers, such as bills of attainder, and "all hands" admitted that "state governments are as liable to attack these invaluable privileges as the general government."[18] Protecting these fundamental liberties, therefore, should not be viewed as a controversial attack upon state sovereignty, but a "cautiously guarded" defense of liberty. Furthermore, Madison added, nearly all states protected these rights in their own declaration of rights, and "he could not see any reason against obtaining a double security." The second proposal that touched upon state sovereignty originated from the "particularly anxious" recommendation of the states that "powers not delegated by this constitution, nor prohibited by it to the states, are reserved to the States respectively." Madison confessed that "words which define this more precisely, that the whole of the instrument now does, may be considered as superfluous," but there was "no harm" in such a definitive statement "if gentlemen will allow that the fact is as stated."[19]

A large portion of Madison's remarks sought to stave off anticipated criticism of his proposals. Those comments reveal Madison's understanding of what the amendments were intended to accomplish. Interestingly, and not without irony, Madison opened by recalling Federalists' ratification arguments against a bill of rights. He said, "It has been said that in the federal government [a bill of rights is] unnecessary, because the powers are enumerated, and it follows that all that are not granted by the constitution are retained." While agreeing with this idea in theory, he added, somewhat optimistically, that "even if government keeps within those limits, it has certain discretionary powers" which could "admit to abuses to a certain extent."[20] Madison pointed specifically to the necessary and proper clause of the constitution. Since Congress would determine for itself what was necessary and proper, his proposal further refined the extent of government's power. Additional limitations upon this controversial power would only reassure the Constitution's critics.

Madison also pointed out that his proposals were not an exhaustive enumeration of the people's rights; they included a provision acknowledging the existence of rights beyond those specified. This amendment insulated the people's liberties in two important ways. First, it allowed "independent tribunals of justice" to act as "an impenetrable bulwark against every assumption of power" by the government. The other layer Madison envisioned for the amendment was telling and pregnant with constitutional implications. Since the "greatest opponents to a federal government admit the state legislature to be sure guardians of the people's liberty," the amendment allowed "state legislatures [to] jealously and closely watch the operation of government" and "resist with more effect every assumption of power." Just how the state legislatures would "resist" a federal power grab Madison did not say, but it is difficult see this as anything but a tacit endorsement of some form of state interposition. Madison clearly believed the states could act to protect their citizens' liberty if threated by the general government. Madison then noted that this particular amendment was "proper in itself, and highly politic, for the tranquility of the public mind, and the stability of the government."[21] Although he did not realize it at the time, he would return often to these thoughts as he fought the constitutional battles of the 1790s.

Madison's hope that proposing amendments would reassure critics that the Federalists kept their promises was realized. In the interval between introducing the amendments and the scheduled date for debates, Madison received word that his efforts had quieted critics who thought Congress was devoting too much time to talk of "rum, sugar, and molasses." Other correspondents reported that Virginia's Anti-Federalists were ready to "acquiesce[e] in whatever may be the fate of the proposed alterations."[22] Perhaps even more pleasing to Madison was the report from William Davie of North Carolina. The Tarheel Federalist informed Madison that his advocacy for amendments in the House had "dispersed almost universal pleasure" throughout the state, and the "honest part of our Anti-Federalists publically expressed great satisfaction on this event." Davie was confident that when North Carolina's second ratification convened in November, Madison's proposals would allow the state to quit being "nominally a foreign state" and join the union.[23]

On July 21, as Madison prepared for the debates on his proposal, Congress had to delay once again. On August 13, three months after Madison had initially suggested consideration for amendments, the House began debate. Four days later, Thomas Tucker, a Virginian representative and Anti-Federalist, moved that Madison's proposal to prohibit the states from infringing on religious thought, speech, and press be stricken from the proposal. The proposal, Tucker noted, was "an interference with the Constitution of the several States," and the "Constitution of the United States interfered too much already."[24] Madison defended the clause as the "most valuable" on the list, reasoning that "if there was any reason to restrain the government of the United States" from "infringing upon these essential rights, it was equally necessary that they should be secured against the state governments."[25] The House sided with Madison. Tucker, however, was not finished. When the House considered Madison's proposal that "powers not delegated by this constitution, nor prohibited by it to the states, are reserved to the States respectively," Tucker moved to add the word "expressly" before "delegated."[26] Such wording would have brought the amendment close to the language of Article II of the Articles of Confederation. Madison again objected, this time arguing how "it was impossible to confine a government to the exercise of express powers." Some degree of implied powers, even if strictly curtailed, was necessary for any government's operation.[27] Once again, the House agreed with Madison's wording but not before it added Elbridge Gerry's proviso "and the people thereof" to the clause.[28]

After the House's approval, the Senate, in the midst of finalizing the Judiciary Act, began consideration of the amendments. Because of the Senate's rule against reporting its debates, the content of those discussions are generally unclear. What is known, however, is that the most fervent Federalists, such as Robert Morris, believed the amendments "nonsense" and a "waste of precious time."[29] Senator William Maclay of Pennsylvania recorded in his diary a telling exchange during Senate debates on the amendments. Senators Ralph Izard, John Langdon, and Robert Morris, strong Federalists all, treated the amendments "contemptuously" and sought to delay consideration until Congress' second session. Morris and Langdon both apparently spoke "angrily" against the bill. The rest of the Senate, however, voted against the Federalist trio.[30] This fleeting glimpse once again shows strong Federalists seeking a delay in fulfilling their ratification promise. However, as the debates transpired, one thing became clear, the Senate dropped Madison's provision against state infringement on religion, press, and speech. Though the reasons remain unclear, it is quite probable that the Anti-Federalist members of the Senate, such as Virginia's Richard Henry Lee and William Grayson, were able to defeat the clause. By the end of September, both houses of Congress had agreed to send twelve amendments to the states for ratification.

Madison's amendments had the intended effect he hoped. In November, North Carolina finally agreed to the Constitution, and, a year later, Rhode Island became the thirteenth state to ratify. Despite these positive developments, not everyone believed the amendments satisfied the various objections raised during ratification. Grayson and Lee, both very

strong Anti-Federalists, believed the amendments were "good for nothing" and, when compared with what many of the states had wanted,
"nothing could be more alike." Both feared that without further and
more explicit protections it was "impossible of us not to see the necessary
consolidation of Empire in the natural operation of the Constitution."[31]
Despite varying degrees of satisfaction with Madison's endeavor, there is
little doubt that Madison's amendments eased most of the fears many
Americans had about the Constitution.

Many scholars assert that the Bill of Rights remained unimportant in
the first decades of the Constitution.[32] This is only partially true. Undoubtedly, the first eight amendments became dramatically more important and significant to American constitutionalism after the Civil War
and into the twentieth and twenty-first centuries. But the last of Madison's amendments, which, when ratified in 1791, became the Tenth
Amendment, would be referred to and used throughout the 1790s as a
weapon to resist federal actions. Although the amendment lacked the
clear and concise language of the Burke Amendment of the Articles of
Confederation, and scholars point to the lack of the term "expressly" as
proof that the amendment carried little constitutional weight, this was
not how Americans of this era understood the amendment. When Tucker
attempted to place "expressly" in the wording of the Tenth Amendment,
Madison noted that Congress should understand his amendment to
mean that the federal government only had express powers and minimal
implied authority. Nor was Madison alone in this reasoning. Throughout
the fight over ratification, Federalists made constant references to how, as
Alexander Hamilton noted during New York's convention, "whatever is
not expressly given to the Federal Head, is reserved to the members."[33]
During South Carolina's convention, Federalist Charles Pinckney told the
Constitution's opponents that "no powers could be executed or assumed,
but such as were expressly delegated."[34] During the Virginia ratification
convention, Federalists had assured critics that the Constitution was an
expressed delegation of power.[35] Madison also endorsed this reasoning
in his June 8 speech introducing the amendments. Since the amendments
were refinements upon government's implied power, the Tenth Amendment, as Madison envisioned it, was a working interpretative guide on
how to construe limitations upon federal actions and powers. When combined with Madison's notion that the states would "jealously and closely
watch the operation of government" and "resist with more effect every
assumption of power," it seems clear that Madison believed that states
could employ the Tenth Amendment in a fashion similar to their invoca-
tion of the Burke Amendment during the confederation period. As the
events of the 1790s unfolded, this is exactly what happened.

At the same time, it bears noting that Madison's herculean efforts
forced Federalists to keep their promises. From the response Madison
received when introducing his proposals, there is very little doubt that

had Madison not forced the issue, the Federalist-dominated Congress would not have considered amendments in its first session, if ever. Because of the importance of the Tenth Amendment in constitutional and political battles in the years following its ratification, it is not too far a stretch to see how the entire political and constitutional history of the 1790s (if not all of American history) might have developed in a vastly different way.

***

Although Madison had forced Federalists to consider a bill of rights with its clause protection of state sovereignty, congressional Federalists showed, for one of the last times in the 1790s, acute sensitivity towards federalism in establishing the federal judiciary. In many ways, it had little choice but to be conscious of state sovereignty on this issue. The vagueness of the Constitution's description of the federal judiciary in Article III left to Congress' discretion nearly all the details and specifics, such as any potential inferior courts or the role the state courts could play. During ratification, Anti-Federalists wrote and spoke more on this article than nearly all other sections. They pounced on Article III's vagueness claiming it the harbinger of consolidation. This was fresh on the minds of congressional members. If they wanted to create a judiciary that supported federal authority but also eased the worries of Anti-Federalists, Congress had to weigh equally both the political and constitutional factors.[36]

The necessary attention Congress devoted to state sovereignty contradicts Alison LaCroix's recent argument that the creation of the federal judiciary in 1789 marked a fundamental change in American federalism. Concerns over "locating the initial source of governmental authority," she claims, gave way to questions "delineating the boundaries among the judicial bodies." Jurisdiction, therefore, became "the defining element of American federalism."[37] Although Congress had to decide how to demarcate judicial power between the state and federal courts, LaCroix conflates the connection between jurisdiction and the settling of federalism during this decade. Questions of sovereignty, that "initial source," did not yield to the judiciary simply because of the Constitution's adoption; they remained at the forefront of many constitutional issues throughout the decade. This is why Congress had little choice but to be sensitive towards state sovereignty: not only was state sovereignty the dominant issue during ratification, but two states had rejected the Constitution because they feared it threatened their sovereignty, and state sovereignty shaped American's perceptions towards a federal judiciary. Pursuing an aggressively nationalistic court system in the first months of the

Constitution's operation would have amounted to little more than the assured failure of the new government and the Constitution.

Soon after reaching its quorum in April 1789, the Senate assumed responsibility for creating the judiciary. The committee formed to draft the initial legislation consisted of a member from each state and included a number of leading figures throughout the states such as William Paterson, Caleb Strong, Oliver Ellsworth, and Richard Henry Lee. Ellsworth apparently took the primary lead in the committee.[38] The committee mixed strong proponents of the Constitution, like Strong and Ellsworth, with stern opponents like Lee, thereby ensuring that any offering from the committee would be the product of debate and compromise. Although little evidence of the committee's debates exists, both Ellsworth and Lee noted that "we have no schism, nor much locality" and that a "spirit [is] prevailing that promises to send this system out free from those vexations and abuses that might have been warranted by the terms of the Constitution."[39]

An important question the Senate's judiciary bill had to settle was whether state courts could participate in "diversity cases." Those cases involved suits whose contesting parties were citizens from different states, or one party was a foreigner. Not surprisingly, American opinion, in and out of the Senate, was divided. Both sides understood that the answer held important constitutional ramifications for the new system. If the state courts played no role in the federal system, it could inflame the still simmering fears that consolidation was the goal of the new government.[40] At the same time, should state courts handle the bulk of federal cases, it could retard attachment to the federal government and hobble it from the outset. The issue was made more complicated since several states, Massachusetts and Virginia especially, forbade state officials from holding national offices. At best, it was dubious whether state judges could even consider being a federal judge. Although Massachusetts wrote this prohibition into its 1780 Constitution and could not have foreseen the Constitution, Virginia's restriction, however, was much more explicit and done with the intent of bolstering the state's belief in its sovereignty.[41] In 1789, and in direct response to its state ratifying the Constitution, the Old Dominion enacted "expedient and necessary" legislation that forbade any state official from holding any office under the Constitution.[42] Ironically, Virginia's intent to trumpet its sovereignty in the face of the Constitution actually weakened the state's attempt to curb the federal judiciary. James Madison worried the act would "oblige the fed[eral] Legislature to extend its [i.e., judiciary's] provisions farther than might otherwise be necessary."[43] The respected Virginian jurist Edmund Pendleton agreed, believing the measure would lead to "those high drawn pictures of War between the foedral [sic] and State Judges, and the Officers of both." Massachusetts Representative Caleb Strong worried that Virginia's action would inspire other states to follow suit.[44]

Debate followed the bill's presentation to the Senate in June. It is difficult to know with certainty the intensity of the debates since the Senate did not report its debates at this time. The best source for those debates is the journal of Pennsylvania senator William Maclay whose biting commentary and dark suspicions of everyone's motivations can sometimes cast doubt regarding the tone or intent of a speaker's comments. However real or imagined the tone, the bill certainly met opposition in the Senate. Most of that debate focused on the bill's particulars. Although some voiced concerns that the bill fulfilled the dark prophecies uttered during the ratification conventions. Maclay himself reported in his diary that the bill was "vile . . . Calculated for Expense, and with a design to draw by degrees all law business into the federal courts." He feared consolidation was the "design of some gentleman." In remarks made on the Senate floor, he worried federal courts would interfere with the federal and state legislatures and "giv[e] more power over the liberty of the Citizen to the former than was usually practiced." Such power would only "sow the seeds of dissension."[45]

Some suggested the state courts should carry the majority of federal cases, claiming it would offset any potential large-scale cost of the court system. More importantly, however, it would provide the state another potential mechanism upon which to limit federal power. It was this second view that guided Richard Henry Lee. On June 22, he proposed an amendment to the bill to limit federal courts to only cases of admiralty and maritime law, and that "federal interference shall be limited to Appeal only from the State Courts to the supreme federal court."[46] It might seem odd that such an amendment came from Lee since he sat on the committee that drafted the bill, spoke in generally positive terms about the bill in private correspondence, and was the senator who presented the bill before the Senate. In presenting his amendment, however, Lee read from Virginia's ratification instrument, which called for confining the federal courts to these two cases.[47] This event is revealing, but it was far from "the unusual step" it has been portrayed.[48] It suggests that Lee might have pushed for—and lost—this provision in the committee's deliberations and was making another attempt to convince the entire Senate. Additionally, and more importantly, by reading from Virginia's ratification instrument, Lee evoked the sovereignty of Virginia and defended its desire to protect that sovereignty. Using the word "interference," therefore, was not accidental; it represented how Lee, Virginia, and many of the Constitution's opponents viewed the court's power. Lee's underlying principle received rhetorical backing from South Carolina Senator Pierce Butler. The "ultimate tendency" of the bill, he charged, was to "destroy, to Cut up at the Root the State Judiciaries[;] to Anhialte [*sic*] their whole system of Jurisprudence" and eventually "[s]wallow up every distinguishing mark of a Distinct Government."[49] Allowing federal courts to hear criminal and civil appeals from the state courts opened citizens to repeated "Counter Act[s]" from their adversaries. This bill only "Sow[ed] the Seeds of Jealousy and destroy[ed] the confidence" of the people in the new government since it made "His Situation . . . more precarious than it was under any System of British Jurisprudence heretofore Established in America."[50]

Lee's motion met opposition from Ellsworth and others, including Maclay, who, despite not liking the bill, pointed out that the Constitution "expressly extended" to the federal judiciary questions of federal law and equity.[51] Many of the bill's supporters in the Senate, though of a general Federalist bent, expressed concerns that Lee's proposal would adversely affect state authority. To allow the state courts to act in a federal capacity would, in the words of Caleb Strong, "mark an inferiority on the State to the federal Courts" when such a relationship did not exist.[52] Not only that, but since state judges were not appointed for life tenure as were federal judges, it created the practical problem of what would happen should a state judge be removed from his state position but still hold federal tenure. Ellsworth agreed with Strong's worries about the practicality of state judges also being federal judges, but added that should state courts deal with the majority of federal cases and meet with frequent reversals by the Supreme Court it "would probably more hurt their feelings and their influence."[53] While it is possible that these remarks were a facade designed to demonstrate sensitivity to the issue while whittling away state authority, the fact that these remarks came in private correspondence suggests that they were real concerns. Also, when these statements are contrasted with the remarks of those Federalists who offered harsh assessments about state involvement in the federal courts, it reveals differing concerns within the Federalists.

Nor was the question of the role of state courts confined solely to the Senate. Like that body, and perhaps even more so, opinion throughout the country was divided. Samuel Huntington argued to William Samuel Johnson and Ellsworth that bridging the state and federal courts would "Inspire a Spirit of Candour and Harmony" between the competing entities and could offset fears of "engrossing or absorbing the Government of the Several States."[54] James Sullivan, the Massachusetts lawyer and qualified supporter of the Constitution, questioned whether state courts hearing federal cases would "mak[e] great approaches towards a Consolidation of all the Governments" since the states were "as Independent of it as any other Government officially."[55] The threat to state sovereignty posed by the judiciary bill brought forth new essays from the pseudonymous "Centinel." In essays appearing in the *Independent Gazetteer* from August to November of 1789, "Centinel" picked up where his last anti-ratification essay left off. He attacked the Federalists for their utopian schemes of consolidation, including the federal judiciary. The potential for the "unlimited jurisdiction of the federal courts," he noted in his essay of August 29, "left nothing to the state courts." He admitted that Congress would limit this jurisdiction by legislation, but this was not a strong enough guarantee; at best, it was a tactic designed to lull the public into complacency, thereby allowing Congress to destroy the states and establish the consolidated government Federalists sought. The only hope, he claimed, was to have more "enlightened republicans as Richard Henry Lee, and a [Thomas] Tucker." [56]

Not surprisingly, many Federalists were less sanguine than Huntington and Sullivan. Underwriting Federalist concerns was the fear that using state courts and judges would weaken the federal government. Fisher Ames told one correspondent that it was "little better than madness" to allow state courts to act as lower level federal courts. This madness would disturb "the public tranquility" from the "clashing of intricate claims of jurisdiction . . . the energy of Gov[ernment]may be impaired by entrusting its powers to those who will see a motive and be furnishing with the means of abusing the trust so far as the union will be endangered by the diversity rule" which would invariably lead to "extinguishing the vital principle" of the government's existence." [57] On the floor of the House of Representatives, Ames delivered a powerful address where he argued for the complete separation of federal and state courts. To Ames, the entire question of jurisdiction was wrapped up in the issue of sovereignty, since the "authority to judge, derived from a superior power." For state courts to consider federal law was to have an inferior act as the superior, and thereby "produce a strong confusion of offices and ideas." Any attempt to create concurrent jurisdictions would generate confusion, clashing of interests, and the subordination of state courts, something, he claimed, he did not wish to see. In other words, Ames understood that a limitation upon the federal courts was a limitation upon its authority.[58] Abiel Foster was even less confident than Ames, telling Oliver Peabody that he had "no confidence" that the state courts would follow the Constitution. State judges were "not amenable to the general government," but depended upon the state governments for their livelihood. When a conflict between federal and state law occurred, Foster was confident that the state judges would side with their particular state and not the federal government. Allowing state judges to act in a federal capacity was placing a "worm at the Root of the general Government which must soon destroy its existence." Benjamin Goodhue, a Federalist who left his politics "undisguised," believed using state courts and judges would do little more than create an *imperium in imperio* and "perpetually existing absurdities." [59]

These conflicting sets of opinion led to a final judiciary act that attempted to bridge the divide. The bill President Washington signed into law on September 24 established a six-bodied Supreme Court, and a three-tiered federal system consisting of district, circuit, and the Supreme Court. The act respected state boundaries by calling for at least one district court per state, including ones for the districts of Kentucky and

Maine. Three circuit courts were established, and were broken into the three main regions of the country, Eastern (i.e., New England), Southern, and Middle. The Judiciary Act settled the contentious issue of state courts by splitting the issue. For criminal cases, the state courts played no role and the federal district courts were to hear all cases arising under federal law where the punishment was limited to thirty stripes [i.e., lashings], a maximum fine of one hundred dollars, or six-month imprisonment. District courts also held original jurisdiction in all cases of admiralty and maritime jurisdiction. On other issues, the state and federal courts shared a concurrent jurisdiction. Either a state or federal circuit could hear cases on civil litigation, violations of the law of nations or a treaty; the defendant could decide where to file the claim. Suits of common law, where the United States sued and the amount did not exceed one hundred dollars, were also of a concurrent jurisdiction. In cases where citizens of the same state held competing land claims and the claim exceeded five hundred dollars, the defendant could remove the case to the circuit court. The Supreme Court was given original (but not exclusive) jurisdiction in civil suits where any state or a foreign power was a party, as well as controversies between a state and a citizen or foreigner. Section 25 of the act allowed the Supreme Court to hear cases on appeal from the decisions rendered by the states' highest court. Although this measure would create a great deal of controversy in the early nineteenth century, it generated very little discussion in the final act.[60]

The Judiciary Act reflected a special concern for both the constitutional and the practical. By limiting the types of cases the federal courts would hear, the committee displayed a concern for the authority of the states. It ensured that the federal courts would hear only the more serious of those cases, leaving the rest to the state courts. In theory, if not in practice, this meant that states would remain the primary repository for sovereign authority since it would be those courts, and not the federal ones, that would hear the majority of the cases that originated from federal law. Today, the process of "federal question jurisdiction" requires that all cases arising from federal law be tried only in a federal court, and the idea that states would hear the bulk of those cases would be shocking—in fact, a great deal of scholarship has attempted to comprehend why such a development did not occur in 1789.[61] Yet, this literature overlooks the constitutional world of 1789, where state sovereignty was the foundation of the constitutional system and remained the primary constitutional concern for most Americans. This also overlooks the intense concern that the federal judiciary would "eventually absorb and swallow up the State judiciaries." If the constitutional beliefs of that world are understood, leaving the bulk of federal cases with the states not only ensured that this foundation remained in place but it clarifies why a "federal question jurisdiction" did not occur. Secondly, the committee's working principles demonstrated a more practical concern: costs. To operate a federal judicial system across a vast, and mostly untamed, continent would require heavy expense. The committee attempted to construct a system "in such a Manner as to be as little expensive as possible." Thus, leaving to the states the bulk of cases kept costs to a minimum. At the same time, the division of American opinion over the nature of the federal judiciary, which the act at least attempted to reconcile in some fashion, reaffirmed how issues of sovereignty—the "source of authority" as LaCroix called it—remained vital to understanding how the Constitution would operate. Questions of jurisdiction, while of great importance, were far from the "central organizing principle—the battlefield" of constitutional politics.[62] Rather, the question of jurisdiction was a skirmish waged upon the larger and decade-long battlefield over the nature of American constitutionalism.

The Constitution opened with many Americans concerned about the future of state sovereignty. To secure ratification, Federalists had promised that the Constitution would not only be limited in its scope and power, but that the first Congress would secure amendments, thereby protecting liberty and securing state sovereignty. Through the efforts of James Madison, Congress submitted the Bill of Rights, with a statement acknowledging the principle of state sovereignty, and, with demonstrable sensitivity toward the constitutional and political realities of the ratification debates, established the federal judiciary. Even as these developments pointed toward the Federalists keeping their promises of having state sovereignty as the bedrock of the constitutional system, there were disturbing signs that these promises might be short-lived.

NOTES

1. George Washington, "First Inaugural Address," April 30, 1789, in Dorothy Twohig, ed., *The Papers of George Washington: Presidential Series*, 17 vols. to date (Charlottesville: University of Virginia Press, 1987), 2: 173–77.

2. Lance Banning, *The Sacred Fire of Liberty: James Madison and the Founding of the Federal Republic* (Ithaca, NY: Cornell University Press, 1995), 275–80.

3. Richard Labinski, *James Madison and the Struggle for the Bill of Rights* (New York: Oxford University Press, 2006), 120–77; Lance Banning, *Jefferson and Madison: Three Conversations from the Founding* (New York: Rowman and Littlefield, 1995), 1–26 and *Sacred Fire of Liberty*, 275–80; Kevin R. C. Gutzman, *James Madison and the Making of America* (New York: St. Martin's Press, 2012), 242–75; Andrew Bernstein and Nancy Isenberg, *Madison and Jefferson* (New York: Random House, 2010), 166–210; and Kenneth Bowling, "'A Tub to the Whale:' The Founding Fathers and Adoption of the Federal Bill of Rights," *Journal of the Early Republic* 8 (Autumn, 1988): 223–51. Scholars continue to debate whether Madison had converted to believing amendments an important protection of civil liberties when he offered his amendments. As is quite often the case in his career, Madison seems to straddle the Federalist and Anti-Federalist position, not believing the amendments fundamental, but at the same time realizing that they would protect liberty while not weakening the new government. Whatever his actual beliefs in 1789, there is little doubt that by the end of the decade he came to appreciate their inclusion in the Constitution.

4. James Jackson, June 8, 1789, in *The Founders' Constitution*, Philip Kurland and Ralph Lerner, eds., 5 vols. (Chicago: University of Chicago Press, 1987; reprint, Indianapolis: Liberty Fund, n.d.), 5: 21. Anti-Federalist Adedanus Burke agreed with Jackson. He is the only Anti-Federalist that I have seen who agreed with the Federalists on this issue.

5. Speeches of James Jackson, Roger Sherman, William Loughton Smith, and John Vining, all June 8, 1789, in Helen E. Veit, Kenneth R. Bowling, and Charlene Bangs Bickford eds., *Creating the Bill of Rights: The Documentary Record from the First Federal Congress* (Baltimore: The Johns Hopkins University Press, 1991), 65, 73–76. These three were not the only objectors, but their arguments are illustrative of the general opposition.

6. Sherman, June 8, 1789, in ibid., 93.

7. Fisher Ames to George Richards Minot, May 29, 1789, and Thomas Dwight, June 11, 1789, both in Seth Ames, ed., *The Work of Fisher Ames*, 2 vols. (Indianapolis: Liberty Fund, 1983), 1; 635–38, 641–42.

8. John Fenno to Joseph Ward, July 5, 1789, in Veit, Bowling, and Bickford, eds., *Creating the Bill of Rights*, 257–59.

9. Theodore Sedgwick to Benjamin Lincoln, July 19,1789, in ibid., 263–64.

10. George Clymer to Richard Peters, June 8, 1789, in ibid., 207.

11. Banning, *Sacred Fire of Liberty*, 286.

12. James Madison, Speech of June 8, 1789, in Charles Hobson, Robert Rutland et al., eds, *The Papers of James Madison*, 17 vols. (Charlottesville: University Press of Virginia, 1962–1991), 12: 196–209, particularly 197–99 [hereafter, Madison, *Papers*].

13. John Page, Speech of June 8, 1789, in Viet, Bowling, and Bickford, eds., *Creating the Bill of Rights*, 75.

14. Thomas Sumter, Speech of June 8, 1789, in ibid., 93–94.

15. Elbridge Gerry, Speech of July 21, 1789, in ibid., 99–100. Also see the remarks of Thomas Tucker, July 21, 1789 in Ibid., 101–102.

16. Bowling, "'A Tub to the Whale'": 230.

17. Madison, June 8, 1789, in Madison, *Papers*, 12: 205–206.

18. Madison, June 8, 1789, in Madison, *Papers*, 12: 205–206

19. Ibid., 209.

20. Ibid., 203–205.

21. Madison, *Papers*, 206–207.

22. John Dawson to James Madison, June 28, 1789, and Edward Carrington to James Madison, September 9, 1789, in Madison, *Papers*, 12: 263–64 and 393.

23. William R. Davie to James Madison, June 10, 1789, in ibid., 210–11.

24. Thomas Tucker, August 17, 1789, in Veit, Bowling, and Bickford, eds., *Creating the Bill of Rights*, 181.

25. Madison, August 17, 1789, in ibid.

26. Tucker as reported in the *Congressional Register*, August 18, 1789, in Veit, Bowling, and Bickford, eds., *Creating the Bill of Rights*, 197.

27. Madison, as reported in the *Congressional Register*, August 18, 1789, in ibid.

28. Elbridge Gerry as reported in the *Congressional Register*, August 21, 1789, in ibid., 199.

29. Robert Morris to Richard Peters, August 24, 1789, in ibid., 288.

30. William Maclay, diary entry for August 25, 1789, in Kenneth Bowling and Helen E. Viet, eds., *The Diary of William Maclay and Other Notes on Senate Debates, March 4, 1789–March 3, 1971* (Baltimore: The John Hopkins University Press, 1988), 133 [hereafter, Maclay, *Diary*].

31. William Grayson and Richard Henry Lee to Patrick Henry, September 28, 1789, in James Ballagh, ed., *The Letters of Richard Henry Lee*, 2 vols. (New York: Macmillan, 1914), 2: 507–508 and Grayson to Henry, September, 29, 1789, in Viet, Bowling, and Bickford, eds., *Creating the Bill of Rights*, 300.

32. The literature on the Bill of Rights is immense. For their supposed relative unimportance in the first decades under the Constitution see Pauline Maier, *Ratifica-*

tion: The People Debate the Constitution (New York: Simon and Schuster, 2011), 459–64; Robert Allen Rutland, *The Birth of the Bill of Rights, 1776–1791* Bicentennial Edition (Boston: Northeastern University Press, 1955; 1991), 219–42; and Akhil Amar, *The Bill of Rights: Creation and Reconstruction* (New Haven: Yale University Press, 2000). As the rest of this book will demonstrate, the First and Tenth Amendments were of immense importance in decade of the 1790s.

33. Alexander Hamilton, speech made during the New York Ratification Convention, June 28, 1788, in Kaminski et al., eds., *Documentary History of the Ratification of the Constitution*, 22: 1982. For a longer examination of how the Founding era assumed and implied "expressly" to the delegation of federal power see the excellent essay by Kurt Lash, "The Original Meaning of an Omission: The Tenth Amendment, Popular Sovereignty and "Expressly" Delegated Power," *Loyola Legal Studies Paper* 2007–31 (October, 2007): 1–54.

34. Charles Pinckney as quoted in Lash, "The Original Meaning of an Omission:," 4.

35. John Kaminiski et al., eds., *The Documentary History of the Ratification of the Constitution*, Volume 10. Also see Kevin R. C. Gutzman, *Virginia's American Revolution: From Dominion to Republic, 1776–1840* (New York: Lexington Books, 2007), 83–112.

36. For an argument that places the emphasis on the political over the constitutional see Maeva Marcus and Natalie Wexler, "The Judiciary Act of 1789: Political Compromise or Constitutional Interpretation," in Maeva Marcus, ed., *Origins of the Federal Judiciary: Essays on the Judiciary Act of 1789* (New York: Oxford University Press, 1992), 13–39. Also see Wythe Holt, " 'To Establish Justice:' Politics, the Judiciary Act of 1789, and the Invention of the Federal Courts," *Duke Law Journal* 38 (1989): 1421–1531.

37. Alison LaCroix, *The Ideological Origins of American Federalism* (Cambridge: Harvard University Press, 2010), 179, 177 and 178.

38. Most of what follows is taken from Maeva Marcus et al., eds., *The Documentary History of the Supreme Court of the United States, 1789–1800*, 7 vols. to date (Columbia: Columbia University Press, 1992, 1986), Volume 4: *Organizing the Federal Judiciary: Legislation and Commentaries*,: 23 [hereafter, Marcus, *Documentary History of the Supreme Court*]. Also extremely useful is Julius Goebel, Jr., *History of the Supreme Court of the United States: Antecedents and Beginnings to 1801*, Volume 1 of the *Oliver Wendell Holmes Device: History of the Supreme Court*, 12 vols. to date (New York: The Macmillan Company, 1971)1: 457–508.

39. Oliver Ellsworth to Oliver Wolcott, Sr., May 30, 1789, in Marcus, *Documentary History of the Supreme Court*, 4: 399, and Richard Henry Lee to Patrick Henry, May 28, 1789, in Ballagh, ed. *The Letters of Richard Henry Lee*, 2: 486–89.

40. Editor's note to the Judiciary Act, in Marcus, *Documentary History of the Supreme Court*, 4: 24–25.

41. Massachusetts Constitution, Part 2, Chapter 6, Article 2.

42. "An Act to Disable Certain Officers under the Continental Government, from Holding Offices under the Authority of this Commonwealth," December 8, 1788, in William Henning, ed., *Statutes at Large: Being a Collection of all the Laws of Virginia from the First Session of the Legislature, in the Year 1619*, 13 vols. (New York, Richmond, and Philadelphia, 1819–1823), 12: 694–95.

43. James Madison to Edmund Pendleton, April 19, 1789, in Marcus, ed., *Documentary History of the Supreme Court*, 4: 375.

44. Edmund Pendleton to James Madison, May 3, 1789, in Madison, *Papers*, 12: 124.

45. McClay, June 29, 1789, in Maclay, *Diary*, 155–56.

46. Lee's motion is mentioned in ibid., and Marcus, *Documentary History of the Supreme Court*, 4: 44.

47. "Virginia Instrument of Ratification," in Kaminski et al., eds., *Documentary History of the Ratification of the Constitution*, 10: 1551–56

48. "Editor's Note on the Judiciary Act," in Marcus, *Documentary History of the Supreme Court*, 4: 31.

49. Pierce Butler as recorded by William Maclay, July 17, 1789, in Maclay, *Diary*, 155–56.

50. Ibid.

51. Maclay, *Diary*, 155–56.

52. Ibid.

53. Oliver Ellsworth to Richard Law, August 4, 1789, in Marcus, *Documetnary History of the Supreme Court*, 4: 495.

54. Samuel Huntington to William Samuel Johnson and Oliver Ellsworth, April 30, 1789, in ibid., 4: 383.

55. James Sullivan to Elbridge Gerry, March 22 and 29, 1789, in ibid., 369 and 372, quote from 369.

56. The "Centenial" essays appeared in the *Independent Gazetteer,* August 27 to November 11, 1789. The quotes are from the August 29 essay.

57. Fisher Ames to John Lowell, July 28, 1789, in Marcus, ed., *Documentary History of the Supreme Court*, 4: 480–83. Also see his July 12, 1789, letter to William Tudor, in ibid., 461, where Ames believes any judiciary bill will be nothing more than "patch work by fanciful amendments," Ames to Theophilus Parsons, August 3, 1789, in ibid., 492.

58. Fisher Ames to John Lowell and Ames to George Richard Minot, September 3, 1789, in ibid., 506–507.

59. Abiel Foster to Oliver Peabody, September 23, 1789, in ibid., 515–17.

60. The text of the Judiciary Act can be found in *Annals of Congress*, 1st Congress, 1st Session, 2239–55. For the nineteenth century debate over this section of the act see F. Thorton Miller, *Juries and Judges Versus the Law: Virginia's Provincial Legal Perspective, 1783–1828* (Charlottesville: University Press of Virginia, 1994), 80–90; Richard E. Ellis, *The Union at Risk: Jacksonian Democracy, States' Rights, and the Nullification Crisis* (New York: Oxford University Press, 1987), 1–40, especially 31; and John C. Calhoun, "A Discourse on the Constitution and Government of the United States," in *Union and Liberty: The Political Philosophy of John C. Calhoun,* Ross M. Lence, ed. (Indianapolis: Liberty Fund, 1992).

61. Charles Warren, "New Light on the History of the Judiciary Act of 1789," *Harvard Law Review* 27 (Nov. 1923): 49–132; Marcus and Wexler, "The Judiciary Act of 1789: Political Compromise or Constitutional Interpretation," and especially Wilfred J. Ritz, *Rewriting the History of Judiciary Act of 1789: Exposing Myths, Challenging Premises, and Using New Evidence*, Wythe Holt and L. H. LaRue, eds., (Norman: Oklahoma Press, 1990), 59–60. Interestingly, and despite my disagreement on her primary argument about the Judiciary Act, LaCroix, *Ideological Origins of American Federalism*, 185, shares my sentiment.

62. LaCroix, *Ideological Origins of American Federalism*, 178.

SIX
===

Breaking the Promise

Hamiltonianism

At the start of 1790, some Anti-Federalists must have been relieved over how Congress had demonstrated noticeable care towards state sovereignty in the addition of the Bill of Rights and the creation of the judicial system. To be sure, the proposed state sovereignty amendment lacked the definitive language of the Burke Amendment, and James Madison had to force Federalists to uphold their promises to amend the Constitution, but it was protection nonetheless. With the federal judiciary, the state courts would play some role in the system thereby curbing some of the potential for mischief from that branch. Thus, all indications pointed toward continued respect for the sovereignty of the states. By the end of the year, however, the growing sense that the Anti-Federalists' prophecies were accurate replaced those hopes and expectations. The Federalists, it seemed, wanted a consolidated government vested with full sovereign power. Proof of this fear, they believed, was found in the economic program of the first secretary of the treasury, Alexander Hamilton.

During the imperial crisis, Hamilton argued forcefully for an imperial Constitution rooted in the idea of Crown-in-Colonial-Assembly, but by the time he accepted Washington's proposal to be the first treasury secretary in 1789, he had long established his nationalist credentials. From his authorship of the "Continentialist" essays and his partnership with Robert Morris and the Nationalist faction in Congress to his defense of the Constitution during New York's ratification debate, Hamilton was a primary leader of the Nationalists. During the ratification convention, Hamilton, like many Federalists, worked to assure critics that the Constitution created a government of limited powers and objectives. In *Federalist* 84, Hamilton argued that not only was a Bill of Rights unnecessary but also "dangerous," because it "would afford a coloruable [*sic*] pretext to claim more than was granted." In other words, and not without a considerable degree of irony, Hamilton believed a bill of rights implicitly endorsed an expansive reading of enumerated powers. Further in the essay, he claimed the Constitution itself was a bill of rights because it "declare[d] and specified the . . . structure and administration of government."[1] According to Hamilton in 1788, the Constitution's sole purpose was to detail the procedural mechanisms of and limitations on power of the federal government. It is hard to know how much Hamilton actually believed what he wrote in this and similar remarks he made during ratification. Just two years later, as treasury secretary, Hamilton responded to Congress' request on how to address the country's fiscal situation by advocating a nationalistic program and reading of the Constitution that contrasted starkly with his writings and arguments of just two years earlier.

Hamilton's answer to Congress' request was the *Report on Public Credit* and *Report on the National Bank*, two of the most important state papers in American history. Both were testaments to Hamilton's undeniable genius and his nationalistic vision. His financial plans sought nothing short of "establishing the economic future and political character of the new republic."[2] In the *Report on Public Credit*, Hamilton proposed a sweeping and complicated overhaul of American finances that revolved around the United States establishing a permanent and funded debt with interest paid through excise taxes and impost duties. The government would always pay the interest of this debt but would never sink the principal. At the same time, he sought to extinguish the old confederation and state bonds through an exchange program that allowed current holders of those bonds to trade them for new bonds at a guaranteed interest rate and the opportunity to purchase western lands at reduced prices. Hamilton also advised that the federal government assume the Revolutionary War debt of individual states and incorporate them into the federal government's debt. In December 1790, in his *Report on the National Bank*, Hamilton advised Congress to establish a Bank of the United States, with the federal government holding 20 percent of the bank's stock. A national bank, he argued, would be an indispensable aid to the national government by providing a depository for federal revenue, a ready source for cash in emergencies such as war, and stabilization of American currency.[3]

Elements of Hamilton's plan were not exactly new; they strongly echoed aspects of Robert Morris' plan from a decade earlier, although they far surpassed the superintendent's in scope and complexity.[4] Like Morris' plan, their nationalistic thrust was undeniable. Hamilton, however, provided very little constitutional justification in either of his reports. He appealed only to the idea that the Constitution was "cloathed [*sic*] with powers competent to calling forth the resources of the community" and required the paying of its debts. He also assumed that it must be constitutional because he thought his plan was in the best interest of the country.

Any constitutional justification Hamilton could offer would have been ancillary to his thinking. He was more concerned with having "all public creditors receive their dues from one source," namely the federal government, and a national bank that would "insinuate itself into every branch of industry" in order to "produce strong prepossession in its favor in all who consider the firm establishment of the national government as necessary to the safety and happiness of the country."[5] In this, Hamilton's ideas were a maturation of those that he first laid out in the early 1780s. He sought to detach Americans, particularly the monied class, from their localism and state interests and bind them to the federal government. In so doing, Hamilton believed the bonds of union would be stronger and the stability of the national government secured. This vision of a robust central government, with its funded debt, national bank, and internal taxation, differed vastly from what most Americans at that time considered necessary or desirable.[6]

As many historians have pointed out, Hamilton sought to refashion the United States into a European-like state, with Britain serving as the preferred model. In the decades following the Glorious Revolution of 1688, England established a fiscal-military state second to none. They achieved this feat by establishing a national bank, a permanent funded debt, a bureaucracy of officials, direct—and heavy—taxation, and a powerful military. Under the leadership of Robert Walpole, the chancellor of the exchequer and England's first prime minister, Parliament became more unified and its politics more stable. Walpole used the powerful influence of the monarchy to offer patronage to members of Parliament (or their family members) in order to secure votes and approval for policy guidelines. In other words, the entirety of the rise of England's fiscal-military state was possible due to a heavily centralized and unified government.[7] Yet, Walpole's plans received criticism. Critics, like the authors of "Cato's Letters," the Viscount Bolingbroke, and James Burgh, commonly referred to as the "Country Opposition," all claimed that Walpole's "Court" policies had corrupted the British government and destroyed the virtue and liberty of the people. Liberty would no longer be the concern of Englishmen, the Country Opposition insisted. Instead, the English would now focus on acquiring more luxury and securing government jobs. Speculators, or "Stockjobbers" as they were derisively called, would seek their self-interest above all else. Through all of this, the government would continue to aggrandize itself. In England, these criticisms came from a distinct, if vocal, minority.[8] In America, however, these ideas galvanized the political resistance to Britain.[9] Although the degree to which Hamilton accepted or even celebrated this English "corruption" remains debatable, what is clear is that the centralizing elements of the fiscal-military state underpinned the plan Hamilton submitted to Congress.[10]

The reports struck Congress like a bolt from a clear sky. Although no one questioned that the United States needed to fund and pay its debts, many doubted Hamilton's proposed method. This concern led to the first true schism in Congress. What concerned many congressmen was Hamilton's plan to exchange the old confederation bonds. Opponents claimed the plan violated the contract offered during the original purchase. The "Constitution has no power to modify it" through legislative action, argued Thomas Hartley.[11] James Jackson of Georgia suggested that England's funding scheme was designed to placate that nation's "monied interest" after the Glorious Revolution. He hoped that America's Constitution was too "firmly established without the assistance of stock-jobbers" and "not depend[ent] upon the support of a party." Such a group would "deceive us, and lead us, and our posterity, into a wilderness of politics, from which we shall never be able to extricate ourselves." He was not willing to take such a "dangerous leap in the dark."[12] In a shock to Hamilton, and in the first open rupture between the two, James Madison sided with the opposition, believing the plan unjust and a payout to the unvirtuous.[13]

Congressmen specifically criticized the assumption proposal on sectional grounds. Southern states, who had mostly paid off their wartime debt, viewed assumption as favoring the eastern states, few of which had paid their debt. It was as unjust, southerners claimed, for their citizens to pay taxes to debts contracted by other states as it would be for eastern states to pay taxes to extinguish southern debts. The taxes needed to pay those debts would not be for the general welfare, they claimed, but to "benefit large cities, like Philadelphia and New York." In turn, this would depress the agricultural economy and hard work of the "remote parts of the continent."[14] This notion of federal taxes levied for special, not national, interests was exactly what Anti-Federalists had warned during the ratification process. Those taxes, Anti-Federalists had argued, would deny states the ability to obtain the revenue they needed, thereby shriveling the state's ability to function. Since it was unknown "how far this government may . . . depress, or injure the individual states; we ought to guard, with the greatest degree of caution, against every danger of such a nature." Otherwise, the entire funding system would "establish a precedent in America . . . that would brin[g] ruin which it has never failed to bring."[15]

In the Senate, William Maclay called the plan a "System of Speculation" with Hamilton "at the head of the Speculators with all the Courtiers, on one side." The whole point of the plan, Maclay confided in his diary, was to "create a mass of debt, which will justify them in seizing all the Sources of Government, thus annihilating the State legislature, and erecting an Empire on the Basis of Consolidation."[16] He noted that some

Senators privately remarked that *"[c]onsolidation* of the different governments" was the primary "[o]bject in the [m]atter" for supporters of Hamilton.[17] Maclay also authored several essays against Hamilton's plan that
appeared anonymously in the *Independent Gazetteer*. In these essays, he
noted that "some individuals," of which he meant Hamilton and the
congressional supporters of his plan, "have endeavored to model the
Constitution of the United States to the standard of the British Monarchy." The first step, Maclay claimed, was to "swallow up the state Legislatures in the federal government." Hamilton's report sought nothing
short of "seiz[ing] all the sources of revenue, and depress[ing] the state
governments; for without reducing them to insignificance, a pompous
Court cannot be established." With that "one stroke," Hamilton's plan
would "reduce us to the beggary of borrowing every shilling." From
there, he continued, the "whole Union" would subsidize New York City
which would, "in a few years equal London or Paris," in size, scope, and
decadence. In short, it would become the center of a highly centralized
and plutocratic empire. Maclay did not surrender to hopelessness, however. One "sure resource" could thwart the Federalists, the "different
State Legislatures." In them the "seeds of a genuine republicanism have
flourished, and brought forth fruit." At the same time, the essays advised
that the state legislatures could not resist individually. They needed to
unite "with firmness and decision, the stations assigned them in the General arrangement of the empire," the United States Senate. Only there
could the "confidence of the people, in the federal government," uphold
the "interests of republicanism."[18]

The plan's supporters in Congress, however, answered the criticism
by establishing, for the first time and only in piecemeal, their thoughts on
the authority of the new government. First, they claimed that the expediency and pragmatism of Hamilton's funding system outweighed all
other considerations. Fears of "Heats and animosities [that would] grow
out of this opposition of sentiment," could "destroy the public tranquility
and blast the hopes and prospects of the people under the government
now so happily established." If Congress adopted the program, it would
diffuse "all the evils of faction, disunion and disappointed expectations
prevented." These calls of crisis and fears of disunion mirrored those
offered by Federalists—many of whom were making these same arguments for Hamilton's program—during ratification. Second, and more
tellingly, they admitted that Hamilton's plan called for the alteration of
the original contracts but maintained that the new government "had a
power to interfere in certain contracts, public as well as private."[19] These
supporters did not address specifically where the government had this
power, but suggested that it derived from "that great object of society . . .
self-preservation." Governments have the responsibility, they claimed,
"to abrogate and set aside" any "measure that has a tendency to destroy
the social compact."[20] Thus, Federalists made their first forays into ar-

guing for an extra-constitutional authority originating from the supposedly teleological nature of the Constitution. Although they did not specify, yet, from where that extra-constitutional authority originated, they
strongly implied that it was an inherent power of sovereignty. This idea
is even more revealing of the Federalist constitutional vision than it
might seem. Recall that during the 1780s, Nationalists had criticized the
states for legislation that altered or abolished contracts. At the Philadelphia Convention, they secured a constitutional prohibition against the
practice. Article I, Section 10 of the Constitution expressly forbade the
states from impairing the obligations of contracts, thereby curbing that
aspect of the states' sovereign authority. Federalists, however, saw no
constitutional problem with the federal government wielding this power,
even without express authority to do so.

Although Hamilton's funding scheme sailed through Congress, his
plan to assume state debts was initially defeated. Only a bargain struck
by Hamilton and Madison, with new Secretary of State Thomas Jefferson,
hosting the two at his residence, saved the assumption plan. In exchange
for the southern states voting to accept assumption, Hamilton pledged to
use his influence to have northern states accept moving the national capital to the swamplands off the Potomac River near the Virginia and Maryland border. With the deal struck, Congress approved the assumption
plan.[21] Nevertheless, the chasm that had been closing between the Federalists and Anti-Federalists in the first year of the Constitution had reopened.

In the winter of 1790, the Patrick Henry-led Virginia legislature sent
Congress a remonstrance protesting the plan. This remonstrance echoed
Henry's famous set of resolutions denouncing the Stamp Act as unconstitutional. Like the 1765 action, these resolutions attacked the centralizing
implications of Hamilton's plan. Troubling Virginia was the "striking
resemblance between this system and that which was introduced into
England at the Revolution of 1688." That "system which has perpetuated
upon that nation an enormous debt, and has, moreover, insinuated into
the hands of the Executive an unbounded influence, which, pervading
every branch of the Government, bears down all opposition, and daily
threatens the destruction of every thing that appertains to English liberty." Hamilton's plan, moreover, concentrated wealth into the hands of
the "monied interests" and threatened the agricultural basis of Virginia.
That action would inevitably lead to one or two courses: a "prostration of
agriculture at the feet of commerce, or a change in the present form of
Federal Government fatal to the existence of American liberty." If the fear
of subverting American liberty in place of a centralized authority did not
change Congress' mind, Virginia reminded them that during ratification
Federalists had:

taught [them] to believe "that every power not granted, was retained"; under this impression, and upon this positive condition, declared in the instrument of ratification, the said Government was adopted by the people of this Commonwealth.

Because the "memorialists can find no clause in the Constitution authorizing Congress to assume debts of the states," Hamilton's program threatened the entire constitutional structure. It thus fell to the states:

> as the guardians, then, of the rights and interests of their constituents; as sentinels placed by them over the ministers of the Federal Government, to shield it from their encroachments, or at least to sound the alarm when it is threatened with invasion; they can never reconcile it to their consciences silently to acquiesce in a measure which violates that hallowed maxim—a maxim, on the truth and sacredness of which, the Federal Government depended for its adoption in this Commonwealth. But this injudicious act not only deserves the censure of the General Assembly, because it is not warranted by the Constitution of the United States, but because it is repugnant to an express provision of that Constitution. This provision is "that all debts contracted, and engagements entered into, before the adoption of this Constitution, shall be as valid against the United States, under this Constitution, as under the Confederation"; which amounts to a Constitutional ratification of the contracts respecting the state debts in the situation in which they existed under the Confederation; and, resorting to that standard, there can be no doubt that, in the present question, the rights of states, as contracting parties with the United States, must be considered as sacred.[22]

The remonstrance was among the first major references to the Revolutionary constitutional settlement made under the Constitution. It would not be the last. The state's reference to itself as the true guardian, "then, of the rights and interests of their constituents; as sentinels placed by them over the ministers of the Federal Government, to shield it from their encroachments, or at least to sound the alarm when it is threatened with invasion," was reminiscent of the arguments that led to the Burke Amendment as well as those made throughout the states during the debates over the implementation of the Treaty of Peace. Nor was the Constitution a reordering of that system. The remonstrance pointed to the Federalists' promise to honor the "hallowed maxim" that the states would retain all the authority not given to the general government in the Constitution. The union the Constitution was attempting to perfect, then, was one where the states had compacted together. With the unconstitutional usurpation of assumption, however, the Federalists had broken that promise. The protest implied that had Virginia realized how quickly Federalists would break their promises, ratification would have failed.[23]

Hamilton fumed at Virginia's protest and the stark reminder of Federalist promises. In two letters, written eighteen months apart, Hamilton defended himself but also revealed the depth of his nationalist vision. In the first letter, written to Chief Justice John Jay in December 1790, Hamilton forwarded copies of Virginia's remonstrance. He added that they were "the first symptom of a spirit which must either be killed, or it will kill the Constitution of the United States." Although he did not specify what those symptoms were, the implications pointed to a constitutional order built upon state sovereignty. He asked Jay to consider how the federal government should respond, offering ominously that perhaps the "collective weight of the different parts of the government to be employed in exploding the principles they contain."[24] As we will see, both would soon attempt to "explode" the principles of state sovereignty embodied in Virginia's protest.

In his second letter, this one written to Edward Carrington in early 1792, Hamilton claimed the "great and real anxiety" was being "able to preserve the national [government] from the too potent and counteracting influence" of state governments, particularly large states like Virginia. He confessed that:

> the prevailing bias of my judgment is that if they [the states] can be circumscribed within bounds, consistent with the preservation of the national government, they will prove useful and salutary. If the States were all of the size of Connecticut, Maryland, or New Jersey, I should decidedly regard the local governments as both safe and useful. As the thing now is, however, I acknowledge the most serious apprehensions, that the government of the United States will not be able to maintain itself against their influence. I see that influence already penetrating into the national councils and preventing their direction.

In other words, Hamilton believed the smaller states posed no real threat to the federal government. Their small size not only rendered them ineffectual, but useful. He seems to have meant the federal government could potentially use them as effective administrative units. This idea was certainly in keeping with what many Nationalists had advocated during the Philadelphia Convention. What the federal government needed to do, what he claimed he was trying to do, was to "erect every fence, to guard it from depredations which is, in my opinion, consistent with Constitutional propriety."[25] Just what those fences were he did not say, but his *Reports* point to a more centralized government that tied all major financial interests to itself.

***

In late 1790, Hamilton began the second phase of his plan when he submitted his *Report on the National Bank.* Although the debt and assumption plan had hinted at the constitutional division between the members, they were just the initial fissures. The final and irreparable rift occurred during the bank debates. Those arguments were the most important political discussions of the place of state sovereignty in the post-Constitution world until 1798. The debates provided Hamilton his chance to "explode" the defenders of state sovereignty. Standard accounts of the event mark it as a battle between "implied powers" or a "strict interpretation" of the necessary and proper clause and over the proper hermeneutics of interpretation.[26] Those issues, important as they were, nevertheless overlook the primary concern underlying the bank debates: the relationship between the Constitution and state sovereignty. The fight over establishing the Bank of the United States was a battle between a nomocratic or teleocratic Constitution. It rekindled, in a way no other issue thus far had, the previous decade's arguments over the nature of sovereignty in the American constitutional order. In particular, the Federalists used the debates to make the final break with their ratification promise that the states would retain most elements of sovereignty. They would articulate a constitutionalism where the federal government was the sovereign power in the American constitutional system. The opponents of the Bank fought to maintain the Revolution's constitutional achievement. Thus, the "the idea that the Bank of the United States threatened to reverse the Revolution still seems ridiculous" is not only inaccurate but a misreading of the true significance of those debates.[27]

Working off Hamilton's opinions in his *Report on the National Bank*, proponents of the bank presented three arguments in support of the measure. First, they claimed the Confederation Congress' creation of the Bank of North America established a precedent for Hamilton's bank. The Articles did not provide explicit authority to charter one, yet the confederation still prescribed it; so too could the new and obviously more powerful federal Congress. Secondly, some argued that because the Constitution granted Congress authority over the national capital, normal constitutional limitations did not apply there. Finally, they linked the utility of a bank to the necessary and proper clause, asserting that the clause permitted "all known and usual means for attainment" of Constitutional powers." From the opening of the new government, Congress had relied upon the necessary and proper clause for a variety of issues, such as lighthouses for navigation and presidential removal power, that many believed they could "scarcely proceed without it."[28] The bank resembled those issues.

Not surprisingly, most of the bank's congressional supporters had consistently supported a stronger and more centralized national government during the confederation and were strong Federalists during the ratification struggle. The diversity of their arguments supporting the bank suggests that the claims they made during ratification—that Congress possessed only delegated powers and the necessary and proper clause provided basic latitude for the executing of those explicit enumerations—was more illusionary than real. The variety of their arguments justifying the bank was more illustrative of their real thought: that the federal government should be sovereign in any issue it deemed fit. In other words, the bank's supporters not only wished to validate the bank, but they also equated the necessary and proper clause with Blackstonian notions of sovereignty. Although hints of this argument were seen in the support of the debt and assumption plans, the bank provided the first serious opportunity for Federalists to claim that implied powers were the means to ensure that the "absolute letter of the Constitution" could never bind the hands of the federal government.

Fisher Ames led the bank's proponents in Congress. In his remarks of February 3rd, Ames offered the first arguments that wedded the implied power to establish a national bank to the Constitution's preamble and the general welfare clause of Article I, Section 8. These two provisions, he claimed, granted government the power "of using every means not positively prohibited by the Constitution to execute the ends for which that government was instituted." Ames never stated explicitly that the federal government was sovereign in all cases whatsoever, but he skirted the edge contending that "Congress may do what is necessary to the end for which the Constitution was adopted, provided it is not repugnant to the natural rights of man or to those which they have expressly reserved to themselves, or to the powers which are assigned to the states."[29] In this claim, Ames was all but indistinguishable from Blackstone, whose *Commentaries* taught that the only limitations upon Parliament's sovereignty were "those rights then which God and nature have established, and are therefore called natural rights . . . no human legislature has power to abridge or destroy."[30]

Ames' address, therefore, including his nod to Blackstone, was an explanation on how the end for which the Constitution was established, as explained in the preamble, was the only limitation upon the new government's power. Under "such rules of interpretation" the Constitution "vested Congress with the authority over all objects of national concern." Ames meant, in other words, that the federal government could exercise any means it deemed necessary to fulfill those objectives as long as the Constitution did not expressly deny the power or violate the "natural rights of man." The paramount importance, then, was ensuring that the federal government met its philosophical ends of the government regardless of their ties to the enumerated powers.[31]

Nor did Ames consider state sovereignty a hindrance to his interpretation. Although he acknowledged that states retained powers the federal government did not wield, he suggested that should the federal government ever deem a state's power necessary and proper, it could simply appropriate it and use the supremacy clause to defend the taking. He hinted at this possibility when he warned that prohibiting the establishment of the bank meant "our social compact [was] incomplete" because it lacked "the means of self preservation." Enacting the bank bill demonstrated that the Constitution included all the power it deemed itself necessary to have to fulfill the Constitution's mission, a complete reversal of the Federalist argument during ratification.[32] New York Representative John Laurance added to Ames' argument maintaining that "as to the great objects for which this government was instituted, it is as full and completed in all its parts . . . a full uncontrollable power to regulate the fiscal concerns of this union." As a result, "it clearly follows, that [the federal government] must possess the power to make every possible arrangement conducive to that great object." Even if the bank interfered with the states since "all interferences of the kind, the particular interest of a state, must give way to the general interest." The proposed Twelfth Amendment, which was still in the process of ratification by the states, would not apply to the debate, claimed Ames and Laurance. "The power of establishing a national bank . . . could not be exercised by the states." It "therefore rested no where but in the federal legislature." Not only that, but as the bank was to be chartered in Philadelphia (the national capital at the time), it did not interfere with the states. Nor did the bank bill force the states to accept the bank's notes, it merely "induced" them to do so. Should the states actually forbid the use of the notes the supremacy clause would override those prohibitions.[33]

The arguments of Ames, Laurance, and others shocked the opposition. Their responses were pointed, and at times, heated, as when James Jackson labeled the bill "illegitimate, a bastard production."[34] They counter-argued, claiming that the precedent of the Bank of North America did not apply to their current context. The dire circumstances of the Revolution produced that bank. Those days were gone, and with them, the desperate need for the bank. They also scoffed at the notion that the bank would not interfere with the states because it was located in the national capital. The bank was supposedly for the common good. Claiming that the bank was not problematic to the states while it operated on the national level amounted to little more than the supporters having their cake and eating it too. Finally, the bank was not necessary and proper for the collection of taxes or regulating currency.

What really concerned the opposition, and what they focused their strongest attacks upon, was how "on the whole [the bank was] a dangerous system—calculated to destroy the state government,—created an all-powerful aristocratical influence and [would] eventually destroy the liberties of the people."[35] Above all else, the opposition sought to defend state sovereignty from Federalists' attempts to aggrandize federal power. Their defense, therefore, focused upon two separate, but related, fronts. First, the opposition, led by Michael Jenifer Stone and William Branch Giles, attacked Ames' philosophical musings by offering their own theoretical responses. Secondly, opponents attempted to protect the Revolutionary constitutional settlement by appealing to the understanding of federal power that emerged from the ratification conventions. On this front, James Madison emerged as the opposition's champion.

The opponents of the bank bill acknowledged that the Constitution stated the proper parameters of the government, but it took explicit care to also "specif[y] the means of execution," in the enumeration of powers. The Constitution was "a solemn compact, that the powers granted shall be made use of to the end thereby specified" rather than being a grant of particular powers "guarded by an implied negative to all others."[36] The opponents indicted the Federalists' claim that the preamble permitted the use of broad, implied powers. Agreeing to such an idea left the Constitution "nothing but a name" and a justification for "the assumption of every power." In a blistering speech, Michael Jenifer Stone explained how "all those that opposed the government [i.e., during ratification], dreaded this doctrine" of implied powers. He noted that during ratification, the Constitution's supporters claimed to be in common "opinion that it ought not to be tolerated," yet they were now using it to "break down every barrier which the federal Constitution had raised against unlimited legislation." Taking a direct shot at Ames, Stone read the preamble aloud and asked if "these gentlemen require anything more respecting the power of Congress, than a description of the ends of government?" If they answered positively, Stone contended, the Constitutional Convention could have stopped its work with the writing of the preamble since "[h]ere was your Constitution!"[37]

Stone took Ames to task for his notion that only natural rights proscribed federal power. In a particularly pointed remark, he noted that:

> [o]ne gentleman [i.e., Ames] has said no implication ought to be made against the law of nature—against rights acquired—or against power pre-occupied by the states; that it is easier to restrain than to give competent powers of execution. Now these notions are hostile to the main principle of our government, which is only a grant of particular portions of power, implying a negative to all others. It has been shown that the ends of government will include everything. If gentlemen are allowed to range in their sober discretion for the means, it is plain they have no limits. By the cabalistical word incident, your Constitution is turned upside down; and instead of being a grant of particular powers, guarded by an implied negative to all others, it is made to imply all powers. But, strange to tell, America forgot to guard it by express negative provisions. Is there any difference in effect between lodging general powers in a government, and permitting the exercise of them by subtle constructions? He said there was a difference—in the one case, the people fairly gave up their liberty, and stood prepared,—in the other, they were unexpectedly tricked out of their Constitution.[38]

Giles followed by offering a more modest and humble understanding of the federal government than that of Ames. He rooted his understanding of the Constitution in the expectations emerging from the ratification debates where the ends of the federal government were only those which the "states or people had expressly delegated." The distribution of authority was not one where the preamble implied that the federal government could wield any authority it wanted unless expressly prohibited by the Constitution or natural rights. Far from containing some grander purpose, "the great object of the Constitution" was the distribution of governmental power between the state and federal government. The Constitution created merely a federal system, and he "was taught to consider this as a federal not as a consolidated government." Any assertion to the contrary was "reasoning . . . with dangerous effects." Relying upon the preamble to defend the creation of the bank not only stripped the Constitution of any real limitation upon its power, but also brought "about a radical change in the nature of our government." The only option, therefore, was to "ultimately discard" the argument before it took root because failing to kill it would destroy any notion that "those powers not delegated to Congress remained with the state or were retained by the people." To accept the Federalists' idea that the preamble led to broad authority not tied to the Constitution was a "mortal stab" to the vitals of state sovereignty. Such a style of government envisioned by the bank's defenders, Giles warned, was one "growing out of a state of society," whereby philosopher-kings divined the limits of federal power in complete contradiction to the understanding—an understanding offered by Federalists during the ratification debates—of the Constitution as one being limited in purpose and power. Yet, the bank's supporters were using the opportunity offered by the bank bill to lay the foundations for making the federal government paramount not only in its enumerated power, but in all things. They sought a "radically subverted" Constitution that destroyed the "dignity and consequence" of the state governments.[39]

Madison opened the opposition's second front by appealing to recent history. Echoing his resistance on constitutional grounds to the Bank of North America of a decade earlier, Madison noted that the Constitution was a "grant of particular power" with the "general mass" left to "other hands." Those powers designed to fulfill the purpose of the union were enumerated and known, and those powers necessary to execute the enumerated powers were "drawn from the nature of each." Since the Philadelphia Convention explicitly rejected the power of incorporation, it was not part of the purpose of the union and therefore a Bank of the United States was not necessary in order to execute the actual purposes of the union.[40]

Madison also explained how the interpretation offered by Ames and others contradicted the very purposes of the Constitution. Although Madison agreed with Giles' more theoretically based argument, he moved his argument to recent events to contend that the proper understanding of federal government derived from the "meaning of the parties of the instrument." In other words, when trying to understand the proper scope of the enumerated powers, Madison argued that the meaning and purpose of the Constitution as understood by the ratification conventions was the "proper guide." Obviously, the ratification conventions never believed they were empowering a federal government to wield unlimited powers of "implications, thus remote and thus multiplied, [that] can be linked together" forming a "chain . . . that will reach every object of legislation, every object in within the whole compass of political economy."[41] Instead, they believed they were creating a limited government with limited powers and purposes.

To prove his argument, Madison read portions of the Pennsylvania, Virginia, and North Carolina ratification conventions (it is not clear which portions) to show "the grounds on which the Constitution had been vindicated by its principles advocates [i.e., Federalists], against a dangerous latitude of its powers, charged on it by its opponents." Thus, the "explanations in the state conventions all turned on the same fundamental principle, and on the principles that the terms necessary and proper gave no additional powers to those enumerated." The interpretation of federal power now offered to support the bank contradicted the very understanding of the Constitution's purpose and powers that had led to its adoption.[42]

Not only did the ratification conventions believe they were adopting a constitution of limited objectives, means, and powers, but they reiterated this understanding through their demands for amendments, particularly their call for a state sovereignty amendment. In particular, Madison noted the Eleventh and Twelfth Amendments (ratified as the Ninth and Tenth) as demonstrable proof of this understanding. The irony of the situation must have frustrated Madison. He repeated the theme of the speech introducing the amendment by explaining to his Federalist colleagues that he designed those amendments to allay the fears that the Constitution required a consolidated government and they were intended to be interpretative guides to the proper understanding of the government's powers. The Ninth Amendment forbade "a latitude of interpretation," such as that offered by the bank's supporters, while the final amendment was for the "excluding [of] every source of power not within the Constitution itself." Thus, ratification conventions and the proposed amendments reflected a Constitution rooted in the constitutional settlement from the Revolution. The arguments of the supporters, however, tried to supplant that settlement and bring the Constitution "under the influence of another set" of ideas that involved "the guilt of usurpation, and establishe[d] a precedent of interpretation, leveling all the barriers which limit the powers of the general government, and protect those of the state governments."[43] Madison summed up his argument:

> It appeared on the whole . . . [t]hat the power exercised by the bill was condemned by the silence of the Constitution; was condemned by the

rule of interpretation arising out of the Constitution; was condemned
by its tendency to destroy the main characteristic of the Constitution;
was condemned by the expositions of the friends of the Constitution;
whilst depending before the public; [and] was condemned by the explanatory amendments proposed by Congress themselves to the Constitution.[44]

In *Original Meanings*, Jack Rakove contends that Madison's "foray in originalism was manifestly a failure."[45] While he credits Madison with operating from long-held principle rather than expediency, he ignores the
broader constitutional context within which Madison operated. The opponents of the bank bill worried that if the Constitution was nothing
more than the philosophical purposes mentioned in the preamble instead
of the bringing the government under the law by distribution of power
between the state and federal government, the constitutional settlement
of the Revolution was truly dead. In its place would be the centralized
power Americans fought a revolution to prevent, and Federalists, including Madison, swore the Constitution would never become and had offered amendments to prevent. Rakove's contention, then, is true only if
the Constitution really was the dawn of a new era, of a new mindset
where federal power, tied to the fulfillment of the preamble, was the
future and state sovereignty the past. This, however, reads twentieth and
twenty-first constitutionalism into the founding era. If we keep in mind
that state sovereignty remained the accepted constitutional norm of this
era, the lens through which most Americans viewed their political order,
and a persistently critical issue throughout the 1790s, Madison's and others' arguments were not forays into a left-behind world, but rather the
defense of a continuing order that the Constitution did not radically alter.

Despite the opponents' efforts, Congress passed the bank bill. The
battle, however, was not over, for President Washington had to sign the
bill. As a member of the Philadelphia Convention, he knew how that
gathering had rejected Madison's attempt to give Congress the power of
establishing corporations. As such, he remained unconvinced about the
bank's constitutionality and asked Madison to draft a veto message.
Madison's draft offered both policy and constitutional reasons for rejection. The veto's policy disagreements rested on the ideas that the bank
favored special, not national, interests and would begin operations before
those who lived far away from the capital could have a chance to "take
advantage of the opportunity."

Although these policy reasons were legitimate enough (and Congress
would eventually remedy them), the veto's real objection rested on constitutional grounds. Madison wrote for Washington that the bill violated
"an essential principle of the Government that powers not delegated by
the Constitution cannot be rightfully exercised." The draft also expressed
concerns Washington could not "satisfy [himself] that it results from any
express power by fair and safe rules of construction."[46] The constitutional

reasons behind the proposed veto succinctly restated Madison's congressional position. Not only did it invoke the idea that the Constitution was
a limited government, but the reference to fair and safe construction indirectly criticized the supporters' arguments for a grander purpose behind
the Constitution. Those ideas were not a safe and fair interpretation of the
Constitution's authority. Instead, they were dangerous and laden with
the potential to subvert both the states and the Constitution's actual and
stated purposes.

Washington, however, remained undecided. He then turned to his
cabinet for further advice. Both Attorney General Edmund Randolph and
Secretary of State Thomas Jefferson objected to the bill. Because historians
too frequently dismiss the attorney general's opinion as a trite restatement of the opponents' argument, they mistakenly overlook how his
opinion most explicitly pronounced this fear of the Federalist interpretation. In many ways, his opinion reflected his qualified support of the
Constitution at the Virginia ratification convention. It was Randolph,
more than any other Federalist at that meeting, including Madison, who
assured Anti-Federalists that the Constitution contained only those powers expressly delegated to it.[47] His opinion to Washington was an elab-
oration and extension of those themes. He advised the president that to
believe the bank was "implied in the nature" of the Constitution was to
"beget a doctrine so indefinite, as to grasp every power." Congress had
"confessed" through the Twelfth Amendment that the theory animating
the Constitution was one "whose powers are described." That amendment "straitens the federal powers" and "opposes an opinion, not unpa-
tronized, that, Congress may exercise all authority, to which the states are
individually competent."[48]

Randolph continued the attack by focusing upon the supporters' reliance of the preamble. He hoped to "once for all" explain that, if the
preamble could "be operative" as a source of power, it was "a full constitution of itself[,] and the body of the Constitution is useless." The purpose of the preamble, he reminded Washington, was "declarative only of
the views of the convention, which they supposed would be left fulfilled
by the powers delineated." Randolph then summarized the various arguments for the bank, but believed he saw a "serious alarm . . . in the
concentrated force of these sentiments." Should Washington approve the
bank, it would open the door to "similar construction on every specified
federal power" and would "stretch the arm of Congress into the whole
circle of State Legislation."[49]

Finally, Randolph turned to the "proper" phrase of the necessary and
proper clause. He argued that "proper" was not a grant of blanket power
for the government. Rather, it was a restriction upon its authority. No
"power [was] to be assumed under the general clause, but such as is not
only necessary but proper." Interestingly, he qualified his argument and
advised both supporters and critics of the bank bill not to read too much

into the clause. Instead, they should use it as an interpretative guide and ask "whether the latitude of construction which they arrogate" to the clause would "not terminate in an unlimited power of Congress."[50]

Jefferson's first real foray into the political and constitutional arguments under the new Constitution was shorter than Randolph's opinion but echoed many of his fellow Virginian's themes. Even more than Randolph, Jefferson offered a more focused constitutional defense of state sovereignty. He opened by declaring that the bank bill altered several elements of state common law, including the laws of mortmain, alienage, descent, distribution, escheat and forfeitures, and monopolies. He then immediately explained that he "considered the foundation of the Constitution" as resting on the Twelfth (Tenth) Amendment. Any attempts to "take a single step beyond" those boundaries were to "take possession of a boundless field of power."[51] The secretary of state then advised how the bank did not qualify under the Constitution's enumeration of powers. The bank did not levy tax, borrow money, or regulate commerce. For those reasons alone, he argued, Washington should veto the bill.

Jefferson devoted the majority of his opinion to attacking the supporters' reliance on the general welfare and necessary and proper clauses. The purpose of the general welfare clause, he argued, was to explain how Congress could lay taxes. In other words, the clause meant Congress could only "lay taxes for the purpose of providing for the general welfare." To detach the clause from its purpose, as the bank's supporters were attempting to do, was to grant Congress "a distinct and independent power to do any act they please, which might be for the good of the Union." This would "render all the proceeding and subsequent enumerations of power completely useless."[52]

The necessary and proper clause was treated much the same. Whereas Randolph hedged his reading of the clause and focused on "proper," Jefferson sided with the bank's opponents and concentrated on the word "necessary." He advised Washington that necessary did not mean convenient, but essential. Jefferson admitted that a bank might "give great facility, or convenience, in the collection of taxes" and that the bank's bills "may be a more convenient vehicle than treasury orders," but that did not make them indispensable. Equating necessary with convenient would "justify the assumption of a non-enumerated power as a means for carrying into effect an enumerated one." Furthermore, should "such a latitude of construction be allowed to this phrase as to give any non-enumerated power, it will go to every one" and "would swallow up all the delegated powers, and reduce the whole to one phrase." All the necessary and proper clause did, Jefferson surmised, was give the "means without which the grant of power [i.e., the Constitution] would be nugatory."[53]

Returning to his list of state common law prohibitions, Jefferson asked a question that struck at the heart of the entire bank debate: was "the

Constitution intended that for a shade or two of convenience, more or less, Congress should be authorized to break down the most ancient and fundamental laws of the several States?" Clearly, this violation of the states' sovereignty was not the purpose of the Constitution, and the foundations it rested upon proved it. Only "a necessity invincible by any other means, [could] justify such a prostitution of laws, which constitute the pillars of our whole system of jurisprudence," Jefferson argued. He wondered if "Congress [would] be too strait-laced to carry the Constitution into honest effect, unless they may pass over the foundation-laws of the State government for the slightest convenience of theirs?" Finally, he advised that one of the several purposes for the veto power was to protect "the States and State legislatures. The present is the case of a right remaining exclusively with the States, and consequently one of those intended by the Constitution to be placed under its protection."[54]

Traditionally, historians have viewed Randolph and Jefferson's opinions—Jefferson's especially—as the classic defense of a "strict" interpretation of the Constitution. Both opinions did this, but it is easy to carry this interpretation too far and attribute to them arguments they did not make. Neither Jefferson nor Randolph sought a crippled federal government unable to wield power, nor one that possessed no degree of implied power. Jefferson made this point clear in the final sentences of his opinion when he advised Washington that if the president remained undecided "his judgment, a just respect for the wisdom of the legislature would naturally decide the balance in favor of their opinion."[55] Thus, while Jefferson was adamant that the bank was unconstitutional, he was willing to accept that others might see incorporation as an implied power. Despite this acceptance of flexibility, neither man embraced the vision of the Constitution offered by Federalists. They used their opinions to warn that taking the Federalists' understanding of the Constitution to its logical limits would radically reorder American constitutionalism by destroying the states and paving the way for consolidation. Both opinions, therefore, were much more than legal briefs that examined legal definitions, they were defenses of the constitutional arrangement as Americans understood it in 1788 and reaffirmed with the Tenth Amendment.

Upon receiving both statements, Washington forwarded them to Hamilton for his thoughts. Hamilton did not waste the opportunity to "explode" the opinions of the Virginians. Hamilton must have certainly had the Virginian Remonstrance in mind when he wrote his opinion because the opinion the president's treasury secretary delivered was the era's most robust and learned arguments of the Federalist understanding of constitutionalism. The entire thrust of his opinion was an argument in defense of the sovereignty of the federal government.

Hamilton told Washington that he believed the "principles of construction like those espoused by the Secretary of State and Attorney General, would be fatal to the just and indispensable authority of the United

States."[56] What troubled Hamilton was his perception that the Virginians' refusal to accept any degree of implied powers, claiming such a restrictive interpretation, would "arrest the motions of government." The potential danger from their interpretation was all too clear to Hamilton. It would "furnish the singular spectacle of a political society without sovereignty, or of a people governed, without government."[57] He admitted to Washington that he accepted the principle contained in the Tenth Amendment, but then dismissed it as "nothing more than a consequence of [the] republican maxim, that all government is a delegation of power." Instead, Hamilton argued that "how much [was] delegated in each case, is a question of fact, to be made out by fair reasoning and construction."[58] The only way to determine this fair reasoning was to use "the general principles and general ends of governments." Tellingly, Hamilton did not rely upon the preamble to note those ends. Instead, he claimed the ends of the government rested upon the broad notion of the "general administration of the affairs of a country, its finances, trade, defense, etc." Supporting these ends justified the "principles of liberal construction" of governmental powers.[59]

After establishing the government on such a broad base, Hamilton then examined the theoretical nature of the federal government. He argued that "every power vested in a Government is in its nature sovereign, and include by force of the term, a right to employ all the means requisite and fairly applicable to the attainment of the ends of such power."[60] The division of power between the state and federal government was not an issue, he maintained, because "each has sovereign power as to certain things, and not as to other things." The sovereignty of the federal government meant, moreover, that "implied powers [were] to be considered [as] delegated equally with express ones."[61] As a result, the power of incorporation was an "incident of sovereign power . . . in relation to the objects instructed to the management of the government."

Hamilton's vision of the federal government's sovereignty flipped the arguments of the bank's opponents who held that the enumeration of powers was the only means to achieve the government's end. To Hamilton this was "a strange fallacy."[62] To show the flaw of Jefferson's argument, he turned to the secretary of state's contention regarding the general welfare clause. Hamilton agreed that the general welfare was the only reason in which the government could raise taxes. The clause simply meant, however, that "Congress [could] be considered as under only one restriction . . . they cannot rightfully apply the money they raise to any purpose merely or purely local."[63] Thus, the general welfare was not the restrictive clause as Jefferson claimed, but a broad grant of taxation power. As such, the sovereignty of the federal government meant that it could exercise nearly every means to achieve its ends. Hamilton offered only three general and somewhat amorphous limitations to the federal government, those "not precluded by restrictions and exceptions specified in the Constitution, or not immoral, or not contrary to the essential ends of governments."[64] Like Ames, Hamilton's understanding of the sovereignty of the federal government was very Blackstonian.

In many ways, Hamilton could have concluded his opinion after establishing the complete sovereignty of the Constitution. If the federal government possessed all power within its spheres of authority—with the few Blackstonian limitations Hamilton pointed to—there was no need to elaborate further. Yet, he continued, and his reasons for doing so became clear. Hamilton proceeded to attack Jefferson's definition of necessary as essential. This definition was "so erroneous a conception," he told Washington, that it "should be exploded."[65] The use of the word "exploded" could not have been coincidental. Clearly, he connected the implication of Jefferson's restrictive definition of necessary to the underlying argument of the Virginia Remonstrance. This, it seems, is why he continued with his opinion. He felt compelled to "kill" the attempts to restrict the Constitution. In his rebuttal, Hamilton admitted that no government could "do merely what it pleases," as that would be an arbitrary tyranny; nevertheless, Jefferson's definition of necessary gave "it a restrictive operation, an idea never before entertained." Such restriction would "beget endless uncertainty and embarrassment." Hamilton noted that common usage of necessary often meant "needful, requisite, incidental, useful, or conducive to." Jefferson's definition, however, would "give it the same force as if the word absolutely or indispensably had been prefixed to it."[66] Instead, the necessity of a measure should be judged by the "relation between the measure and the end; between the nature of the mean employed toward the execution of power." Hamilton also appealed to the convention, noting that the necessary and proper clause "indicates that" the convention intended to "give a liberal latitude to the exercise of the specified power."[67] This appeal to the intent of the convention was interesting. Earlier in this opinion, Hamilton chastised Jefferson for relying upon the convention's rejection of a power to establish corporations, claiming that "arguments drawn from extrinsic circumstances regarding the intention of the convention must be rejected."[68] Hamilton did not explain why one appeal must trump the other, but his reasoning was obvious.

Hamilton devoted considerable space in his lengthy opinion to address the question of the degree of interferences the bank posed to state sovereignty. Not surprisingly, he rejected the claims of Jefferson and Randolph, asserting that the states themselves had altered Jefferson's list of state laws so often that "it is not conceived how anything can be called the fundamental law of a State government" if it was so easily amendable. Reliance upon arguments that a federal law would alter state law could "never be good reasoning" because "it must be shown that the act which makes the alteration is unconstitutional on other accounts, not because it makes the alteration."[69] Still, Hamilton was willing to admit that "difficulties on this point are inherent in the nature of the Federal Constitution; they result inevitably from a division of the legislative power."[70] There were—or would be—cases where the federal government was clearly operating within or against its powers, but also a "third class, which will leave room for controversy and difference of opinion."[71] In those cases, a "reasonable latitude of judgment must be allowed." Hamilton's opinion implies that when those judgments must be settled, the federal government should be the victor since "there is a clause of its Constitution which would be decisive," the supremacy clause.[72]

Hamilton consistently endorsed nationalism after the Revolution. His support of a Blackstonian sovereignty for the federal government during the bank debates corresponded to the ideas in his writings of the early 1780s. The Constitution had not altered Hamilton's vision. The national government, including that of the old the Articles or the Constitution, possessed a purpose beyond its expressed limitations. Hamilton appreciated the Constitution because it offered a clearer source for which to justify his long-held desires.

In the end, Washington sided with Hamilton. Whether Hamilton's opinion played the definitive role in that decision remains unclear, although it is probable. Whatever Washington's reasoning, when he signed the Bank of the United States into existence on February 25, 1791, he also endorsed the Federalists' understanding of the Constitution. The creation of the Bank of the United States represented the breaking point in American politics. The constitutional differences between the Federalists and their opponents, which seemed to have been narrowing after the first year of the Constitution, had reopened wider than ever. Their separate and competing understandings of what the American constitutional order was had become a chasm too great to bridge.

NOTES

1. Alexander Hamilton, *Federalist* 84, in George W. Carey and James McClellan, eds., *The Federalist: The Gideon Edition* (Indianapolis: Liberty Fund, 2001), 442–51.

2. Lance Banning, *The Jeffersonian Persuasion: Evolution of a Party Ideology* (Ithaca: Cornell University Press, 1978), 129.

3. Alexander Hamilton, *Report on Public Credit* and *Report on the National Bank*, both in Harold Syrett and Jacob Cooke, eds., *The Papers of Alexander Hamilton*, 26 vols. (Columbia: University of Columbia Press, 1961–1981), 6: 65–168; 7: 305–42 [hereafter, Hamilton, *Papers*]. My summation is borrowed from Forrest McDonald, *The Presidency of George Washington* (Lawrence: University Press of Kansas, 1974), 58–62.

4. E. James Ferguson, *The Power of the Purse: A History of American Public Finance, 1776–1790* (Chapel Hill: University of North Carolina Press, 1961), part 2 and, more recently, Max M. Edling, *A Revolution in Favor of Government: Origins of the U.S. Constitution and the Making of the American State* (Oxford: Oxford University Press, 2003).

5. Alexander Hamilton, *Report on Public Credit*, and Hamilton to George Washington, "Notes on the Advantages of a National Bank," March 27, 1791, both in Harold Syrett and Jacob Cooke, eds., *The Papers of Alexander Hamilton*, 26 vols. (Columbia:

University of Columbia Press, 1961–1981), 6: 80 and 8: 223 [hereafter, Hamilton, *Papers*].

6. Gordon Wood, *Empire of Liberty: A History of the Early Republic, 1789–1815* (New York: Oxford University Press, 2009), 95–140.

7. John Brewer, *The Sinews of Power: War, Money, and the English State, 1688–1783* (Cambridge: Harvard University Press, 1990).

8. J. G. A. Pocock, *The Machiavellian Moment: Florentine Political Thought and the Atlantic Tradition* (Princeton: Princeton University Press, 1975), 423–505; Caroline Robbins, *The Eighteenth-Century Commonwealthman: Studies in the Transmission, Development, and Circumstance of the English Liberal Thoughts from the Restoration of Charles II until the War with the Thirteen Colonies* (Cambridge: Harvard University Press, 1959; reprint, Indianapolis: Liberty Fund, 2004).

9. Bernard Bailyn, *The Ideological Origins of the American Revolution*, enlarged ed. (Cambridge: Harvard University Press, 1967 and 1992); Gordon Wood, *Creation of the American Republic, 1776–1787* (Chapel Hill: University of North Carolina Press, 1969); and Banning, *Jeffersonian Persuasion*.

10. On Hamilton's possible belief on the necessity of corruption, the best starting point remains Gerald Stourzh, *Alexander Hamilton and the Idea of Republican Government* (Stanford: Stanford University Press, 1970), 38–76. Also valuable is Forrest McDonald, *Alexander Hamilton: A Biography* (New York: Norton, 1979), *passim* and *Presidency of George Washington* 58 where McDonald notes that Hamilton "cast his lot unequivocally with Walpole"; Banning, *Jeffersonian Persuasion*, 126–40. For the fiscal-military elements of Hamilton's plan see Edling, *A Revolution in Favor of Government*, 149–218.

11. Thomas Hartley, as reported in *The New York Daily Gazette*, February 12, 1790 in Helen Viet, Charlene Bangs Bickford, Kenneth Bowling, and William Charles DiGiacomantonio, eds., *The Documentary History of the First Federal Congress* 18 vols. to date, Volume 12, *Debates in the House of Representatives, Second Session,: January-March, 1790* (Baltimore: The Johns Hopkins University Press, 1977-), 12: 241 [hereafter, Viet, et al., eds, *Documentary History of the First Federal Congress*].

12. James Jackson, as reported in *Congressional Register*, February 10, 1790 in Ibid., 260–62.

13. Lance Banning, *The Sacred Fire of Liberty: James Madison and the Founding of the Federal Republic* (Ithaca, NY: Cornell University Press, 1995), 293–324.

14. Jackson, as reported in *Congressional Register*, February 9, 1790, in Viet et al., eds, *Documentary History of the First Federal Congress*, 207.

15. James Jackson, Ibid. Also see James Monroe to Thomas Jefferson, July 18, 1790 in Julian P. Boyd, ed., *The Papers of Thomas Jefferson* 30 volumes (Princeton: Princeton University Press, 1962), 17: 221–23. [hereafter, Jefferson, *Papers*]

16. William Maclay, Diary entry for February 15 and April 10, 1790 in Kenneth Bowling and Helen E. Viet, eds., *The Diary of William Maclay and Other Notes on Senate Debates, March 4, 1789-March 3, 1971* (Baltimore: The John Hopkins University Press, 1988), 203.

17. Maclay entry for April 27, 1790 in Ibid., 254. The Senator who Maclay claimed made this remark was John Langdon of New Hampshire. Emphasis in the original.

18. Maclay, "Political, The Budget Opened, Object," and untitled essay both printed in *The Independent Gazetteer*, February 6 and 20 in Ibid., 410–11, 413–14.

19. Theodore Sedgwick reported in *The New York Daily Gazette*, February 12, 1790 in Viet, et al., eds, *DHFFC*, 12: 248.

20. Ibid.

21. Jacob E. Cooke, "The Compromise of 1790" *William and Mary Quarterly* 27 (November, 1970): 523–45 and Kenneth Bowling, "Dinner at Jefferson's: A Note on Jacob E. Cooke's 'The Compromise of 1790'" *William and Mary Quarterly* 28 (October 1971): 629–48; Wood, *Empire of Liberty*, 143–45.

22. Virginia "Remonstrance against the Assumption of State Debts" December 16, 1791 in Lance Banning, ed., *Liberty and Order: The First American Party Struggle* (Indianapolis: Liberty Fund, 2004), 68–70.

23. On this point also see Kevin R. C. Gutzman, *Virginia's American Revolution: From Dominion to Republic, 1776–1840* (Lanham: Lexington Books, 2007), 116–17.

24. Alexander Hamilton to John Jay, November 28, 1790, in Hamilton, *Papers*, 7: 166–67.

25. Alexander Hamilton to Edward Carrington, May 26, 1792, in Hamilton, ibid., 11: 426–45.

26. John C. Miller, *The Federalist Era, 1789–1801* (New York: Harper and Row, 1960), 55–69; Stanley Elkins and Eric McKitrick, *The Age of Federalism: The Early American Republic, 1788–1800* (New York: Oxford University Press, 1993), 226–34; and James Rogers Sharp, *American Politics in the Early Republic: The New Nation in Crisis* (New Haven: Yale University Press, 1993), 38–41. For the debate over the proper hermeneutics see exchange, carried out in several essays, between H. Jefferson Powell, "The Original Understanding of Original Intent"; Charles A. Lofgren, "The Original Understanding of Original Intent?" both in Jack N. Rakove, ed., *Interpreting the Constitution: The Debate over Original Intent* (Boston: Northeastern University Press, 1990), 53–150; and Raoul Berger, *Federalism: The Founders' Design* (Norman: University of Oklahoma Press, 1987); "The Founders' Views—According to Jefferson Powell," *Texas Law Review* 67 (1988–1989): 1033–96; "Jack Rakove's Rendition of Original Meaning," *Indiana Law Journal* 72 (Issue 3, 1997): 619–49. See Powell's response to Berger in "The Modern Misunderstanding of Original Intent," *The University of Chicago Law Review* 54 (Autumn, 1987): 1513–1544.

27. Quote is from Richard J. Buel, *Securing the Revolution: Ideology in American Politics, 1789–1800* (Ithaca: Cornell University Press, 1972), 19.

28. Fisher Ames, February 3, 1791, in *Annals of Congress*, 1st Congress, 3rd session, 1955.

29. Ibid., 1955–56.

30. William Blackstone, *Commentaries on the Laws of England,* Stanley Kurtz, ed., 4 vols. (Oxford: Clarendon Press, 1765; Chicago: University of Chicago Press, 1979), 1: 54.

31. Ames, 1st Congress, 3rd session, 1956.

32. Ibid., 1957.

33. John Laurance, February 4, 1791, in ibid., 1965–67.

34. James Jackson, February 4, 1791, reported in *Gazette of the United States*, found in Viet et al., *Documentary History of the First Federal Congress*, 14: 376.

35. James Jackson, February 4, 1791, reported in *Gazette of the United States*, found in ibid., 376.

36. Michael Jenifer Stone, February 4, 1791, in ibid., 425.

37. Michael St. Jennifer, February 4, 1791, in ibid., 1982–83.

38. Ibid., 1983.

39. William Branch Giles, February 7, 1791, in *Annals* 1st Congress, 3rd session, 1993–1994.

40. James Madison, February 2, 1791, in ibid., 1945.

41. Ibid., 1951.

42. Ibid., 1951.

43. Ibid.

44. Ibid.

45. Jack Rakove, *Original Meanings: Politics and Ideas in the Making of the Constitution* (New York: Knopf, 1996), 354.

46. James Madison to George Washington, February 21, 1791, in Dorothy Twohig, ed., *The Papers of George Washington: Presidential Series*, 16 vols. to date (Charlottesville: University of Virginia Press, 1987–), 7: 395 [hereafter, Washington, *Papers*]. For the measure that corrected Madison's policy objections see "An Act Supplementary to the Act Initutled [*sic*] 'An Act to Incorporate the Subscribers to the Bank of the United States," in Richard Peters, ed., *Public Statues at Large of the United States: 1789–1845*, 8 vols. (Boston: Charles C. Little and James Brown, 1845), 1: 196–97.

47. Gutzman, *Virginia's American Revolution*, 115, and Gutzman, *James Madison and the Making of America* (New York: St. Martin's Press, 2012), 212–36.

48. Edmund Randolph, "Opinion on the Constitutionality of the Bank," February 12, 1791, in Washington, *Papers*, 7: 331–36, quotes on 332–33; Walter Dellinger and H. Jefferson Powell, "The Constitutionality of the Bank Bill: The Attorney General's First Constitutional Law Opinions," *Duke Law Journal* 44 (1994): 110–33.

49. Randolph, "Opinion on the Constitutionality of the Bank," ibid.

50. Ibid., 337.

51. Thomas Jefferson, "Opinion on the Constitutionality of the Bank," February 15, 1791, in ibid., 348–53, quotes on 349.

52. Ibid., 350.

53. Ibid., 351–52.

54. Ibid. 353.

55. Ibid.

56. Alexander Hamilton, "Opinion on the Constitutionality of an Act to Establish a Bank," February 23, 1791, in ibid., 425–52; quote on 425.

57. Ibid., 426.

58. Ibid., 427

59. Ibid., 430.

60. Ibid., 425.

61. Ibid., 426.

62. Ibid., 428.

63. Ibid., 447.

64. Ibid., 425.

65. Ibid., 429.

66. Ibid.

67. Ibid.

68. Ibid., 435–35.

69. Ibid., 432–33.

70. Ibid., 431.

71. Ibid.

72. Ibid., 426.

SEVEN

The Settlement Defended

Republican Counterattack and the Eleventh Amendment

The early 1790s were years of victory for the Federalists. Not only had they passed Hamilton's economic program, but they had also begun the successful implementation of their constitutional vision of a sovereign federal government. The constitutional future, it seemed, lay with them and not with state sovereignty. This optimism, however justified, was misguided. What the Federalists did not anticipate was the degree to which their opponents would fight back. By 1792, the Federalists' opponents would start organizing themselves around Thomas Jefferson and James Madison. Calling themselves Republicans and drawing from the ideas of the Country Opposition thinkers, they feared that the Federalists' broken promises pointed in the direction of erasing the American Revolution and establishing a consolidated monarchy. The Republicans, therefore, took it as their mission to halt the Federalist advancement by restoring American constitutionalism to its Revolutionary roots. The next two chapters explore how Republicans accomplished that task. This chapter explains how Republicans defended the Revolution's constitutionalism settlement by resisting Federalists' arguments and fighting a Federalist-controlled Supreme Court bent on establishing a national popular sovereignty. The Republican's task was daunting, but, by 1800, they had accomplished their goal.

To stop the Federalists, Republicans had to first articulate their constitutional vision. Prior to the early 1790s, they had expressed this vision only in the bits and pieces of congressional debates. These intermittent speeches were useful, but they were not enough. Republicans believed that they needed a more coherent and systematic appeal to the public. Just three days after Washington signed the bank bill, Jefferson and Madison took the first steps in this direction when they hired Madison's former college classmate, Phillip Freneau, to be a translator in the State Department. Freneau's real mission, however, was to establish the *National Gazette*, a newspaper from which the Federalists' opponents could express their concerns about Hamilton's program and advance the cause of the emerging Republicans. In this plan, however, the Federalists had already beaten them to the punch.[1] In early 1790, Hamilton had created the *Gazette of the United States*. Each issue praised Hamilton and his economic plan and damned those who opposed him. Such praise frustrated Jefferson who labeled the *Gazette* "a paper of pure Toryism, disseminating the doctrine of monarchy, aristocracy, and the exclusion of the influence of the people."[2]

As the *National Gazette* began operation, Madison entered the fray by publishing the first of eighteen essays. Known collectively as the "*National Gazette* essays," each self-contained essay addressed a singular topic. Most essays did not directly address Hamilton or the Federalists, but the timing of the essays made it clear that they were his targets. Madison threaded the essays with the theme of republican self-government and the threat posed to it by Hamilton and the Federalists. While it is not clear exactly when Madison wrote the essays, there is little doubt that he hoped they would counteract the growing power of the Federalists.[3]

Several of Madison's essays are critical to note. In his essay on "Charters," published in January of 1792, Madison praised Americans for their adherence to written constitutions. Madison reminded readers that history had demonstrated that all the evils of despotism emerged when power remained unfettered by the "solemnity of the act proclaiming the will and authenticated by the seal of the people." Madison urged his readers to remain vigilant about establishing the efficacy of the Constitution and to "defending liberty against power and power against licentiousness; and in keeping every portion of power within its proper limits." Doing so "means discomfiting the parti[s]an of anti-republican contrivances." Just who those partisans were was obvious.[4] Madison furthered his attacks on Hamilton's scheme in his essay "Property." Madison noted that the protection of private property was "the end of government that alone is a just government which impartially secures to every man whatever is his own." There could be no "just security to property if it is not afforded by that government under which unequal taxes oppress one species of property and reward another species."[5] In this, Madison echoed the congressional criticism offered against Hamilton's scheme. Opponents attacked it for its unequal taxation of southern states to pay for northern wartime debt and its enrichment of speculators at the expense of burdening agricultural laborers.

In two critical essays, "Government of the United States" and "Consolidation," Madison not only touched on the core issues dividing the Federalists and Republicans but also issued a clarion call for resistance to the Federalists. The federal structure and the separation of powers, wrote Madison in "Government of the United States," made the United States unique. The division of government between state and union provided a "security against power."[6] Maintaining this federalism was difficult because of the need to "discriminate by precise enumerations one class of legislative power . . . [w]hen the powers being more kindred nature, their boundaries are more obscure and run more into each other." Despite this problem, that separation must "by no means be abandoned."[7] Those, like the Federalists, "who would pronounce" federalism "impossible offer no alternative . . . but schism or consolidation." That was the "high road to monarchy." It was the responsibility of those "who love their country," therefore, to "avoid the alternative, by elucidating and guarding the limits which define the two governments." Defenders of federalism must be "ready to make their voice to pronounce and their arm to repel or repair aggression on the authority of their constitution."[8] Nor should Americans scoff at the threat of consolidation; it was all too real. Should the "state governments [be] abolished, the same space of country that would produce an undue growth of the executive power would prevent that control on the legislative body which is essential to a faithful discharge of its trust." Should consolidation destroy the "local organs" of the state government, the "universal silence and insensibility" would place the federal government on a "self-directed" course towards arbitrary government.[9]

The federalism Madison offered in these essays was one where the state governments remained the primary entity of self-government and the best protection of liberty. But he warned that the permanency of the state governments should not be taken for granted. Threats abounded to both the Constitution and the federal scheme. Again, the context surrounding those essays made it clear that Madison saw those threats as emanating from the Federalists. Should their plans continue apace, the entire constitutional system would be overturned and replaced with monarchy and tyranny.

Madison feared the Federalists' triumph would not be stopped until the public was made aware. Madison was also clear that his calls toward vigilance were not attempts to establish a political party. In the eighteenth century, Americans viewed political parties as evils to be avoided at all cost. To have a party signified a sickness in the body politic. In his essay "Parties," Madison admitted that political parties were "unavoidable," but the people should combat them at all times. The sources of these parties, he concluded, derived from when one set attempted to increase unnatural inequalities, such as wealth and privileges. Taking a direct shot at Hamilton's economic program (although he did not mention it by name), he noted that "the great art of politicians lies in making them [i.e., wealth and privileges] checks and balances to each other."[10] In other words, Madison accused Hamilton and his program of creating the party. By attaching the monied classes to the federal government, Hamilton sought a party to aggrandize itself at the expense of everyone else. This sophistry, Madison noted, was no less "absurd than it would be, in ethics, to say that new vices ought to be promoted, where they would counteract each other, because this use may be made of existing vices."[11]

One other important fact surrounds Madison's essays. They represent his final and decisive break from the Federalists. Although Madison was a vocal champion of the Constitution, and had allied with the Nationalists during the 1780s, his nationalism was always different from that of Hamilton and Ames. Whereas they, and many other Federalists, championed the sovereignty of the federal government, and saw the Constitution as a means to an end, Madison's federalism was one of balance. He accepted and endorsed the constitutional settlement that left the main bulk of sovereignty with the states. The Constitution was not a radical refounding; it was, instead, limited in its powers and objectives. The federal government gained power but the sovereignty of the states remained. To him, the Constitution was the end, and the enumeration of powers the means to achieve that end. Hamilton's program, however, threatened to destroy that settlement and replace it with a consolidated government. The differences between him and the Federalists became increasingly clear during the first years of the Constitution's operation. The first clear step in his break, although no one at the time realized it, came when he forced the Federalists to honor their promise to consider a bill of rights. From there, Hamilton's program only accelerated his divergence. By 1791, the break was complete.[12]

Hamilton, for his part, was stunned by what he perceived as Madison's abandonment. In the same letter to Edward Carrington where he reported his preference for smaller states that would serve as the administrative arm of the federal government, Hamilton told his friend he thought he knew "for a certainty it was a primary article in [Madison's] creed that the real danger in our system was the subversion of the national authority by the preponderancy of the state governments. All his measures have proceeded on an opposite direction."[13] Not only had Madison seemingly changed his mind, but he and Jefferson were at "the head of a faction decidedly hostile to me and my administration, and actuated by views in my judgment subversive of the principles of good government and dangerous to the union, peace and happiness of the Country."[14] From nearly every measure of government, they "have been found among those who were disposed to narrow the Federal authority." Madison, in particular "lost no opportunity of sounding the alarm with great affected solemnity at encroachments meditated on the rights of the states, & of holding up the bugbear of a faction in the government having designs unfriendly to liberty." Not only had they dared resist Hamilton in the councils of government, but they had become "coadjustor" of Freneau's paper that is "generally unfriendly to the Government of the U States."

Hamilton believed Madison had either fallen under Jefferson's influence or was "seduced by the expectation of popularity" in Virginia. Nor did Hamilton's letter betray any affection for Jefferson. Hamilton believed Jefferson's resistance originated from his jealousy at "not [being] in the first instance cordially acquiesced in the new government," and that, as the confederation's minister to France, he never "experienced the imbecilities" of the Articles of Confederation. Jefferson's time in France colored his political views, Hamilton claimed. Jefferson "saw government only on the side of its abuses" because he had drunk "deeply of the French Philosophy."[15] Although he returned to head a major office under the new government, Jefferson was disappointed he did not "have greater share in the direction of our councils." Hamilton attributed Jefferson's opposition to personal ambition: he desired the "Presidential Chair." Whatever the motivations of the duo, Hamilton believed their ultimate goal was to "effect a change" in government, starting with him. So desirous was their goal, he believed they were willing to "risk rendering the Government itself odious." The duo was working to "strength[en]" the "organized rivalry of state government," and once they turned the people against the federal government that animosity "will be kept so by these powerful [and] indefatigable enemies." But Hamilton warned that Jefferson and Madison "forget an old but very just, though a coarse, saying— That it is much easier to raise the Devil than to lay him."[16]

***

The separation between Madison and Hamilton was emblematic of the wider political division that occurred throughout the early 1790s. Historians often point to growing sectionalism as one of the primary culprits behind the gulf between Republicans and Federalists. There is some truth to this. Northerners and southerners certainly viewed themselves as different, but it is easy to exaggerate the extent to which this fueled the rift in the 1790s.[17] While many southerners resisted Hamilton's assumption plan because they had paid their wartime debt, they did not act as a collective section. The sectional identity that many associate with the South was much more of a nineteenth-century development. Furthermore, in the early days of the Revolution, Americans had recognized quickly the differences between the northerners and southerners. Those distinctions persisted well into the post-independence era. Additionally, the vast number of Federalists in the South and Republicans in the North suggests that these differences were not as sectional as they might seem. Nor did the political divide the result from Republicans not understanding Hamiltonian economics, as historians sometimes claim.[18] There is little evidence to support this claim. Hamilton's program was certainly complex and intricate, but the debates over the program reveal that the Republicans understood all too well not only how those details were to operate but, more importantly, exactly what Hamilton's program was attempting to achieve.

Federalism divided the Federalists and the Republicans. The Federalists, despite their promises during ratification, had advanced an understanding of the Constitution at odds with the American constitutional experience. To them, the Constitution had created a new civil society, national in scope and characteristics. Everyone should focus their attention on this new society; not only should this society be paramount to the distinct societies of the states, but it needed to meld them together. Because the Constitution created a new civil society, the national government had to exercise powers beyond those enumerated in the document; it was the only way to ensure the stability of the society. Federalists made repeated appeals to extra-constitutional power precisely because of this belief in a new society; without those powers, they claimed, the civil compact was incomplete. In many ways, then, the constitutionalism to which the Federalists subscribed reflected the premodern understanding of what constitutions were. From the classical era to the eighteenth century, the terms constitution and society were intertwined. Society was the manner in which life was lived with the constitution describing "what that life should be like and the institutions by means of which will be achieved that way of life." [19] In other words, the Federalists viewed the Constitution as a means to a much greater end: the establishment and stability of civil society. When the Federalists reacted harshly to the Republicans' appeals to state sovereignty, they did so because they viewed those appeals as life threatening to the new order.

By 1792, the Republicans were not only cognizant of the Federalists' ideas, but they considered them a betrayal of the Revolution's primary accomplishment, republican self-government in the form of distinct sovereign states. To Republicans, the Constitution did not establish a civil society; civil society already existed in the separate states. The only way to create the national society envisioned by the Federalists was to tear down those distinctions and consolidate them into one. The first step in this consolidation was to destroy the state governments. The constitutionalism of the Republicans, then, aligned closer to the more recent understanding of the word, which held "something distinct from and superior to the entire government including even the legislative representatives of the people." [20] This adherence to modern constitutionalism helps explain why the Anti-Federalists, who by-and-large became Republicans, fought so strenuously for a state sovereignty amendment. A stated protection of state sovereignty would be superior to any legislative action that could threaten the states and their societies. It also helps clarify the Republicans' reliance upon "strict" construction of the Constitution.

Strict construction provided the interpretative means to prevent threats to the internal societies or governments of the states. The Republicans, moreover, understood the constitutional arrangement as a union of distinct sovereign states. Union, to the Republicans, was the preferable and logical outgrowth of having such small and geographically close states. Union was what the Articles of Confederation had created and the Constitution was trying to perfect. Thus, Republicans viewed the Constitution as the end—creating a better functioning union—and the enumeration of powers as the means to achieve that end. What is more, they originally thought Federalists shared this belief. As Republicans became more aware of the Federalists' real goal, however, they reacted by appealing to the Revolution's constitutional settlement.

No Republican appealed more frequently to state sovereignty than the Virginian John Taylor of Caroline. An Anti-Federalist during ratification, Taylor originally opposed the adoption of the Constitution on grounds that it would destroy state sovereignty. Throughout the 1790s, Taylor returned to these themes repeatedly in several well-circulated pamphlets. In an age when pamphlets were the primary means of disseminating information, Taylor was the Republicans' premier pamphleteer.[21] His works are not always the easiest to read, however. As Kevin R. C. Gutzman has explained, Taylor's works were "masterpieces of sometimes inspired, sometimes befuddled opposition to Federalism."[22] Nevertheless, and despite the awkwardness of his prose, Taylor used his writings to accuse Hamilton's program of introducing "principles dangerous to the rights and interests of the community" with the sole purpose of "undermining the great pillars of the government."[23] Taylor worried that Federalists' schemes would turn Americans away from republican self-government and induce a laziness in order to introduce "monarchical ingredients" into the constitutional system.

Taylor had a particular hatred for the Bank of the United States, devoting his pamphlet *An Enquiry into the Principles and Tendency of Certain Public Measures* to attacking the institution. The bank was "the master key of that system, which governs the administration." The bank allowed Hamilton to create a "class of men . . . dangerous to the general welfare" and a threat to the morality of the people."[24] It opened the door for the Federalists to enact taxes designed to benefit a single group at the expense of the general welfare. None of this would have been possible had the Federalists not created the bank through an "express violation" of the government's power and the "principles of the constitution." No "trace of such an idea" as a national bank was found in the Constitution; instead the bank's supporters were "reduced to the narrow ground of asserting that a power is tacitly implied, conflicting and subverting the most fundamental principles, early and loudly express[ed]."[25] By this, he meant that reliance upon implied powers to achieve extra-constitutional powers violated the idea that the states retained all powers not given by the Constitution.

Taylor informed his readers that two remedies existed to thwart the Federalists. The first, which he admitted would take time, was to elect members of Congress who shared "a familiarity of interests—of—burthens—of benefits and of habits with the electors." His second suggestion was to go "through the organs of state legislatures." Those bodies were the best "security for liberty of the happiest texture which could have been devised." Taylor advised turning to the state governments because they were "the people themselves." Because of annual elections state legislators were more accountable to the people. Since they elected the members of the federal Senate, they could "operate decisively upon the general government." Finally, he noted, but did not elaborate, that the state legislatures "have at least as good a right to judge of every infraction of the constitution as Congress itself."[26]

The idea of the state legislatures judging the constitutionality of federal measures was not unique to Taylor. States used the Burke Amendment in the 1780s in a similar fashion, and Virginia's 1790 Remonstrance also argued for the power. But Taylor was the first to give it popular credence. He developed this idea further in his 1795 work, *An Argument Respecting the Constitutionality of the Carriage Tax*. Part of Hamilton's financial plan levied an excise tax on carriages. The tax affected southern planters more than any other group. In his pamphlet, Taylor charged that the federal tax was so unequal that it rendered southerners to slaves. "States which impose unequal taxes are master; those which pay them, slaves."[27] The Constitution, he asserted, "was designed to preserve certain rights." Yet, if no remedy to this unconstitutional "tribute" could be found, "America possesses only an Utopian Constitution." The Constitution's framers surely did not intend to create an instrument "by which a faction could seduce—corrupt—and divide the states!" Indeed, they did not, Taylor claimed. Instead, the Constitution was "not a compact of individuals it is a compact of the states." Individuals were required to obey both the state and federal legislatures, but only "whilst legislating with the pale of the Constitution."[28] When the federal government violated the constitution by interfering with power of the states, the states had to respond, as the federal government had "no control over the latter." It was this last point that allowed the states to judge for themselves the constitutionality of measures. Who else but the states could determine if a federal action interfered with state authority or threatened the liberty of their citizens? In the years that followed Taylor's pamphlet, the states would invoke this power to judge the constitutionality of federal actions.

***

Even as Republicans began their public push back they also had to contend with the Federalists on another front, the judiciary. In particular, they had to address the question of state sovereign immunity. Not long after the creation of the courts the question of state sovereign immunity, of whether individuals from one state could sue a state government, became the judiciary's most important issue. It was also an issue of singular importance because it touched upon the very nature of American constitutionalism. If a citizen of one state could sue an entire state, it begged the questions, how truly sovereign did the states remain after the adoption of the Constitution and whether the Constitution established a union of states or a consolidated republic? How the participants and unfolding events the 1790s answered both questions provided a clear guide to the understanding of the nature of American constitutionalism and of the union that emerged out of 1787. Although the question had been perennial since the proposal of the Constitution, when the Supreme Court maintained the Constitution formed a consolidated republic rooted in a national popular sovereignty, the subsequent response was a resounding and unmistakable affirmation of state sovereignty in the form of the Eleventh Amendment.

Originating in medieval England, sovereign immunity, the idea that the crown was protected from most forms of legal actions since sovereignty rested with the king, was well-known in colonial America.[29] Several colonies, however, permitted lawsuits against their colonial governments. With the declaring of independence, several states maintained this practice explicitly with constitutional provisions, but, for the most part, the concept was not discussed. It is difficult to ascertain whether this silence implied an endorsement or rejection of sovereign immunity. It seems likely that this silence was a tacit endorsement. Given the large amount of prewar debt held by British and Loyalist creditors, a silent rejection of sovereign versus a constitutional or statutory allowance would have made acquiring payment of the debts easier. In many ways, the various state laws passed during and following the war forbidding or limiting the form of how these debts were paid flowed from an implied understanding sovereign immunity. This implicit understanding can also help further explain why states reacted in anger to Articles Four and Five of the Treaty of Peace; the Treaty, from its opponent's views, mocked state sovereignty. Interestingly, however, during the Constitutional Convention the Committee of Detail included state suability in Section 2 of Article III of the Constitution. It passed without any debate or consideration.[30] Nevertheless, the explicit lack of protection for state sovereignty immunity was a featured critique of Anti-Federalists, who saw it and the judicial branch in general as tools to weaken the states at the expense of federal power. Federalists assured critics that since "it is inherent in the nature of sovereignty not to be amenable to the suit of an individual without its consent" the provision of Article III applied only when the state was a plaintiff.[31] Despite these assurances, Virginia and New York both suggested amendments that would have forbidden individuals from other states suing another state.[32] Finally, Congress defeated the efforts of Virginia representative Thomas Tucker to add his state's recommendation to the list of amendments that eventually became the Bill of Rights.[33]

Unsurprisingly, the question of state sovereign immunity and its implications for state sovereignty remained contentious. When the Supreme Court opened its inaugural session in 1791, it already had cases that centered upon the issue. In *Van Staphort v. Maryland, Oswald v. New York*, and *Hollingsworth v. Virginia*, all of which involved wartime debts contracted by the states, the Supreme Court summoned each state to appear before the Supreme Court.[34] Citing their status as sovereigns, each state initially refused to attend. Maryland eventually appeared before the Court but settled the case rather than "permit a precedent to be established" that would adversely "affect the political rights of this state, as an independent member of the union."[35] The Van Staphort lawyer, Pierce Butler, advised taking the state's offer lest the court decide in favor of Maryland. In *Oswald v. New York*, New York refused to appear on the grounds that "being so free, sovereign, and independent, [it] cannot or ought to be drawn or compelled against the Will therefore to appear."[36] Virginia was even more forceful. When the Supreme Court ordered a federal marshal to deliver a summons to Virginia, the state refused to be "involuntarily dragged" before the Supreme Court and considered the action "an unauthorized, and dangerous Assumption of power which if established may give birth to a Series of pernicious, and disgraceful consequences, to this Country."[37] Its House of Delegates rebuffed the Supreme Court's summons as "incompatible with, and dangerous to the sovereignty and independence of the individual states, as the same tends to a general consolidation of these confederated republics."[38] In another set of resolutions, the entire Virginia legislature notified the Court that the state would not appear before it since the state had settled the issues surrounding the *Hollingsworth* case in 1779 when the Articles of Confederation "expressly guaranteed perfected and unimpaired sovereignty as to all matters of internal Government to all the State leagued under it."[39]

These robust invocations of state sovereignty—and—Virginia and New York's close paraphrase of the Burke Amendment was not coincidental—signified that the issue of sovereignty and sovereign immunity would make deciding the case difficult. By invoking state sovereignty, the states assumed their sovereignty remained as intact in the 1790s as it did a decade earlier. In other words, the states believed the union was a collection of republican states in league with one another. The Constitution may have strengthened and even rearranged elements of that bond, but it did erase the sovereignty of the states.

Newspapers and pamphleteers paid particular attention to the cases and the constitutional issue involved. Some newspapers editorialized that the *Van Staphorst* case could "settle" whether "several states, have relinquished all their SOVEREIGNTIES, and have become mere corporations."[40] Others claimed the states were overreacting; sounding a false alarm over the issue of the threat to state sovereignty posed by the cases. "Enthusiasm," wrote one anonymous essayist, "has very frequently created within the minds of men, fears, which, like mere phantoms, have neither body nor basis to support them."[41]

The potential implications of the *Van Straphorst* case inspired James Sullivan, Massachusetts' Attorney General, to author a widely-read pamphlet, *Observations on the Government of the United States*. Despite the wide-ranging title, Sullivan focused his lengthy *Observations* upon the issue of state sovereign immunity. Siding with Maryland, the Massachusetts jurist explained that the crux of the case centered upon "whether we are an assemblage of republics, held together as a nation by the form of government of the United States, or one great republic, made up of divers corporations?"[42] Invoking the arguments first made by Americans during the imperial crisis, Sullivan claimed that prior to independence the colonies possessed an independent measure of sovereignty apart from that of Britain. When independence broke formal ties to Britain, the states assumed all elements of sovereignty. States surrendered some powers, but not their sovereignty, to the Articles of Confederation. Article II of the articles reaffirmed state sovereignty in strong, indisputable language. Even the term "state," while maintaining a geographical element, retained its ancient definition as an "empire, kingdom or commonwealth possessing sovereign power."[43] By grounding his argument in an overview of the development of state sovereignty, Sullivan opined that the Constitution of 1787, was a "system of government which would firmly and indissolubly unite all states" for their general interest and not a consolidated nation. This "revision" of the constitutional system remained "quite compatible with each state's retaining a sovereignty," while preventing "the great evils" that often accompanied a change of government. In other words, the states had transferred to the Constitution the powers needed to maintain a union, but had reserved their sovereignty.[44]

Establishing that the sovereignty of the states remained essentially unaltered allowed Sullivan to defend the sovereign immunity of the states. It seemed obvious to him that from the start of the new government the "states, as states were not liable to the civil process" of the federal judiciary. "There can be nothing," he added, "more absurd and ridiculous than to suppose the government existing as separate governments, and yet to suppose them amendable before a civil tribunal, of any kind, upon mean process." Such an action flew in the face of history and

seemingly settled debate. The only cases states could have before the
Supreme Court were those where the state was the plaintiff or a dispute
arose over boundaries between two or more states. Otherwise, "a sovereign can never consent to become a party before a foreign tribunal."[45]

Sullivan's argument endorsed two critical, but long-standing constitutional ideas. First, the Constitution was a compact between the several
states. The history of the sovereignty of the colonies, and now states,
made this point clear to Sullivan. Any attempt by the United States
government to force any state to be defendant was "inconsistent with
every idea of any kind of sovereignty." Second, since the states retained
their sovereignty, they had to consent before being a defendant in any
judicial action. Sullivan asserted that the states had consented to the Constitution but not to allowing individuals of another state to sue them.
Since neither the states, nor the people of the states, consented to give the
Constitution coercive powers over the states, the Supreme Court could
not force a state to defend its sovereign actions.

Timothy Ford, a South Carolina Federalist, published a lengthy response to Sullivan's argument. Sullivan's great oversight, Ford argued,
was "placing every state superior to the jurisdiction or control of the
supreme court of the union." Ford restated the Federalist position that
"arms" or a "civil war" would be the only possible remedy for disputes if
Sullivan and the states had their way. Ford also critiqued Sullivan on the
more solid ground of the Constitution's language. He accused Sullivan of
wishing for the Constitution as it "ought to be," rather than "what it is."[46]
Ford followed Sullivan by retracing the history of the confederation but
arrived at a different conclusion. The term confederation, he noted, signified an agreement amongst powers. The late confederation may have
had a "federal head," but it was little more than "ad deliberandum," with
nearly all power contained with the states. The states had so jealously
protected their sovereignty that they destroyed the confederation and the
union. The Constitution however, saved the union by establishing an
actual government that derived its authority from, and operated upon,
individuals and not states. The powers of the federal government could
not have sprung from the states, as the states were never sovereign. Rather, the federal government derived its power from the sovereignty of the
people of the entire United States, whom, he added, also chose to make
those powers the supreme law of the land.[47] Thus, the Constitution was
not a reformulated confederation, but rather a national government that
wielded the power of the sovereign people of America.

Talk of state sovereignty, Ford claimed, ignored the Constitution's
provisions making the states clear "subordinates." Operating as it did
upon both individuals and states (with the states retaining only limited
elements sovereign power) eliminated the worst elements of both consolidated government and confederations. Yet, when states ignored the
summons of the Supreme Court, they embraced the worst traits that de-

stroyed the confederation. Furthermore, refusing to be a defendant before the Supreme Court established a dangerous precedent that would disrupt the new system in its infancy and make the states the clear superior to the federal government. Quoting from *Federalist 32*, the South Carolina pamphleteer noted that bringing an exclusive and uniform rule was necessary for constitutional stability. Thus, states refusing to be defendants before the Supreme Court not only denied justice, but also the spirit, purpose, and plain language of the Constitution.[48]

By 1792, the public and legislative positions on the issue of state sovereign immunity were well entrenched, but the court itself did not consider the issue until hearing *Chisholm v. Georgia*. Like the earlier cases, the *Chisholm* case revolved around a wartime contractual debt. During the war, South Carolina resident Robert Farquhar sold products and goods to Georgia. After the war's conclusion, Georgia failed to pay its debt. Subsequently, Farquhar died, and by the time Alexander Chisholm became Farquhar's executor, the Constitution and federal courts had been established. In 1791, at roughly the same time the *Van Straphort, Oswald*, and *Hollingsworth* cases began generating controversy Chisholm sued Georgia. After the Federal Southern Circuit Court dismissed the case on grounds that it lacked jurisdiction, the Supreme Court decided to hear the case during its next term.[49]

Like the other states before it, Georgia demurred. Thomas Carnes and John Noel, the attorney generals for the state, advised Governor Edward Telfair that although the Constitution empowered the Supreme Court to hear cases between a state and citizens from another state, it "can never convey the idea that a free sovereign and independent State shall be subject to the impleaded in such courts." Rather, because the Constitution was a "Federal Compact," Article III of the Constitution "suppose[d] the State or States in such cases [were] always plaintiffs or petitioners."[50] Governor Telfair took his counsel's advice and informed the Court in late 1791 that since Georgia was a "free, sovereign, and independent State," and was so at the time of the contract between it and Farquhar, Georgia could not "be drawn or compelled, to answer against the will of the said State of Georgia before any Justices of the Federal Circuit Court . . . or before any Justices of any Court of Law or Equity whatever."[51] The state held true to his word and refused to appear before the Supreme Court during the August 1792 session. Edmund Randolph, Chisholm's attorney (and the United States Attorney General), requested the Court either compel the state's attendance or decide the case with Georgia *in absentia* and award judgment to Chisholm. The Court, probably realizing that such unilateral action would only further inflame Georgia and other states, balked at Randolph's suggestion. Instead, they postponed hearing the case until the February 1793 term.[52]

The Court's delay only intensified Georgia's resolve. Its House of Representatives passed resolutions describing the case as the final step in a process to "effectually destroy the retained sovereignty of the states" and "annihilate the very shadow of state government, and to render them but tributary corporations to the government of the United States." This process, which began with the "injustice of the funding system of the United States," would "perplex the citizens of Georgia with perpetual taxes" due to the resulting "numberless law-suits" should Georgia lose the case and its sovereignty. Governor Telfair sent the resolution to Georgia's legal agent in Philadelphia in hopes that he would read it before the Court.[53]

When the Court reconvened in February 1793, Georgia's official agents James Dallas and Jared Ingersoll read the House resolution before the Court but refused further participation in the case. Randolph's defense of Chisholm addressed four questions the Court had asked him to consider.[54] The attorney general answered the first query, of whether Georgia, "being one of the United States," could be a defendant in "any" case, by appealing to the language of the Constitution. Although he would "always contend that the states were sovereigns," in this instance the Constitution "produced a new order of things." The Constitution simply mentioned cases "between" a state and a citizen of another state; it did not distinguish between a defendant or plaintiff. The Constitution, furthermore, through prohibitions on habeas corpus, *ex post facto* laws, and bills of attainder, also protected individuals from state actions; the only way to stop this violation of the federal Constitution was to sue the state in federal court. Thus, an individual's constitutional ability to sue, Randolph claimed, was a critical check upon state power. From this position, Randolph dispatched the remaining questions, answering that states could have an action of assumpit (i.e., debt collection) against it, that the governor should represent the state in lawsuits, and, finally, since there was no law determining how the Court could compel state attendance before the court, it was up to the Justices to determine the proper procedure. Randolph, well-aware both of the public's attention to the case and the larger constitutional and political context involved, "personally assure[d] them [i.e., the states], that the prostration of State-rights is no object with me; but that I remain in perfect confidence, that with the power, which the people and the Legislatures of the States indirectly hold over almost every movement of the National Government, the States need not fear an assault from bold ambition, or any approaches of covered stratagem."[55]

Two weeks after Randolph's remarks, the Justices delivered their opinions. The case was decided four to one in favor of Chisholm. At the time the Justices delivered their opinions *seriatim*, or individually; there was no single majority opinion. The opinions of Justices William Cushing and John Blair were simple and direct. Relying upon the language of the Constitution, both asserted that Georgia—and by implication the other states—had no choice but to be appear before the court. If they could be plaintiffs, they could also be defendants.[56] The other two majority opinions by James Wilson and John Jay were much more elaborate and touched upon the underlying constitutional issues of the case. Both offered stridently Nationalistic defenses of the Constitution.

Wilson's opinion reflected the Nationalistic position he had held since before the drafting of the Articles of Confederation. Recall that it was Wilson who, in 1776, first asserted that the Continental Congress was a national government representing the entire American people. Although the instruments of government had changed in the intervening two-decades, his opinion had not. In his learned, markedly philosophical, and somewhat snobbish opinion, Wilson again invoked the idea that a national popular sovereignty created a national government.

Wilson devoted significant space to the natural law idea that "Man, fearfully and wonderfully made, is the workmanship of his all perfect Creator: A State; useful and valuable as the contrivance is, is the inferior contrivance of man; and from his native dignity derives all its acquired importance."[57] To Wilson, this is the original and proper notion of sovereignty, as power and autonomy resting in the individual, who upon a mutual agreement with others, formed states (i.e., society) and governments. Historical development, however, like the serpent in the garden, had perverted this perfect sovereignty into two notions that acted "against the natural order of things, and an inconsiderate or an interested disposition to sacrifice the end to the means." The first developed when governments claimed dominion over both the society and the individual. The second, and by far worse, definition of sovereignty grew out of the noxious notions of feudalism. This sovereignty permitted governments to "usur[p] equally the property of land, and the administration of justice," while denying the people the right to seek justice against their actions. This feudal notion, Wilson claimed, "furnishe[d] a basis for what I presume to be one of the principal objections against the jurisdiction of this Court over the State of Georgia."[58]

Wilson admitted that governments had powers, rights, and responsibilities but they did not override the natural sovereignty of the people. Starting his Nationalistic crescendo, Wilson noted that states frequently "assumed a supercilious preeminence above the people, who have formed it: Hence the haughty notions of state independence, state sovereignty and state supremacy."[59] Although the people of Georgia certainly made the state of Georgia a republican state, the entire American people formed the United States. In fact, precisely because Georgia was republican, with its power deriving from the people of that state, meant "Georgia has no claim upon her own citizens."[60] Extending the logic of this thought, Wilson claimed that since the United States was a national republic, with national popular sovereignty as the font of its authority, also meant Georgia (and, by extension any other state) "can have no claim upon the citizens of another State." Wilson therefore found "nothing, which tends to evince an exemption of the State of Georgia, from the jurisdiction of the Court." Instead, he found "a contrary tendency." Wilson then offered a lamentation against how:

> the states, rather than the People, for whose sakes the States exist, are
> frequently the objects which attract and arrest our principal attention.
> This, I believe, has produced much of the confusion and perplexity,
> which have appeared in several proceedings and several publications
> on state-politics, and on the politics, too, of the United States. Senti-
> ments and expressions of this inaccurate kind prevail in our common,
> even in our convivial, language. Is a toast asked? "The United States,"
> instead of the "People of the United States," is the toast given. This is
> not politically correct. The toast is meant to present the view of the first
> great object in the Union. It presents only the second. It presents only
> the artificial person, instead of the natural persons, who spoke it into
> existence. A State I cheerfully fully admit, is the noblest work of Man.
> But, Man himself, free and honest, is, I speak as to this world, the
> noblest work of God.[61]

To Wilson, then, the people of the several states, acting in concert at the various state ratification conventions, did not adopt the Constitution. Rather, he imagined it as a popular sovereignty of the collective whole, as a national body untethered to state boundaries. When this collective "acted upon the large scale of the Union, as a part of the 'People of the United States,'" it siphoned not just the powers of the states but also their sovereignty and placed it firmly in the Constitution. "As to the purposes of the Union, therefore, Georgia is not a sovereign State," Wilson opined. By "institute[ing], for such purposes, a national Government, complete in all its parts," Wilson continued, "we may then infer, that the people of the United States intended to bind the several States, by the Legislative power of the national Government." Thus, when the language of Article III failed to distinguish whether states could only be plaintiffs, clear and easy deduction pointed to states being defendants. If nothing else, Wilson claimed, the preamble to the Constitution, with its calls for justice and domestic tranquility, empowered the federal government to "bind" Georgia.[62]

Wilson's use of the word "bind" is of particular importance to his nationalist argument and reveals his concept of the relationship between the states and the constitution. Wilson must have realized that by claiming "certain laws of the States are declared to be subject to the revision and control of the Congress," and that the "United States intend[ed] to bind the several States by the Executive power of the national Government," he echoed Parliament's assertion in the Declaratory Act to "bind the colonies in all cases whatsoever." Yet, this seems to be exactly what Wilson was arguing. While his concept of sovereignty differed from Parliament's in that it rested within a supposed national popular sovereignty, nevertheless, his conception of the federal government's sovereignty was as final and absolute as that of Parliament. State sovereignty, therefore, was essentially non-existent to Wilson's thinking. To be sure, the people of Georgia could do what they wanted with the state of Georgia, but final, complete, and decisive sovereignty rested in the United States government.

One final element of Wilson's opinion bears mentioning: its contradiction to his primary claim in his famous "State Courthouse speech" in October 1787. In those remarks, Wilson acknowledged popular sovereignty at the state and national level, and in this, his *Chisholm* decision simply restated that long-held belief. Yet, in 1787, he labeled the proposed constitution a "positive grant expressed in the instrument of the union. Hence, it is evident, that in the former case everything which is not reserved is given; but in the latter the reserve of the proposition prevails, and everything which is not given is reserved." The state governments would not only continue to wield the predominance of power, but "upon their existence depends the existence of the Federal plan." [63] This sentiment did not appear in his *Chisholm* opinion, however. Wilson's federal government was a full sovereign empowered by the preamble and natural rights philosophy to bind the states in any manner it best saw fit. So much for specific grants of power with ungranted powers reserved to the states.

Jay's opinion, while agreeing that Georgia's claim to sovereignty rested upon "feudal principles," lacked Wilson's intensity or appeals to natural law and political philosophy. Yet, it was no less as nationalistic. Jay argued for the existence of a pre-independence popular sovereignty. To prove his argument, he appealed to recent history.[64] Yet, his historical account was so at odds with actual events that one wonders if Jay knowingly twisted historical facts to fit his ideological argument. In fact, Jay's opinion contradicted his own revolutionary writings. In 1779, Jay, as a member of the Continental Congress, penned a Circular letter to the states where he proclaimed that the Declaration "did, in the name of the people of the Thirteen United Colonies, declare them to be free and independent States." Not only did Jay fail to mention a preexisting national popular sovereignty, but his letter also explicitly endorsed the idea that the Declaration created thirteen distinct sovereigns. Fifteen years later, however, Jay now argued that the Declaration of Independence transferred the sovereignty of the British crown to the entire American people. How such a transfer occurred, he did not say. Jay claimed that at the time of the Declaration:

> it was then not an uncommon opinion, that the unappropriated lands, which belonged to that crown, passed not to the people of the Colony or States within whose limits they were situated, but to the whole people; on whatever principles this opinion rested, it did not give way to the other, and thirteen sovereignties were considered as emerged from the principles of the Revolution, combined with local convenience

and considerations; the people nevertheless continued to consider themselves, in a national point of view, as one people.[65]

Continuing with his defense of national popular sovereignty, Jay maintained that the American people formed the Articles of Confederation. This statement, offered as fact by Jay, was clearly contradicted in the actual drafting and acceptance of that document as well as the plain language of Articles II and III of the Articles of Confederation. Even Nationalists of the 1780s accepted that the Articles as a treaty amongst the states; it was why they wanted to reform the Articles. They considered its structure too protecting of state sovereignty. When the American people found the Articles insufficient, Jay continued, they replaced it with the Constitution. "Here we see," Jay proclaimed, "the people acting as sovereigns of the whole country; and in the language of sovereignty, establishing a Constitution by which it was their will, that the State Governments should be bound, and to which the State Constitutions should be made to conform. Every State Constitution is a compact made by and between the citizens of a State to govern themselves in a certain manner; and the Constitution of the United States is likewise a compact made by the people of the United States to govern themselves as to general objects, in a certain manner" as demonstrated by the Constitution's preamble.[66] This national popular sovereignty, which Jay claimed predated the existence of the states, meant that states had to appear before the Supreme Court since the sovereignty of national people overrode the sovereignty of people of a state.

Turning to the language of the Constitution, Jay noted that if the clause was to have any real meaning the Court had to "liberally" construe its remedial power to hear cases between a state and a citizen. If a state could be plaintiff, it could be a defendant. To argue as Georgia—and other states—had was to "contradict and do violence to the great and leading principles of a free and equal national government, one of the great objects of which is, to ensure justice to all: To the few against the many, as well as to the many against the few." Since the people formed the Constitution on the principles that "every free Government makes to every free citizen, of equal justice and protection," Jay believed Georgia had no authority to limit this standard. Finally, Jay noted how "Georgia has in strong language advocated the cause of republican equality," but he hoped that "the people of that State will yet perceive that it would not have been consistent with that equality, to have exempted the body of her citizens from that suability, which they are at this moment exercising against citizens of another State."[67]

James Iredell offered the lone dissent to the nationalist panegyric. Although Iredell was a leading proponent of the Constitution in the North Carolina ratifying conventions, he was also a defender of state sovereignty. During his state's ratification debates, Iredell claimed that "if anything in this Constitution tended to the annihilation of the state government, instead of exciting the admiration of any man, it ought to excite the resentment of exaction. No such wicked intention ought to be suffered."[68] His opinion in the *Chisholm* case reflected those concerns, and while he did not directly address Wilson and Jay, his opinion clearly responded to their ideas.

Iredell's thinking on the overall issue is much more important than most scholars have claimed. It is likely that Iredell's published opinion did not reflect everything he said in his oral remarks on the case. During the controversy over the *Chisholm* case, Iredell prepared a memorandum, "Observations on This Great Constitutional Question." Elements of this memorandum were apparently read before the Court, and sections were actually incorporated into the published opinion.[69] Iredell's "Observations" and published opinion not only endorsed the Constitution as a compact of the people of the several states, but it was also an exercise of constitutional restraint and warnings against liberal interpretations of power. Iredell cautioned against any "consequences ensu[ing] from one construction, inconsistent with the known basis on which the Constitution was formed and adopted, that construction shall not be received, if there be another at least equally natural and more consistent with the principles of the Constitution, which can take place." He offered an interpretation of Article III that was narrower than that of Wilson and Jay, asserting that "where every word can be fully satisfied, without implying a grant of a very high authority, that authority ought not to be understood to convey."[70] In other words, Iredell ignored Wilson's genuflection toward natural law and Jay's appeals to an imagined preexisting popular sovereignty. His argument closely paralleled that offered by the Federalists during ratification and reaffirmed with the Tenth Amendment:

> [E]very State in the Union in every instance where its sovereignty has not been delegated to the United States, I consider to be as completely sovereign, as the United States are in respect to the powers surrendered. The United States are sovereign as to all the powers of Government actually surrendered: Each State in the Union is sovereign as to all the powers reserved. It must necessarily be so, because the United States have no claim to any authority but such as the States have surrendered to them.[71]

At no point, Iredell asserted, had Georgia — or any other state — consented that a citizen of another state could sue it. Considering the constitutional import of sovereign immunity, had the Constitution intended for members of another state to sue a state without its consent, it required "greater clearness in the expression." The lack of clarity, and of a clear transference of sovereign power from the states to the Constitution, meant, therefore, that state sovereign immunity remained one of the powers not delegated to the national government. In other words, if the Constitution did not explicitly grant the federal government this power, it could not enjoy such power. Iredell took Randolph to task for saying that the courts could rely upon its inherent power to force states to comply. The courts did not have any authority, in either the Constitution or the Judiciary Act; to wield such power was to act with the "high authority" he worried about in his memorandum. As such, Georgia's appeal to its sovereignty kept with the American constitutional tradition.[72]

Once the decision reached the public, the reaction was swift. The initial reporting of the case in newspapers described majority decisions, particularly that of Wilson and Jay, as "elegant, learned, and contained sentiments highly republican." Jay's opinion, in particular, was singled out as "one of the most clear, profound and elegant arguments perhaps ever given in a court of judicature."[73] Yet, that opinion was the distinct minority; the general reaction was overwhelmingly unfavorable. William Few reported to Governor Telfair that "Gentlemen of the first information . . . reprobated" the decision because "if the principle is admitted it will evidently tend to exterminate the small remainder of State sovereignties."[74] Edmund Pendleton told his nephew that Wilson and Jay's "reprehensible" opinions were nothing more than "tending to prove the Fed[er]al to be a consolidated Government for all Americans, and to Annihilate those of the States." Should the case remain a precedent its underlying "Principle . . . would make that Constitution as great a curse as I have hitherto thought it a blessing." Pendleton also attacked Wilson and Jay's idea of national popular sovereignty. The Constitution was a "grant by the People, not by the States true, but how did the people Act in making the Grant? Not individually through America, but by a voted taken in each state." All it took for the Constitution to be defeated, he noted, was for the "Majority of the people in the five of the smallest states" or no more than "1/10 of the whole people" to have "voted against the adoption of the Constitution, [and] there had been an end to it."[75] Thus, to Pendleton, the Constitution was not an agreement of a supposed national popular sovereignty, but rather a compact of the people of the several states. To endorse Wilson and Jay's notions threatened the constitutional order.

Few and Pendleton's remarks, made in private, were echoed publicly in a series of essays by "The True Federalist" that appeared in the Boston newspaper, *Independent Chronicle*, in early 1794. Although the author of the essays remains unknown, it seems likely that James Sullivan authored them as they touched upon many of the same issues discussed in his "Observations" of three years earlier. The essays embraced the idea that the Constitution was a compact of the several states and castigated the Court and Randolph both for their disregard of state sovereignty and their distortion of history to support a national popular sovereignty. The Constitution as a compact of the sovereign states, the essayist claimed, was rooted in the history of the imperial crisis and the declaring of independence. The controversy with Britain, he claimed, was over the "preeminence in legislation, over individuals of each colony," whether "Parliament could bind the people in all cases whatever in their individual capacity. Although the Declaratory Act had used the word colonies, "yet by it was intended nothing but the people of the same in the natural individual capacity." The essay challenged Wilson and Jay's position that the Declaration of Independence created or reinforced a national people. The Declaration, instead, "made every one of the thirteen Provinces, Free, Sovereign and Independent States."[76] They were independent states until the Articles of Confederation united them in 1781. Yet, the Articles did not affect the preexisting sovereignty because the "2nd article expressly provide[d]" that the states "retain[ed] its Sovereignty, Freedom, and Independence." Even the preamble, which many claimed as a source for broad grants of power and a national popular sovereignty, pointed to a union of the states and not broad authority or national popular sovereignty. "Was this, or was it not a union of States? And if it was a union of States, will not a destruction of these communities, destroy the Union?"[77] The author focused particular ire at Wilson calling notions of state independence and sovereignty "haughty." This passage in Wilson's opinion was "well calculated to render all kinds of sovereignty detestable and contemptible; and yet . . . it is contending for the exercises of a much higher, and more absolute act of sovereignty." In a passage dripping with sarcasm, "True Federalist" believed it odd how "the word sovereignty may have something terrible in it when applied to the several States, but when applied to the United States, in order to give pre-eminence to the Judicial of that government over communities, confessedly sovereign, there does not appear to be anything very dreadful in it."[78] Finally, the essay noted how, when the Constitution was brought before the people of Massachusetts for ratification, "some men in whom the people had placed confidence openly and solemnly declared" that the states could never be sued. "Some of them, for reasons very obvious to their fellow-citizens, have altered their opinions, and other openly confess, that they thought it best to deceive the people into the measure of adopting the plan proposed." This "breach of trust" was "much more criminal, in my opinion, than that of subduing them by force."[79]

Nor were reactions confined to correspondence and essays. Immediately after the decision, states began calling for a constitutional amendment to override the decision that seemed "so incompatible with the operations of Government, and the intentions of the framers of the Constitution."[80] Interestingly, Massachusetts led the way. While the *Chisholm* case was before the Court, Massachusetts awaited its outcome since it had a similar case, *Vassal v. Massachusetts*, on the Court's docket.[81] One day after the *Chisholm* decision, Theodore Sedgewick, a Massachusetts congressman and noted Federalist, proposed before the House of Representatives an amendment to the Constitution that stated:

[t]hat no state shall be liable to be made a party defendant, in any of the judicial courts, established, or which shall be abolished under the authority of the United States, at the suit of any person or person, whether a citizen or citizens, foreigner or foreign, or any body politic or corporate, whether within or without the United States.[82]

The following day, Massachusetts senator Caleb Strong made a separate proposed amendment. Simpler in form and language it stated that:

[t]he Judicial Power of the United States shall not extend to any suits in law or equity commenced or prosecuted against any one of the United States by Citizens of another State or by Citizens of any foreign State.[83]

The speed upon which these two proposals appeared before Congress was indicative of the reaction to the *Chisholm* case. At the same time, Virginia's governor, Henry Lee, who had already pushed for an amendment, requested his state's senators, James Monroe and John Taylor, propose their own amendment. When they reported back that it was too late in the Senate's session to propose one, but assured they would in next session, they also added that they would propose one to curb the "exercise of construe powers particularly, and as exemplified in the establishment of the Bank." Congress' session ended before it could consider Sedgewick and Strong's proposals.[84]

In the intervening months, the Massachusetts government reacted. A series of resolutions adopted by the Massachusetts House of Representative rejected the *Chisholm*, labeling it "very different from the ideas which the Citizens of this Commonwealth entertained of it at the time it was adopted." A constitutional amendment was of paramount concern to reaffirm that "Federal Constitution necessarily involved component parts, consisting of distinct and separate Governments."[85] Although the general court was to consider the matter more fully in January 1794, Governor John Hancock, worried about the *Vassal* and the constitutional implications of the *Chisholm* decision, believed the matter was too urgent for delay. He summoned a special session of the general court to meet in September. Addressing his legislature, Hancock, who would die just six weeks after the general court's convening, sounded the same alarm he raised during the waning days of the Massachusetts ratification convention. A "consolidation of all the States into one Government," he warned, "would at once endanger the Nation as Republic, and eventually divide the States united, or eradicate the principles which we have contended for. It was much less hazardous to prevent the establishment of a dangerous precedent, that to attempt an abolition of it, after it has obtained a place in a civil institution."[86] Embracing Hancock's reasoning, the general court formally rejected the Court's opinions as "dangerous to the peace, safety and independence of the several States and repugnant to the first principles of the Federal Government."[87] The legislature then repeated its call for its federal representatives to propose an amendment to the Constitution to preserve the sovereignty of the states.

Georgia did not formally respond to the case until early 1794. As expected, it reacted by condemning the decision, but pushed the matter even further by approving legislation prohibiting, on pain of death, federal marshals or anyone else who attempted to carry out the Court's order.[88] The legislation, which the Georgia Senate let quietly die, provoked a stinging rebuke by an essayist in the *American Minerva*. The Georgia legislators, the essayist noted, "are all sworn to support the constitution of the United States" and the "Supreme Court has deliberately decided" that Article III includes allowing a person to sue a state. "This decision is then a law of the United States, or rather a part of the constitution, and binding on every citizen until unaltered." The "passion and fury" of Georgia's "intemperate resolutions can come only from men who are accustomed to brandish a whip over slavery; men who are tyrants in domestic life, and levelers in political." The state, the essayist noted, should be ashamed of immodesty and should follow the other states who have calmly called for a constitutional amendment.[89]

Between Massachusetts taking the lead and Georgia's surprisingly belated response to the case, Virginia, New York, Connecticut, and Maryland called for a constitutional amendment. By the time all of these states had responded, however, Congress had reconvened and with it Sedgewick and Strong's amendments. For reasons that remain unclear, Sedgewick's amendment went nowhere in the House of Representatives. Strong's proposal, which now included a slight rewording to prohibit "construing" the judicial power to include suits against states by a single individual, passed both houses of Congress on January 14, 1794. By 1795, three-fourths of the states had ratified the Eleventh Amendment. Despite this quick ratification, it was not until 1798 that President John Adams proclaimed the amendment officially ratified.[90]

Most accounts of the Eleventh Amendment assert that it was little more than a self-interested reaction to the case, of the states' way to prohibit continuous litigation from Loyalists and other wartime contracts.[91] While the states were certainly worried about continuous litigation that could result from the *Chisholm* case, the amendment addressed broader concerns about state sovereignty. The entire issue surrounding *Chisholm* and the amendment operated within a larger political and constitutional context. Arising as it did during ratification, the issue of state suability touched directly upon the very foundations of the constitutional system, which is why many Federalists tried to assuage Anti-Federalist worries by promising that states could not be sued without their consent. Those promises, as the *Chisholm* case made clear, were not kept. Thus, the Eleventh Amendment wove those promises into the constitutional fabric. An important element often overlooked was how opposition to state suability crossed geographic regions or partisan politics.

Federalist strongholds like Massachusetts were just as concerned as Republican bastions like Georgia. Furthermore, both Sedgewick and Strong, the two members of Congress who proposed the amendments (and Strong's being the one accepted), were noted Federalists. Clearly, then, the issue of state sovereignty during was no mere sectional or partisan weapon. Some Federalists still accepted state sovereignty as the foundational element its constitutional order. At the same time, scholars often overlook how the issue of state sovereign immunity and state sovereignty in general, which the amendment protected, occurred within the context of the debates over the Tenth Amendment and its limits to the Constitution. Both amendments, which had widespread support, should be viewed as endorsements of the idea that the Constitution was not a full-scale revolution in American constitutionalism but rather that state sovereignty remained the cornerstone the constitutional system. In some ways, of the two, the Eleventh Amendment was the more explicit endorsement of state sovereignty as the foundation of the American constitutional system. By protecting the states' sovereign immunity, it rejected the more extreme Federalists' idea of a national popular sovereignty, and especially the notion that this national popular sovereignty predated the states, independence, or the Constitution. Unlike the Tenth Amendment, which even supporters claimed left room for debating the real limitation of federal power, the Eleventh Amendment explicitly endorsed and protected state sovereignty. In stating that the "judicial power of the United States shall not be construed to extend to any suit in law or equity, commenced or prosecuted against one of the United States by citizens of another state, or by citizens or subjects of any foreign state," the amendment shut any potential backdoor attempt to consolidate the states through the federal judiciary. In short, the Eleventh Amendment was a powerful curtailment of federal power and a strong reinforcing of state sovereignty.

The Eleventh Amendment was another step in securing state sovereignty's nomocratic position as the foundation of American constitutional order. During the first half of the 1790s, the Republican Party had turned to the public in order to counterattack the Federalists' constitutional vision of a powerful central government. In newspapers and pamphlets, the Republican arguments centered on how the Federalists' policies and constitutionalism was the path of monarchy and that resisting the Federalist required a strong embracement of state sovereignty. Yet, securing public opinion was only part of the battle. They had to fight against a Supreme Court that endorsed the Federalist view of federal power and a notion that a national popular sovereignty had preexisted the states and the declaring of independence. Only through the securing of the Eleventh Amendment were those arguments turned aside and repealed. As the next chapter will demonstrate, the battle over America's constitutional order was not over. In fact, by the end of the decade, both

Federalists and Republicans would provide the fullest expressions of their competing constitutional visions.

NOTES

1. Lance Banning, *The Sacred Fire of Liberty: James Madison and the Founding of the Federal Republic* (Ithaca: Cornell University Press, 1995), 340–43; Kevin R. C. Gutzman, *James Madison and the Making of America* (New York: St. Martin's Press, 2012), 262–63.

2. Thomas Jefferson to Thomas Mann Randolph, Jr., May 15, 1791, in Julian P. Boyd, ed., *The Papers of Thomas Jefferson*, 38 vols. to date (Princeton: Princeton University Press, 1950–2011), 20: 416.

3. Banning, *Sacred Fire of Liberty*, 348–65; Colleen A. Sheehan, *James Madison and the Spirit of Republican Self-Government* (Cambridge: Cambridge University Press, 2009) is the first book length treatment on the essays as a deeper reflection of Madison's political thought. Also see Denver Brunsman, "James Madison and the *National Gazette* Essays: The Birth of a Party Politician," in Stuart Leibiger, ed., *A Companion to James Madison and James Monroe* (Malden, MA: Wiley-Blackwell, 2013): 143–58.

4. James Madison, "Charters," January 18, 1792, in Lance Banning, ed., *Liberty and Order: The First American Party Struggle* (Indianapolis: Liberty Fund, 2004), 103–104.

5. James Madison, "Property," March 27, 1792, in ibid., 107.

6. James Madison, "Government of the United States," February 4, 1792, in ibid., 105.

7. Ibid.

8. James Madison, "Consolidation," December 3, 1791, in ibid., 102–103.

9. Ibid.

10. James Madison, "Parties," January 23, 1792, in ibid., 105.

11. Ibid.

12. For an argument that the break occurred earlier and was the result of Hamilton's arguments in *The Federalist* see Michael Schwarz, "The Great Divergence Reconsidered: Hamilton, Madison, and U.S.-British Relations, 1783–1789," *Journal of the Early Republic* 27 (Fall 2007): 407–36.

13. Alexander Hamilton to Edward Carrington, May 26, 1792, in Harold Syrett and Jacob Cooke, eds., *The Papers of Alexander Hamilton*, 26 vols. (Columbia: University of Columbia Press, 1961–1981), 11:

14. Ibid.

15. Ibid.

16. Ibid.

17. James Roger Sharp, *American Politics in the Early Republic: The New Nation in Crisis* (New Haven, CT: Yale University Press, 1993), 34, says that "[s]ectionalism . . . was the main catalyst inciting political conflict"; and Gordon Wood, *Empire of Liberty: A History of the Early Republic, 1789–1815* (New York: Oxford University Press, 2009), 164–73.

18. This is especially true of Wood, *Empire of Liberty*, 140–73.

19. Donald Lutz, *Origins of American Constitutionalism* (Baton Rouge: Louisiana State University Press, 1988), 13. Also see Michael Oakeshott, *On Human Conduct* (Oxford: Oxford University Press, 1991).

20. Gordon Wood, *Creation of the American Republic, 1776–1787* (Chapel Hill: University of North Carolina Press, 1970), 266.

21. Lance Banning, *The Jeffersonian Persuasion: The Evolution of a Party Ideology* (Ithaca: Cornell University Press, 1978), 192–201.

22. Kevin R. C. Gutzman, *Virginia's American Revolution: From Dominion to Republic, 1776–1840* (Lanham, MD: Lexington Books, 2007), 117. Also see Adam Tate, *Conservatism and Southern Intellectuals1789–1861* (Columbia: University of Missouri Press, 2005), 8–20.

23. John Taylor of Caroline, "An Examination of the Late Proceedings in Congress Respecting the Official Conduct of the Secretary of the Treasury" (Richmond: n.p., 1793), 26–27.

24. Ibid.; John Taylor of Caroline, "An Enquiry into the Principles and Tendency of Certain Public Measures" (Philadelphia: Dobson, 1794), 2.

25. Taylor, "Enquiry," 36.

26. Ibid., 54–56.

27. John Taylor, "An Argument Respecting the Constitutionality of the Carriage Tax" (Richmond: Augustine Davis, 1795), 17.

28. Ibid., 4.

29. "Introduction" in Maeva Marcus, ed., *The Documentary History of the Supreme Court of the United States, 1789–1800*, 8 vols. (New York: Columbia University Press, 1986–2007), 5: 1. The remaining part of this chapter relies heavily upon the sources contained in that volume.

30. Ibid., 2.

31. Alexander Hamilton, *Federalist 81*, in George W. Carey and James McClellan, eds., *The Federalist: The Gideon Edition* (Indianapolis: Liberty Fund, 2001), 422.

32. Virginia Instrument of Ratification and New York Instrument of Ratification both in Kaminski et al., eds., *Documentary History of the Ratification of the Constitution* 10: 1551–56 and 23: 2326–34

33. "Tucker Amendments" in Helen E. Veit, Kenneth R. Bowling, and Charlene Bangs Bickford, eds., *Creating the Bill of Rights: The Documentary Record from the First Federal Congress* (Baltimore: The Johns Hopkins University Press, 1991), 35.

34. "Introduction," in Marcus, ed., *Documentary History of the Supreme Court*, 5: 18, 58–60, 282–84.

35. Maryland House of Delegates, Report of the Ways and Means Committee, December 13, 1791, in ibid., 34–35.

36. Pierce Butler to Messrs. Van Staphorts and Hubbard, September 23, 1791, and Jared Ingersoll, "Plea to the Jurisdiction, in Oswald v. New York," August 5, 1783, both in ibid., 5: 34 and 92.

37. James Innes to Henry Lee, November 10, 1792, in ibid., 320.

38. Proceedings of the Virginia House of Delegates, November 28, 1793, in ibid., 338.

39. Proceedings of the Virginia House of Delegates, December 18, 1792, in ibid., 332.

40. Anonymous essay, *Independent Chronicle*, July 7, 1791, in ibid., 21.

41. Anonymous essay, *Columbian Sentential*, September 7, 1791, in ibid., 32–33.

42. James Sullivan, "Observations on the Government of the United States" (Boston: Samuel Hale, 1791), vii.

43. Ibid., 23–37, quote on 26.

44. Ibid., 15.

45. Ibid., vii, 30, and 37.

46. Timothy Ford, "An Enquiry into the Constitutional Authority of the Supreme Federal Court" (Charleston: Young, 1792), 5–6.

47. Ibid. 8–20, 24.

48. Ibid., 20.

49. Marcus, ed., *Documentary History of the Supreme Court*, 5: 127–37.

50. Thomas P. Carnes and John Y. Noel to Edward Telfair, March 31, 1791, in ibid., 140–41.

51. "Plea to the Jurisdiction in Chisholm v. Georgia" October 17, 1791, in ibid., 143.

52. John Wereat to Edward Telfair, August 13 and 14, 1792, in ibid., 159–60.

53. Proceedings of the Georgia House of Representatives, December 14, 1792, in ibid., 161–62.

54. *Chisholm v. Georgia*, February 18, 1793, in James Alexander Dallas, *Reports of the Cases Ruled and Adjudged in the Courts of Pennsylvania, Before and Since the Revolution*, 3 vols. (Philadelphia: T. Bradford, 1790–1799), 2: 419.

55. Ibid., 419–29.

56. For Blair and Cushing's opinions see ibid., 450–53 and 466–69.

57. James Wilson, "Opinion in *Chisholm v. Georgia*," ibid., 455. For Wilson's reliance upon the natural law in the *Chisholm* case also see William R. Casto, *The Supreme Court in the Early Republic: The Chief Justiceships of John Jay and Oliver Ellsworth* (Columbia: University of South Carolina Press, 1995), 193; Julius Goebel, Jr., *History of the Supreme Court of the United States: Antecedents and Beginnings to 1801*, Volume 1 of the *Oliver Wendell Holmes Device: History of the Supreme Court*, 12 vols. to date (New York: The Macmillan Company, 1971), 1: 731.

58. Ibid., 457–58, 460–61.

59. Ibid., 461.

60. Ibid., 463–64.

61. Ibid., 462–63.

62. Ibid., 463–64, quote on 463.

63. James Wilson, "Speech in the State House Yard," October 6, 1787, in Kaminiski et al., eds., *Documentary History of the Ratification of the Constitution*, 2: 167–68.

64. John Jay, "Circular to the States," September 13, 1779, in Worthington C. Ford, ed., *Journals of the Continental Congress*, 34 vols. (Washington, DC: Government Printing Office, 1904–1937), 15: 1058.

65. Ibid., 470.

66. Ibid., 471.

67. Ibid., 477–79.

68. James Iredell, "Speech at the North Carolina Ratification Convention," July 25, 1788, in Jonathan Elliot, ed., *The Debates in the Several Conventions on the Adoption of the Constitution* 5 volumes (Washington, DC: n.p., 1836) 4: 53.

69. James Iredell, "Observations on This Great Constitutional Question," in Marcus, ed., *Documentary History of the Supreme Court*, 5: 186–93. For his reading elements of the "Observations" in the *Chisholm* decision see Kurt T. Lash, "Leaving the *Chisholm* Trail: The Eleventh Amendment and the Background Principle of Strict Construction," *Loyola, Legal Studies Paper 2008–18* (June 2008): 44–45.

70. Iredell, "Observations," ibid., 187.

71. Iredell, "Opinion in *Chisholm*," in Dallas, *Reports*, 2: 435.

72. Iredell, "Observations," in Marcus, ed., *Documentary History of the Supreme Court*, 5: 187; "Opinion in *Chisholm*," in ibid., 429–34.

73. *Dunlap's American Daily Advertiser* in Ibid., 5: 219.

74. William Few to Edward Telfair, February 19, 1793, in ibid., 221.

75. Edmund Pendleton to Nathaniel Pendleton, August 10, 1793, in ibid., 232–33.

76. The True Federalist," No. 2, in ibid., 243–45.

77. Ibid., 245.

78. Ibid., 245 and 247.

79. Ibid., 247–48.

80. Few to Telfair, February 19, 1793, in ibid., 221.

81. The details of *Vassal v. Massachusetts* are covered in ibid., 354–69.

82. Proceedings of the United States House of Representatives, in ibid., 605–606.

83. Resolution of the United States Senate, in ibid., 607–608.

84. James Monroe an John Taylor to Henry Lee, February 20 and March 2, 1793, in ibid., 606, 608.

85. Report of a Joint Committee of the Massachusetts General Court, June 20, 1793, in ibid., 230–31.

86. John Hancock to the Massachusetts General Court, September 18, 1793, in ibid., 418–19.

87. Report on the Joint Committee of the Massachusetts General Court, September 23, 1793, in ibid., 424.

88. Proceedings of the Georgia House of Representatives, November 19, 1793, in ibid., 236.

89. *American Minerva*, January 15, 1794, in ibid., 237–38.

90. For these accounts see ibid., 609–17, 636–37.

91. Calvin R. Massey, "State Sovereignty and the Tenth and Eleventh Amendments," *University of Chicago Law Review* 56 (1989): 61–151; Carlos Manuel Vazquez, "What is Eleventh Amendment Immunity?" *Yale Law Journal* 106 (1997): 1683–806. For a counterargument to this literature see Lash, "Off the Chisholm Trail," and Bradford R. Clark, "The Eleventh Amendment and the Nature of the Union," in *Harvard Law Review* 123 (June 2010): 1817–918.

EIGHT

The Settlement Secured

*Kentucky and Virginia Resolutions
and the Defeat of the Federal Common Law*

By the middle of the 1790s, Republicans had achieved some success at counteracting the Federalists' argument for sovereignty in the federal government. With the combination of the Tenth and Eleventh Amendments, state sovereignty was the most secured it had been since the Articles of Confederation. The Republicans had not achieved a total victory, however. The Federalist threat to the Revolution's constitutionalism remained. In last years of the decade, and during the most important international crisis since the Revolution, the Federalists and Republicans would clash a final time over the nature of the American constitutional order. Federalists seized upon the growing Franco-American crisis and attempted to clinch their constitutional transformation through the Alien and Sedition Acts. Their advocacy for a federal common law and sovereignty of the federal government was the maturation of a constitutionalism first advanced by the Nationalists and developed throughout the 1790s. When the Republicans fought back, most famously in the Kentucky and Virginia Resolutions of 1798, they drew upon and restated the arguments for decentralization that fueled the Revolution and made state sovereignty the primary principle of the constitutional arrangement. In recalling and applying these arguments, the Republicans articulated the most comprehensive understanding and defense of state sovereignty. The contest between Federalists and Republicans in the last two years of the 1790s, therefore, became the culmination of a two-decade-long struggle over competing visions of the location of sovereignty and the nomocratic or teleocatic nature of American constitutionalism. The stakes of this final battle were high. Each side believed that the winner would determine whether the future of American constitutionalism rested on the Revolution's foundation of state sovereignty or upon sovereignty in a national government. When the Republicans emerged victorious in 1801, they achieved more than just a political victory, they had preserved the Revolution's constitutional settlement.

When John Adams became the second president on March 4, 1797, he inherited a growing foreign policy crisis.[1] Relations with America's one-time ally, France, had deteriorated precipitously since 1793 when revolutionary France declared war against its ancient enemy, England. The Washington administration angered both European powers by declaring neutrality.[2] The Jay Treaty of 1795 between England and the United States only added to France's anger. Although the treaty's purpose was settling issues that dated back to the end of Revolutionary War as well as British actions against the American neutral shipping, Britain's modest trade concessions to the United States caused France to view the agreement as an Anglo-American alliance. After 1795, France began a campaign of harassment against American merchants, and in 1796 attempted to influence the presidential election by defeating John Adams and the Federalist Party.[3] Nor did Americans sit idly as these events unfurled. Although most Americans celebrated the early stages of France's revolution, seeing it as the offspring of their own Revolution, those celebrations turned to skepticism and horror as the French Revolution spiraled into bloodshed and civil destruction. The growing rift in America's domestic politics over the constitutional implications of Alexander Hamilton's economic program soon incorporated divisions over the direction of the French Revolution. In general, Federalists viewed the radicalism of the French Revolution as demonstrable proof of what happens when a people abandon the pillars of civilization and embrace democratic licentiousness. Their sympathies in the European conflict, therefore, rested with Britain. Republicans, while shocked and disappointed at the extreme violence, nevertheless remained optimistic that France's bloodletting would cease and eventually be another example of republican virtue and self-government. Federalists viewed Republican celebrations of France and its revolution with suspicion, believing that they sought to bring its licentiousness to American shores. Republicans, for their part, claimed Federalists were closeted Monarchists who desired a formal alliance with England in order to restore monarchy to republican America. The Neutrality Proclamation and the Jay Treaty, both major Federalist political victories, were just the first steps in realizing those dreams. Neither side was correct, but as domestic issues became increasingly filtered through these divergent views of the French Revolution, both sides believed they had reason to fear that the other sought the destruction of the American constitutional order. This is the political context John Adams inherited in 1797.[4] It was not an enviable position.

Adams was no celebrant of the French Revolution, but he also had no love for Britain (despite Republican claims to the contrary). As such, he sought a middle path. He wanted peace and normal relations with France but not at the expense of an alliance with Britain. Soon after taking office, he dispatched John Marshall, Charles Cotesworth Pinckney, and Elbridge Gerry on a special diplomatic mission to France, hoping their trip would result in a treaty of peace. Adams had initially wanted to send Vice President Thomas Jefferson and James Madison to France as a goodwill gesture, but both declined his offer.[5] Any hopes that his commissioners would achieve peace were dashed when dispatches he received from the trio reported that France would negotiate only if the Americans first paid a bribe to three secretaries of France's foreign minister, Francois Talleyrand. As Adams weighed his actions, Republicans accused the president of purposefully withholding the news as evidence of his disappointment that France had offered Americans favorable terms. When they pressed Adams to release the messages, he obliged but removed the names of the French secretaries replacing them with X, Y, and Z.[6]

The Republican gambit failed miserably. The public reaction to the XYZ Affair (as it came to be called) was swift and ferocious. As Americans rallied to President Adams, he called for the increased defense of American ports, a reinvigoration of the American navy, and a dramatic increase in the size of the military.[7] As petitions of support flooded his desk, he responded with clarion calls for "Character, moral, political, and martial" spirit to offset the French depredations. He lectured the American people that "if the object of France, in her revolution, ever was liberty, it was a liberty very ill defined and never understood."[8] The Federalist-controlled Congress responded to Adams' bellicosity by granting Adams' wishes. They increased port defenses, established a formal navy, and increased the size of the American army. On this last point, they far exceeded Adams' recommendation of a force of 10,000 by growing the military to 50,000. To pay for this military buildup, Congress enacted the first direct taxes ever imposed by the federal government. Adams then summoned Washington out of retirement to lead the army, but when Washington agreed to lead the force only if a French invasion occurred, Adams' cabinet, with assistance from the retired president, forced Adams to accept Alexander Hamilton, whom Adams despised, as the second in command.[9]

The military measures were not the only items on the Federalist agenda, however. The crisis brought them the opportunity to destroy their political adversaries. In the summer of 1798, as public support for the Federalist Party was at its zenith, congressional Federalists proposed the Alien and Sedition Acts. The partisan nature of these measures was obvious. The intended targets were the Republican press and the large and recent influx of aliens who fled the French revolutionary wars and supported the Republicans. Sweeping in their scope and objectives, the measures amounted to little more than the Federalists trying to remove Republicans from the political arena.

The Alien Act was actually four separate pieces of legislation. In the Naturalization Act, the Federalists repealed the milder and more liberal naturalization laws of 1790 and 1795. The new measure, which applied only to aliens from nations in which the United States was not at war, required a fourteen-year residency in the United States before becoming a naturalized citizen. Aliens were required to announce their intent to file for naturalization at least five years prior to obtaining their citizenship. The other two measures, the Alien Friends and Alien Enemies Acts, were even more restrictive and applied to those aliens from nations in a declared war with the United States. Although Federalists had originally proposed both measures as one bill, the Republicans separated the bill into two measures and secured a provision that allowed those aliens "not chargeable with actual hostility" to have time "for the recovering, disposal, and removal of their goods and effects." [10] All other aliens wishing to stay in the country had to obtain special permission from the executive branch. Even then, both measures empowered President Adams to deport without a trial any alien he deemed a threat to the safety of the United States. The Alien Acts forced aliens to register with the federal government, demanded any ship—including an American vessel—to inform customs officials of any alien on board or face detainment, and permitted the government to maintain surveillance on all alien residents. [11]

While Federalists aimed the Alien Acts at nonnaturalized residents, the Sedition Act applied to everyone, at least nominally. The real targets of the law were Republican newspapers like the Philadelphia *Aurora*. Headed by Benjamin Franklin's grandson, Benjamin Franklin Bache, the *Aurora* published scathing attacks on the Washington and Adams administrations and the Federalists in general. [12] The measure punished with a maximum 5,000 dollar fine and six-month to five-year imprisonment any person who wrote, printed, uttered, or published "any false, scandalous and malicious writing or writings" with the "intent to defame" the government, Congress, or president. The measure's third section allowed defendants to use the "truth of the matter" in their defense. This meant that if a defendant could demonstrate to a jury that the reason for their writing or utterance was based upon a truth they could be found not guilty of sedition. The Sedition Act also applied the standard eighteenth-century norm of allowing juries to determine both the law and the facts of the case. This permitted the juries to determine not just whether the defendant actually said or printed the controversial words, but also to decide if the law applied in that particular case thereby removing potentially biased federal judges from making that determination. Yet, the partisan nature of the measure became clear when Federalists set the expiration date of the Sedition Act for March 3, 1801, the last full of day of

President Adams' first (and, subsequently only) term. At the same time, the Sedition Act excluded the other elected member of the federal government, the vice president, who just happened to be the Republican leader, Thomas Jefferson.[13]

Although the growing partisanship between the Republicans and Federalists, coupled with the hysteria surrounding the XYZ Affair and potential war with France, drove the adoption of the measures, it was the Federalists' conception of the sovereignty of the federal government that made them believe they could enact the measures. While the Federalists believed the Alien and Sedition Acts were constitutional, the details of the measures offer only glimpses behind that reasoning. The acts made no mention of the Bill of Rights prohibition against denying the due process of law, trial by jury or the First Amendment's statement that "Congress shall make no law abridging the freedom of speech . . . press," even though both measures touched directly upon those amendments. The Federalists considered the prohibitions contained in the Bill of Rights as inapplicable to these acts.

In congressional speeches and numerous pamphlets and essays over the next two years, Federalists defended the Alien and Sedition measures as the actions of a sovereign government. These arguments were little more than a restatement of the arguments Federalists used in explaining the constitutionality of Hamilton's economic program earlier in the decade. Federalists, like Harrison Gray Otis of Massachusetts, invoked the general welfare and common defense statements of both the preamble to the Constitution and Article I, Section 8. These two "very general power[s]," Otis noted, were "the great objects forming" the Constitution and thus the Alien and Sedition measures were yet another means by which to fulfill its purpose. Although the Constitution did not explicitly empower Congress to pass either piece of legislation, the "time [was] full of danger, and it would be the height of madness not to take every precaution in our power."[14]

Defending the Alien and Sedition Acts through the text of the Constitution was of secondary importance to the Federalists. Of greater significance to them was their dual claims on the sovereign nature of the federal government and its relationship to a national society. That the federal government possessed a Blackstonian sovereignty was a foregone conclusion to the Federalists by 1798. In the defense of the measures, Federalists made repeated references to Blackstone's *Commentaries* on Parliament's authority to punish seditious publications and regulate alien activities within a nation.[15] In the fourth volume of his *Commentaries*, Blackstone noted that one of basic elements of sovereignty was to punish sedition speech or writings in order to preserve the "public peace."[16] Thus, to the Federalists, the United States was not a collection of sovereign states that formed a Constitution for limited purposes and objectives. Instead, it was a sovereign nation-state in the fullest sense. At the same time, the Federalists connected their belief in the Blackstonian sovereignty of the federal government to their idea that the Constitution created a distinct national society. Nationalists had first broached the idea of a national society—and national popular sovereignty—as early as 1776 and throughout the 1780s. In the first years of the Constitution, the Federalists had maintained the notion and had based the *Chisholm* decision upon the idea. It was during the controversy over the Alien and Sedition Acts, however, that the idea took on a new emphasis in Federalist thinking in the form of a national common law.

The Federalists' notions of the common law mirrored English legal thinkers of the seventeenth and eighteenth centuries. Best expressed in the works of Sir Edward Coke and Blackstone, these English thinkers maintained that the common law was the distillation of centuries of a society's experience, customs, reason, and traditions.[17] It was, as James Wilson called it, "a social system of jurisprudence."[18] English writers celebrated the common law's unwritten and organic nature, claiming that the common law adapted to changes of circumstances and customs, thereby making it the perfect reflection of society. Anchored as it was in well-developed ideas and practices, and continued over long and uninterrupted stretches of time, most commentators held the common law as the embodiment, protector, and best expression of natural law. This conclusion led common law advocates to an important conclusion: the common law was the supreme law of society, including any written law.

One element of the common law that drew increasing attention in the eighteenth century, and would be a mainstay of Federalist thought on the common law foundations of the Alien and Sedition Acts, was the law of nations. Developed in the seventeenth and eighteenth centuries by Hugo Grotius, Burlamaqui, Samuel von Pufendorf, and, most importantly, Emer de Vattel, and incorporated into English common law by Blackstone, the law of nations was an attempt to bring the concepts of natural law into the relationships between nations.[19] If nations adhered to the natural law in their dealings with one another, these writers argued, civilization and justice would flourish.

The ideas of the common law deeply influenced Federalists, such as Wilson, Zephaniah Swift, James Kent, and Joseph Addison.[20] All were instrumental in establishing the intellectual groundwork for the Federalists' assertions that the common law applied to the federal government. In a series of legal lectures at the start of the 1790s, Wilson explained how the common law was "accommodated to the circumstances, the exigencies, and conveniences of the people, by whom it is appointed." As these changed, "a proportional change, in time and in degree, must take place in the accommodated system." Even with these gradual changes, however, the principles of the common law, established since time immemorial, "have not been overturned by successive invasion, migrations or revolutions." These principles endured, Wilson noted, because they were rules drawn from the "fountain of justice" and thus contained "the common dictates of nature, refined by wisdom and experience."[21] Swift agreed with Wilson, adding that because the common law reflected the eternal truths established by God and derived from immemorial usage, it was a "highly improved system of reason, founded on the nature and fitness of things, and furnishes the best standard of civil conduct."[22] Addison followed this line of thinking, adding that the common law was "founded on the law of nature and the revelation of God . . . which have long prevailed, and been sanctioned by judicial authority.[23]

Wilson, Kent, and Addison also explained the connection between the common law and the law of nations. All agreed that "the law of nature, when applied to states or political societies" was "of obligation indispensable: the law of nations, as well as the law of nature, is of origin divine."[24] Under the law of nations, nations had "a right" and were "under obligation to preserve itself and its members." This right of self-preservation provided the nation to "do every thing, which, without injuring others, it can do, in order to accomplish and secure those objects."[25] Like the common law, the foundations of the law of nations rested upon the "rules which reason and custom have established among civilized nations of Europe."[26] Designed as it was to "preserve peace . . . and good faith" between nations, it was the duty of the state to refrain from "inciting disturbances in another" and "seducing its Citizens."[27] As the common law dealt with the relationship of man to man, the law of nations was a nation's relationship to other nations.

To Wilson, Swift, Kent, and Addison, then, the common law and the law of nations represented norms and behaviors that predated government. Because their principles were divine and immutable, they reflected the very nature of humanity and formed the bedrock of civil society. The particular governmental structure that a society decided it wanted was of secondary importance to these Federalist writers. What did matter was that whatever government the society chose had to follow and operate within the confines of this higher law. This line of thinking, moreover, adds a layer of explanation behind why the Federalists of the 1790s were so willing to abandon their ratification promises for a government of proscribed and limited powers. As they argued during the debates over the Bank of the United States and during the *Chisholm* decision, an American society preexisted the Constitution. To maintain a government based upon strict limitations would be abandoning the natural law that made the common law not only possible, but also higher than that of any written law.

In the years prior to the Alien and Sedition Acts, Federalist judges employed this idea of federal common law several times. In *Henfield v. United States*, which dealt with a violation of Washington's 1793 Proclamation of Neutrality, Wilson, one of the judges who presided over the case, lifted passages from his own law lectures to inform the jury that the common law was "one of the noblest births of time."[28] He asserted that "its principle and many of its more minute particulars" was "now received in America." Exactly how or when the United States had received the law of nations, Wilson did not clarify. His remarks suggested that he believed he did not have to because of the "many and binding laws" that Henfield violated the first and most important was that of the law of nations, which "was in existence long before Gideon Henfield existed."[29] Thus, by simply being a sovereign nation, the United States had automatically received the law of nations.

The second and more important case where Federalists invoked a federal common law was *United States v. Worrall*.[30] This case involved Robert Worrall's attempt to bribe Tench Coxe, the commissioner of the revenue of the United States. Although no congressional statue existed to punish bribery, Worrall was arrested on the grounds that his "evil example" was offensive "against the peace and dignity of the said United States" and violated the common law prohibition against crimes.[31] During the trial, the government's attorney, William Rawle, argued that the case touched upon "the whole system of national government" because Worrall's actions were in "opposition to the pure, regular, and efficient administration of government." Drawing upon *Henfield* and several other cases, the government based its prosecution of Worrall on the "principles of the common law." In essence, the fact that the federal government was a constituted government meant that it absorbed the common law. Rawle insisted that since the office of the commissioner of revenue existed, the common law crime of bribery existed to punish offenses against the position.[32]

Justice Samuel Peters agreed with Rawle, holding that Worrall's actions were intended to "obstruct and pervert the administration" of good government. The federal government, Peters maintained, was "constitutionally possessed" of "common law power" to punish bribery. "Whenever a government has been established," wrote Peters, "a power to preserve itself was a necessary, and inseparable, concomitant." To allow a bribery attempt to go unpunished stripped the federal government of its status as an "independent government." As such, even though Congress had not made bribery of a federal officer a statutory crime, it could be "enforced in a course of [j]udicial proceeding." Worrall's action, moreover, was "an offense against the well-being of the United States; from its very nature, it [was] cognizable under their authority; and, consequently, it is within the jurisdiction of this court." The court ordered Worrall's imprisonment for three months and forced him to pay a 200.00 dollar fine.[33]

The Federalist idea of a federal common law was the last and most important element in their decade-long argument that the Constitution was the structural means to a teleological end, namely the sovereignty of the federal government and existence of a national people. In their pronouncements on federal common law, they tore down the strictures placed upon federal power within the Constitution.[34] They would refer to those listed powers when they believed it necessary to do so, but, as the 1790s continued, those references became more of a pretense than an actual concern. As the *Worrall* case made clear, the lack of a specific law or enumerated power was not enough to prohibit an action the Federalists believed was inherent in the very sovereign nature of the federal government. Thus the argument for a federal common law allowed Federalists to abandon the idea of *inclusio unius est exclusio alterius*, or, what is not given is retained, that Wilson and other Federalists had defended during ratification. At the same time, the argument for a national common law also reinforced the Federalists' adherence to the traditional idea that a constitution was a reflection of society. Since the common law supposedly predated any established government, and only an established society could exercise those powers, it meant that a national society predated the Constitution.

Federalist apologists relied heavily on the existence of a federal common law to defend the Alien and Sedition Acts. Those defenses crystallized, in a manner no other debate had, the Federalists' belief in the federal government's sovereignty. Both measures, they argued, reflected the most primal element of the natural law, the right of self-preservation. Since the United States was on the brink of war with France, the government had the responsibility to remove aliens who could subvert the government and war effort from within. It should not matter, Federalists argued, that the Constitution did not grant this power. The United States was of the same "sovereign power of every nation," noted Representative William Gordon, and, consequently, it possessed the inherent right of self-preservation. It was "absurd to say, at a time when the United States are about to enter upon a war, and the country is filled with the natives of the enemy-country, that we do not possess power to send them out of the country." Should Congress "make the express letter of the Constitution the rule of their power," rather than the common law right of self-protection, the government would fail in its duty to protect its citizens.[35] Harrison Gray Otis took the argument even further. It would have been better that "the Federal compact . . . have never been made" than to deny that that it was "prevented from exercising an authority which may be necessary to its existence, is not better than no Government at all." Claiming that the federal government lacked the "power of self-defense" was allowing "the knife of the traitor [to be] held at our throats."[36]

Out of Congress, Federalist defenders echoed their congressional allies. Charles Lee, Adams' attorney general, argued that refusing the federal government the power to remove enemy aliens was a denial that the "[C]onstitution possess every essential power of a complete government."[37] The lack of enumerated power to remove aliens did not concern Lee. "The legislative power need not on this occasion, to be enumerated," he wrote, because Congress had the power to pass "all laws necessary and proper"; the executive had to faithfully execute the laws; and the judicial power extended to "all cases in law." This final clause, he argued, "understood" to mean "all cases at common law arising under the [C]onstitution."[38] Lee also connected the common law origins of the Alien Act to Article IV, Section 4 of the Constitution in which the federal government guaranteed the states would maintain a republican form of government. Since alien enemies may be living in the country, and could work to overthrow the state and national government, the alien law was necessary and proper in order to secure that constitutional promise.[39]

Thomas Evans of Virginia offered one of the most stark and robust defenses of a federal common law. He asked "[a]re not we, the people of the United States of America, a sovereign and independent nation?"[40] Since the United States was sovereign, it contained "all the rights pertaining to that state, equally with any other nation." It was an "essential and inherent authority and power" of sovereign states to determine how they would interact with other nations. The idea that the Constitution did not provide the authority to protect the country turned the document into "a set of shackles to bind up our hand from the natural and inherent power of self-defense."[41] Better than perhaps any other Federalist, Evans connected the structural elements of Constitution to its supposed greater purpose. Instead of being a limitation of the government's power the Constitution was:

> a shield to *protect* and *aid* in the *assertion of our pre existent national rights,* in relation both to ourselves and to others: it is not a set of shackles to *abridge* in any manner whatever, the power of asserting those rights.[42]

Like practically all Federalists, Evans argued that the Constitution's primary objectives were contained within the preamble. Whereas Federalists in the earlier part of the decade used the preamble to justify an expansive reading of federal power, Evans took their argument one step further. The objectives listed in the preamble were important, but were "subordinate" to the "chief ends" of preservation.[43] Thus, to Evans—and the rest of the Federalists—an expansive use of federal power might be the means to achieve the Constitution's sovereignty, but that sovereignty served the even higher and more important ends of the common law.

Along with dispensing with the Constitution's enumeration of powers, the Federalists also had to explain why the Alien Act was not an issue for the states to decide. That the Federalists had to offer an argument against state involvement demonstrates the degree to which state sovereignty was embedded in the constitutional system. Additionally, while the Constitution empowered Congress to pass naturalization laws, it said nothing about how to handle aliens during either peacetime or war. Practically every state had laws that handled those issues. By arguing for a federal common law that tied to the sovereignty of the federal government, the Federalists hoped to circumvent the states. Only the federal government could address the issue of aliens, Federalists claimed, because the measures were linked to the war power of Congress via the use of implied powers. Federalists were not claiming that the Alien Acts were only temporary measures resulting from the exigencies of the crisis with France; only the Alien Friends Act had an expiration date. Rather, they meant that since the Alien Acts were attempts to defend the country, the federal government was assuming permanent control over the issue.

The accumulation of extra-constitutional authority via implied power originated with the Nationalists of the 1780s and reemerged again with the Federalists' arguments over the Bank of the United States. It was also one of the great fears of the Anti-Federalists and one of the key reasons behind the clamor for a state sovereignty amendment. With the growing crisis and potential for war, however, the Federalists made their greatest and most assertive use of the doctrine. By combining implied powers and a federal common law, the Federalists' vision of the federal government as a complete sovereign was becoming reality. This explains why the Federalists had to circumvent the states and assume their authority over aliens. As Otis explained during the debates over the Alien Acts in Congress, "the great objects of peace and war, negotiations with foreign countries, the general peace and welfare of the United States, must be provided for and maintained by the National Government; no other authority is competent to these great duties." Therefore, "if Congress has the right to defend the Union, it certainly has the right to prepare for defense," and any state laws regarding aliens "must vanish before the obligation of the General Government to provide for the common defense."[44] Thomas Evans was just as explicit about the minimalist role of the states. Offering an argument that was reminiscent of Alexander Hamilton's "Contientialist" essays of the early 1780s, Evans argued that since the *"chief end* of the [C]onstitution of the United States" was the establishment of a sovereignty with the power to protect the country, a "reference to the same end all its parts ought to be construed."[45] In other words, if the sovereignty of the federal government was to have any real meaning, its powers needed a liberal construction. Nor should the states object to this power. As Evans explained, the states dealt only with "the internal, local, and municipal affairs of the people." While the federal government might not address those issues, should a local issue touch upon the Constitution's *"chief end . . .* [the] rational and found construction must extend" federal sovereignty to that issue. Otherwise, "we mean to be guilty of the absurdity of proposing to attain the most important of all political ends, *the preservation of our national existence,* without adequate means."[46] In short, the states dealt with local issues only because the federal government permitted it and only until they believed the matter touched a national concern.

Federalists would apply the argument of a federal common law with even greater force in their defenses of the Sedition Act. Unlike the Alien Acts, which the Federalists connected to common law through the law of nations, the Sedition Act illustrated Federalists' connections between federal sovereignty to an American society. Commentators have noted how the Federalists improved upon the English common law idea of sedition by making truth a defense at trial.[47] While this is true, it nevertheless overlooks why the Federalists believed in the necessity of the measure in the first place and how the Sedition Act did not violate the seemingly explicit language of the First Amendment. The Federalists believed the Sedition Act was an internal self-defense measure to protect society from the ravages of licentiousness.

To understand properly what the Federalists meant, it is necessary to understand why they feared licentiousness. To most Americans of the eighteenth century, whether Federalist or Republican, licentiousness was the "bane of liberty" because it was the absence of order.[48] Liberty, Americans believed, could not exist without order. Should the people ever remove the restraints of order, licentiousness would overcome liberty and chaos would ensue. During the 1780s, Nationalists had believed that licentiousness was taking root in the state governments. Only the empowerment of the federal government, they argued, could stop the slide. During the 1790s, the Federalists considered the bloody excesses of the French Revolution as proof of what happened when a people destroyed constitutional and societal order and overindulged in liberty. To Federalists, the Republicans' celebration of the French Revolution was an endorsement of societal overthrow, political revolution, and licentiousness. The harsh and unrelenting attacks on Federalists and the Adams administration by Republican newspapers such as the *Aurora* only confirmed this fear. The Sedition Act was nothing short of a measure to save American society from the Republicans.

In Congress, Federalists gave full vent to their fears of the licentiousness of the Republican press, asking "how [was] society aided by the gross and monstrous outrages upon truth and honor, and public character and private peace which inundate the country?"[49] Reading passages from the *Aurora* on the floor of Congress, Federalists concluded that the Republicans' attacks were "calculated to freeze the very blood in our veins" and "destroy all confidence between man and man" and tear "asunder every ligament that unites man to his family, man to his neighbor, man to society, and to Government."[50] Federalists accused Republicans of "planting [the] thorns" of civil war. These "base calumniators" were in the minority at that moment, another Federalist argued, but by sowing malignant falsehood amongst the people, it would not take long before the whole people turned against the government. Thus, there was "no reason why we should not harbor traitors in our bosom." Only with the "coat of mail" in the form of the Sedition Act could the government "turn away the point of some dagger aimed at the heart of the Government."[51]

The falsehoods and venom of the Republican press, claimed Massachusetts Federalist John Allen, mirrored what French Jacobins had done in the other nations of Europe. These "loud and enthusiastic advocates for liberty and equality" had all used the press as the first line of attack in their efforts to overthrow the established order. The "baneful effects" of their licentious writings were aimed at making the "poor, the ignorant, the passionate, and the vicious" the "tools of faction and ambition."[52] With so many emigrants flooding the country, the "Jacobins in our country" were attempting to execute the plans that had worked so well in Europe. It was the Federalists' responsibility to "wrest it from them."[53]

Nor was the First Amendment's prohibition an obstacle to the Sedition Act. Not only did the measure allow truth as a defense, but the amendment did not protect against licentious printing. Did "gentlemen seriously think," asked one Federalist, that the amendment "authorize[ed] such publications" as contained in Republican newspapers?[54] Simply because the amendment protected the freedom of the press did not mean it provided the liberty to "falsely call you a thief, murderer, [or] an atheist . . . the freedom of the press and opinions was never understood to give the right of publishing falsehoods and slanders, nor exciting sedition, insurrection, and slaughter with impunity."[55] Charles Lee made a similar argument. "The freedom of the press differs from the licentiousness of the press," he argued. Laws against publishing sedition would "always be found to affirm and preserve the former." Without a sedition law, Lee continued, the Constitution and American society would be "undermined and subverted" by a Republican press that sowed "contempt and hatred among the people by means of malicious and false stories."[56] Thomas Evans, like many Federalists, relied upon Blackstone to defend the Sedition Act. Evans quoted Blackstone passages on sedition in the *Commentaries*. Sedition left the "liberty of private sentiment" intact, but punished "bad sentiments, destructive of the ends of society."[57] Therefore, the intertwining of the Constitution and American society authorized the federal government to punish seditious publication in order to protect the society. When Congress "concurred in recommending" the First Amendment, Evans noted, "they ratified and approved that article intend[ing] to provide an exemption" from licentious and seditious writings.[58]

Federalists invoked Blackstone for more than just explaining how sedition did not apply to the First Amendment; they used him to anchor the Sedition Act to the common law. "That the principles and doctrines of the common law of England form the basis of our laws," wrote Evans. Since the common law doctrines of "liberty" and "freedom of the press" had "received definite meaning . . . long prior to the establishment of the [C]onstitution," the Constitution absorbed that long-held understanding.[59] In other words, Evans established the syllogism of since sedition was a crime punishable under the common law, and since the federal government assumed the common law upon the Constitution's adoption, the national government had the power to punish sedition. Otis reinforced Evans' argument by noting in congressional debates that "[w]hen the people of the United States convened for the purpose of framing a federal compact, they were all habituated to this common law." Hence, it was:

> natural to conclude that, in forming the Constitution, they kept in view the model of the common law, and that a safe recourse may be had to it all cases that would otherwise be doubtful . . . It was, therefore, most evident to his mind, that the Constitution of the United States, prior to the amendments that have been added to it, secured to the National Government the cognizance of all the crimes enumerated in the bill [i.e., the Sedition Act], and it only remained to be consider where those amendments divested it of this power.[60]

Addison's argument was even more explicit. Since the formation of the colonies, he wrote, the colonies took "with them the laws, rights, and duties of the mother country."[61] While they applied the common law to their particular circumstances, they nevertheless "carried with them all the common law of England" with England serving as the "general superintending government." Even the declaring of independence did not end the American reliance upon the common law. "There was a common law in each state before the declaring of independence, and it remained after this declaration," he wrote, since independence did not dissolve societal bonds. With the adoption of the Constitution and the establishment of a national society the common law was received through Article III of the Constitution, which stated that the "judicial power shall extend to all cases in law and equity."[62] The only definition that could extend to this phrase, he concluded, was that the Constitution intended to embrace and follow the common law.

The connection to this assumption of the common law by the Constitution meant, therefore, that the First Amendment did not protect against "false, malicious and seditious expressions, whether spoken or written."[63] As Addison argued, "Government, the sovereignty, [was] as it were, the *person* of civil society."[64] Since it violated the common law to libel an individual, so too was it a crime to libel the government. To Federalists, a denial of this basic fact was to reject nature itself. The nation's right to "defend itself against injuries and outrages" originated from the "nature of things" and "resulted from the spirit of the Constitution."[65] John Allen agreed, noting that very nature of federal government's sovereignty meant that it had the power to punish sedition, "for no government can exist without it; it is inherent in every government; because it is necessary to its preservation."[66] Lee, in summarizing the

Federalist argument, argued that since sedition was a common law crime, the Sedition Act was not even necessary. "Perhaps the law was not indispensably necessary," he wrote, "because without it the same misdemeanor were punishable" and would remain so "after its expiration."[67]

The Alien and Sedition Acts represented the apogee of the Federalists' constitutionalism. As their arguments made abundantly clear, the federal government was far more than what the Federalists of 1788 had promised, a limited government established for limited objectives. Instead, it was a fully fledged sovereign on par with any traditional nation-state. It could wield any power the Federalists believed necessary to fulfill and protect the federal government's real purpose, the establishment of an American society. Nor was the enumeration of federal power in the Constitution an impediment to the Federalists. As they argued, the Constitution was more than just the document itself; it was the means to the greater end of establishing the federal government's sovereignty and the protection of a national society. Ratifying the Constitution and, with it, creating a national society and sovereignty, transcended the document's limitations via enumerations of power and the Bill of Rights by infusing the federal government with the extra-constitutional and higher law authority of the common law.

***

Although the irony of this constitutional position—that the extra-constitutional power of the common law superseded the enumeration of powers and the Bill of Rights—was lost on the Federalists, the Republicans realized it. "It sh[owed] that gentlemen were ready to defend not only existing violations of the federal constitution, but any infractions, which might hereafter be committed upon it," noted one Republican.[68] "Of all the doctrines which have ever been broached by the federal government," wrote Jefferson in the summer of 1799, "the novel one of the common law being in force [and] cognizable as an existing law in their courts, is to me the most formidable."[69] The formidability of the Federalists' argument derived from the Republican belief that it represented the final "link in a chain of events leading to the most serious of consequences . . . a practical change in our Government."[70]

For most of the 1790s, they had waged a constitutional and public relations battle to stop the Federalists and their constitutionalism, but the battle over the common law would be different because of the "audacious, barefaced and sweeping pretension to a system of law for the US. without the adoption of their legislature and so infinitely beyond their power to adopt."[71] Although their own intense partisanship surrounding the XYZ Affair was partially responsible for heightened tensions, they were shocked and demoralized by the Alien and Sedition Acts, and espe-

cially the constitutional theory that underlay them. The Republicans saw
those ideas as the antithesis of the Revolution's efforts of establishing a
state-sovereignty constitutional order. Thus, they believed the fight over
the common law and the Alien and Sedition Acts was nothing short of a
battle over the fate of the American experiment in self-governance. If they
did not fight the Federalists, the future of American governance was
consolidation and monarchy.

Before examining the Republicans' resistance to the Alien and Sedition Acts, it is important to note that in one area, the idea that the federal
government possessed the law of nations, the Republicans and the Federalists were in some constitutional agreement. The Republicans believed
that in the realm of domestic issues the sovereignty of the federal government was limited strictly to those areas enumerated in the Constitution.
In the realm of international relations, however, the federal government
was the only sovereign. While Republicans often disagreed with Federalists "over the nature, scope, and application" of that sovereignty, they
nevertheless believed sovereignty existed. The handling of the international relations by the general government was one of the primary reasons behind the union, the Articles of the Confederation, and the Constitution.[72]

In accepting this idea, the Republicans were furthering the constitutional argument first established during the imperial crisis by authors
such as John Dickinson and John Adams. During those debates, colonial
Americans had accepted that King-in-Parliament possessed the authority
to regulate the external issues of the empire, such as international trade
and war and peace. As the colonies had consented to this arrangement, so
too had the states in the formation of the confederation and, later, the
Constitution. The Republicans not only accepted the sovereignty of the
federal government on external issues, but they believed that Americans
had an obligation to follow the federal government's decisions in that
area. In 1790, Congress passed, with overwhelming support, the "Act for
the Punishment of Certain Crimes." The measure codified infractions
against the law of nations such as "offering violence to the person of an
ambassador or other public minister."[73]

The Republicans further revealed their belief in the law of nations
during the controversy over Washington's neutrality proclamation. Although most Republicans were uncomfortable with the proclamation's
implications for executive power, they nevertheless believed that it represented the state of American relations until Congress acted.[74] As Jefferson put it, Washington's actions reminded Americans that the United
States was "in a state of peace with all the parties, admonishing the
people to do nothing contravening it, and putting them on their guard as
to contraband."[75] This explains why many Republicans did not protest
when the federal government arrested Henfield for violating the neutrality proclamation. Americans, they believed, had an obligation to follow

the proclamation because it embodied the law of nations. When French ambassador Edmund Genet protested the proclamation, Henfield's imprisonment, and the American refusal to support France, Jefferson's retort amply explained the American position. "You think, Sir," that the proclamation was "contrary to the law of nature and usage of nations. We are of the opinion that it is dictated by that law and usage."[76]

By the time of the crisis over the Alien and Sedition Acts, the Republicans had long accepted the idea that the federal government was not only sovereign in foreign affairs but also possessed the unwritten authority of the law of nations. Yet, when Federalists proposed the Alien Acts in the summer of 1798, the Republicans universally condemned the measures as unconstitutional and tyrannical. At first glance, their opposition to the Alien Acts might seem hypocritical or irreconcilable with their previous positions, but it was not. If the Republican understanding of the external and internal dichotomy of constitutional sovereignty is kept in mind, their opposition becomes clear.[77]

Of the three measures that made up the Alien Acts, the only one the Republicans accepted as constitutional was the Alien Enemies Act. That measure, recall, operated only when the United States was in an officially declared war. A declared war, they argued, triggered the law of nations' power to expel any enemy alien from the country, and since only the federal government possessed the authority over the law of nations, only the federal government could act on alien enemies. Indeed, as one Republican noted, as soon as war was declared "by the law of nations, alien enemies become prisoners of war" and Congress had the only "right to say what may be done with these prisoners."[78] In Congress, Albert Gallatin, who had assumed leadership of congressional Republicans upon Madison's retirement in 1796, noted that the federal government could punish alien enemies because of the "principle which existed prior to the Constitution, and coeval with the law of nations."[79] The only hesitation the Republicans expressed over the Alien Enemies Act was over executive power. They were troubled that the measure violated the separation of powers by empowering the President to remove the enemy aliens. Nevertheless, and despite this caution, they supported the measure.

This dichotomy also explains why the Republicans objected strenuously to the Alien Friends Act. While a declared war empowered the federal government to use the law of nations to expel the enemies of the union, nowhere did the Constitution empower the federal government to handle relations with aliens from nations who were friendly to the United States. Since the states were their own self-governing society, when peaceful immigrants migrated to a state, they were joining that state's distinct polity. Therefore, it was left to the sovereignty of the states to determine how to deal with friendly aliens. Any attempt by the federal government to regulate the activity of alien friends violated the Constitution's strict limitations of congressional power over domestic issues and the sovereignty of the states. When the Federalists declared that the necessary and proper clause infused the federal government with sovereignty over all aliens, the Republicans responded by noting how the Tenth Amendment prohibited that interpretation. That amendment, noted Gallatin, prohibited such "improper use" of the "sweeping clause." If the Federalists' reading of the necessary and proper clause to the law of nations power were accepted, "this amendment would have no application." Showing the Republicans' division over the external and internal sovereignty of the federal government, Gallatin argued that the Federalists' argument for the implied power over alien friends was "flatly contradicted by the Constitution, as it recognizes a division of powers between the General and State Government."[80] Tying the "power for providing for the common defense" to the necessary and proper clause in order to regulate alien friends was nothing more than a ruse to "absorb all other powers." Indeed, the Federalists' doctrine that "all power should be vested in the Government, because it is possible that occurrences may arise which will call for the exercise of them . . . [was] contrary to the Constitution, for that has put limits to the powers of the Government."[81] Gallatin finished by noting that since the Alien Friends bill was "of more a local than of a general nature," the "States and State Judiciary would, indeed they *must* declare it unconstitutional."[82] Although Gallatin did not clarify how the state was to make that declaration, the Republicans would soon explain.

Although the Republicans willingly accepted both the idea of the federal government's sovereignty over external issues, including the use of the implied powers under the law of nations, they rejected any such authority over domestic issues. In particular, the Republicans focused heavily upon the Federalists' notions of a federal common law of crimes. To accept a common law for the federal government was to erase the enumeration of powers and accept that the American Congress was merely Parliament reborn. If the Republicans were to stop the Federalists, they would have to devise a strategy that resisted the federal government, while, at the same time, protecting themselves from the Federalist persecution under the Sedition Act. Making the task all the more difficult was the dramatic rise in the Federalists' popularity resulting from the XYZ Affair. The Republicans would have to expose the implications of the Federalists' ideas in hopes that a "little patience, and we shall see the reign of witches pass over, their spells dissolve, and the people, recovering their true sight, restore their government to its true principles."[83]

The first two hints of how the Republicans would resist the Sedition Acts occurred within a year of the measure's passage. The first came from Justice Samuel Chase in the *Worrall* case. In the midst of Rawle's defense of a federal common law, Chase interrupted to note that the government's common law indictment could not stand. Equating the "silence of the Constitution and Statutes of the Union," he said, mocked the Constitution's foundation of not assuming "any power, that is not expressly granted by that instrument." At no point could anyone "trace when, or how, the system [of the common law] was adopted, or introduced" at the federal level. The states, however, had clearly adopted it, but they had only absorbed those elements of the common law that fit their circumstances. The reality, Chase concluded, was that the "Constitution does not create" the common law "and no act of Congress ha[d] assumed it;" therefore, the federal government could not wield common law powers.[84]

The second hint towards Republican resistance occurred in the late summer of 1797 when Jefferson authored an anonymous petition to the Virginia legislature denouncing the federal grand jury indictment of Republican Congressman Samuel J. Cabell (Jefferson's congressional representative), on the grounds that he violated the federal common law crime of sedition. Cabell's crime, as it was, centered on sending his constituents letters that, during "a time of real public danger," supposedly contained "unfounded calumnies against the happy government of the United States."[85] His prosecution represented the first significant application of the idea of a federal common law against sedition.[86]

Jefferson's petition attacked Cabell's indictment on several grounds. It violated the tenets of republican representation by censoring the free communication between the people and its chosen representative. It was a "natural right" for a "good and dutiful representative," to communicate often and freely with constituents. A people's representative should not fear "the cognizance or coercion of its co-ordinate branches Judiciary and Executive." The interference by those branches, Jefferson wrote, constituted a dangerous violation of the separation of powers. The only remedy to the indictment, Jefferson argued, was for the Virginia legislature to intervene, impeach, and punish the members of the federal grand jury for committing a crime of "high and extraordinary procedure."[87] To Jefferson, impeaching and punishing the federal grand jury for violating a nonstatutory law was no hypocritical reliance upon the common law. As he noted in the petition, the Virginia constitution of 1776 explicitly adopted the common law, thereby making it the "law of this land." The Virginia constitution also provided the state legislature the power of impeaching offensives committed against the state, and since their constitution recognized the common law right of constituent communication, the federal grand jury had violated the rights of the people of the Commonwealth of Virginia.[88]

Jefferson's petition, and its strong implication of state sovereignty and interposition, was a calculated political move based upon his constitutional principles. As he informed James Monroe, since the "system of the General government [was] to seize all doubtful ground," it was necessary to petition the state legislature in order to "join the scramble or get nothing." In essence, then, the petition was a move to secure the sovereignty of Virginia, since "first occupancy is to give a right." [89] What Jefferson meant was that if the federal government claimed the common law right of punishing sedition—a right it did claim in 1798—without any opposition, the power would become a part of the federal government. Not only was the petition designed to challenge the idea of a federal common law, but more importantly, it was intended to empower the Virginia legislature to protect the rights of its citizens. "It was of immense consequence that the States retain as complete authority as possible over their own citizens." To turn to the "foreign jurisdiction" of the federal courts ran the risk of losing their liberty. The entire reasoning for the petition, Jefferson concluded, was not to rectify the "breach of Mr. Cabell's privilege." Instead, it was to correct "the wrong done to the citizens of our district." [90] In other words, the federal government's indictment of Cabell represented a direct threat to the liberties and natural rights of the citizens of Virginia. The only method to preserve those rights was state interposition.

Chase's remarks at the Worrall trial and Jefferson's anonymous petition to the Virginia legislature revealed the Republican strategy in their fight against the Federalists. They would rely upon the sovereignty of the state governments and the use of interposition to defend the people, the states, and the union from the Federalists. In the summer and fall of 1798, however, Republicans remained unsure if they should use the state governments in attacking only the Alien and Sedition Acts or the entirety of the Federalist program. The Republican pamphleteer, John Taylor of Caroline, recalling the arguments of his essays, urged that the Republicans fight the entirety of the Federalist program. The current crisis, he argued to Jefferson, "arises from political causes." [91] In particular, Taylor wanted the Republicans to fight the direct taxes Federalists had enacted to support the military buildup against the French. "Standing Armies are one cause of oppressive taxes" but were "only temporary, lest they [the Federalists] perpetuate oppressive taxes." Taxation, he continued, corrupted and putrefied the body politic because it "transfers wealth from a mass to a selection. It destroys political Equality, which alone can save liberty." Any government endowed "with a right to transfer, bestow, and monopolize wealth in perpetuity is in fact, unlimited" and "soon becomes a feudal lord over a nation in villenage." If the "the right of the State governments to expound the [C]onstitution" could be turned to the issue of limiting the Federalists' access to the people's wealth, the Federalist program, including the Alien and Sedition Acts, could come crashing down. Should the states fail to intervene and the federal government's "habit of peeping into private letters" continue, Taylor hinted that perhaps the union would break apart. [92]

Jefferson's response to Taylor urged calmness and prudence. That Federalists were attempting to "divide certain parts of the Union, so as to make use of them to govern the whole," was the "old practice of despots." Simply because a "temporary superiority of the one party" was working its machinations against the people was not reason enough to "resort to a scission of the union." That would unleash unforeseen evils worse than what the Federalists were attempting to accomplish, Jefferson wrote. The situation, while "insulting to our feelings as well as exhausting to our strength and substance," was not as dire as it might seem, Jefferson told Taylor. The "body of our countrymen is substantially republican through every part of the union," and with "a little patience" the disease that Taylor saw in the Federalists' taxation would be cured.[93] Already, Jefferson counseled, the "Doctor [was] now on his way to cure it, in the guise of a taxgatherer." With the Federalist tax collectors administering the cure against taxes, Jefferson preferred to devote Republican energies towards "resolving the alien and sedition laws."[94] He agreed with Taylor on turning to the state governments. It was "a singular phenomenon that while our state governments are the *very best in the world* without exception or comparison, our general government has, in the rapid course of 9 or 10 years, become more arbitrary, and has swallowed more of the public liberty than even that of England." Because of the Federalists' decade-long hold over the federal government, Jefferson believed the federal government could not and would not fix the situation. Only the states, then, could declare the Alien and Sedition Acts as "against the [C]onstitution and merely void."[95]

While Republicans set about turning to the states, those Republicans in and out of Congress attacked the Sedition Act. Congressional Republicans, realizing they had little hope of stopping the passage of the Act—the Federalists were too popular and emboldened—nevertheless used their argument to establish the framework of the greater Republican counterattack. In Congress, Republicans restated the arguments of the past decade to attack the idea of a federal common law as a violation of the principles upon which the people of the states had ratified the Constitution.

Gallatin opened the attacks by noting how "there [was] not any such thing as a common law of the United States."[96] Only the states possessed the common law, and while its principles were the same, its application varied from state to state because each state was its own polity. The Federalists' claim that the United States was a collective unit with a national government possessing the full powers of sovereignty was false. The "Government of the Union" was "only a federal one, vested with specific powers, defined by the Constitution." As a result, the "people of the United States" were under the authority of "two distinct Governments" charged with very different responsibilities.[97] The states had general legislative powers, including those found in the common law, because the states had to protect their societies. The federal government, by contrast, had no "undefined general legislative power," only those granted to it. The clear language of the Tenth Amendment embodied that principle and prohibited the Federalists' connection of the common law to the necessary and proper clause. Finally, Gallatin claimed that only a "party in the United States, feeling that they had more power, [and] were not afraid of passing such law" could pass such a "preposterous" and "insulting evasion of the Constitution" like the Sedition Act. In their haughtiness and desire for power, Gallatin asserted, the Federalists were claiming that plain language of the First Amendment, "Congress shall make no law abridging the freedom of the press," meant that "you may write and publish what you please, but if you publish anything against us, we will punish you for it."[98]

Wilson Cary Nicholas and Nathaniel Macon were more forceful. Both followed Gallatin in asserting that the Constitution lacked any express common law authority, but each tied the argument against the common law to the understanding of the Constitution at the time of its ratification. Nicholas asked the simple question of whether "gentlemen supposed that, in adopting the Constitution, the United States adopted the common law of all the states?" He answered his question by reading a selection from Virginia's instrument of ratification that stated that Virginia adopted the Constitution on the understanding that "every power not granted thereby, remains with" the state and that "among other essential rights . . . the liberty of the press cannot be cancelled, abridged or restrained or modified by any authority of the United States." This was proof, he told Congress, that even before the writing and adoption of the First Amendment "the understanding of the members of the convention was complete," that the federal government could not interfere with the liberty of the press.[99] Macon followed by noting that the "best way of coming at the truth of any construction of the Constitution, was, by examining the opinions that were held respecting it when it was under discussion in the different states." Macon then read from the "opinions of the leading members in several of the State conventions," including remarks made by the current Federalist members of Congress, to show how the common law of "prosecutions for libel could take under the general government."[100]

Republicans outside of Congress also appealed to the limited nature of the Constitution to deny the existence of a federal common law. In Jefferson's home county of Albemarle, Virginia, a committee published a remonstrance to Congress. The petition reminded Congress that when "we were called upon to ratify the [C]onstitution, an alarm was given" that "the states might be swept away by an encroaching construction." Yet, promises offered by the Constitution's supporters quieted those fears and were "afterwards totally banished" by language of the Tenth Amendment. That language demonstrated that Congress had no authority over alien friends or the punishment of sedition. With the Alien and Sedition Acts, however, Congress was threatening the arrangements made during ratification of the Tenth Amendment.[101] John Page, in a campaign pamphlet, paraphrased the Burke Amendment by noting that the Alien and Sedition Acts struck at the heart of the "freedom, the happiness, the sovereignty, and independence" of Virginia and the rest of the states.[102]

Among the more learned attacks on the Alien and Sedition Acts came from the Virginia jurist St. George Tucker. A prominent lawyer, law professor, and judge, Tucker was perhaps the Republicans' most important legal thinker.[103] In 1799, he published "Of the Unwritten, or Common Law of England; And Its Introduction into, and Authority within the United American States," a rebuttal to the Federalist arguments of Wilson, Evans, and Addison. Tucker's detailed analysis of the historical background of common law and its diverse development in the colonies and states led him to conclude the common law could not exist at the federal level. Although the states had adopted the common law, they did so in acutely diverse ways. The common law of Virginia, for example, was not necessarily the common law of Massachusetts or even neighboring Maryland. For the federal government to adopt the common law was to impose a uniform system that contradicted the reasons why the states adopted only those elements of the common law they believed best for their state.[104] Not only would it destroy the diversity of the common law, but it would undermine the very nature of the constitutional order. The federal government could not adopt the common law because its powers were limited to only "certain determined objects . . . leaving the administration of their internal, and domestic concerns, to the absolute and uncontrollable jurisdiction of the states."[105] While this argument was not unique to Tucker, what was different was his unattributed application of Blackstone's phrase, "absolute and uncontrollable," to define the state sovereignty. Stealing Blackstone's well-known definition of sovereignty from the Federalists allowed him to express in terms uncharacteristically bold for the Republicans their belief that state sovereignty was the foundation of the constitutional order. Nor was using Blackstone to demonstrate state sovereignty the only instance where he turned the Federalists' arguments against themselves. The incorporation of the Tenth Amendment, he claimed, was "nothing more than an express recognition of the law of nations" as elaborated upon by great law of nations theorist Vattel, another favorite of the Federalists.[106]

Tucker used Blackstone and Vattel for more than rhetorical tricks. By referring to these authors, Tucker was establishing the nature of state sovereignty in relation to the federal government. In this, he sounded like a State Sovereigntist of the early 1780s, and an Anti-Federalist of 1788, because what Tucker argued was that the Constitution was nothing more than a better established confederation of states. Much like the confederation, the "powers delegated to Congress," such as declaring war, raising armies, and barrowing money, have "usually supposed to belong to the executive department." To Tucker, this meant the states were still the primary holders of sovereign authority, while the federal government was bounded to only those powers granted to it by the people of the several states. The "grant of powers to the federal government operat[ed] only by way of enumeration," which weakened any Federalist claims to use powers not enumerated. Even the necessary and proper clause was "calculated to restrain the federal government from the exercise of any power, not *necessarily* an *appendage* to, and *consequence* of some power particularly *enumerated*." [107] When the states adopted the Constitution, they did not establish a "general consolidated government, which should swallow up the state sovereignties, and annihilate their several jurisdictions." [108]

Yet, destroying state sovereignty was exactly what the Federalists were attempting by calling for a federal common law. Since the Constitution did not grant the power to use the common law, Federalists could only claim it through the "dangerous" doctrine of implication. The Tenth Amendment, however, "was proposed, adopted and ratified, for the express purpose of rebutting, this doctrine of grant by implication." [109] Even if that fact were not so plainly true, he continued, it would be an "absurdity in the extreme" to think that the federal government could, through the power of implication, "revive, and enforce such parts of the common law" that the states had explicitly rejected as "incompatible" with republican self-government. This led Tucker to conclude that the Federalists' argument represented "probably the first instance in which it has been supposed that sovereign and independent states can be abridged of their rights, as sovereign states, by *implication* only." [110] If the Federalist construction of federal common law power was established, the consequence would be "but at one stroke, to annihilate the states altogether" since the "common law of England, be *paramount*" to the states. Yet, Tucker concluded, since "it [was] impossible to trace, when, or how, the system was adopted, or introduced" to the federal government, a federal common law simply did not exist. [111]

The claims of Tucker and other Republicans that a federal common law was the antithesis of the constitutional system reflected their constitutionalism. Yet, scholars often ignore this connection leading to the false conclusion that Republicans were opposed to the general idea of sedition. No Republican claimed that seditious libel could not be punished, only that the federal government could not punish it. The responsibility for punishing seditious libel fell to the states alone, because only they had adopted the common law. What the Republicans argued, then, flowed directly from their belief in a state sovereignty-centered constitutional order. To Republicans, the Federalist syllogism that since the common law existed, and the states wielded the common law, the assumption that the federal government did too was false. It conflated the nature of the federal government by treating that government as the same as the state governments. Thus, the Republicans' appeals to state sovereignty, the text of the Constitution, the Tenth Amendment, and the promises made during ratification were all demonstrations that the federal government was not a government similar to the states.

The most important Republican attacks against the Alien and Sedition Acts came from the pens of Jefferson and Madison. During a meeting at Jefferson's Monticello in the fall of 1798, the two Republican leaders decided to turn to the state legislatures of Kentucky and Virginia to defeat the Federalists' plans and constitutionalism. Yet, their decision was not born from pragmatism or lack of other options. Not only had state interposition been used throughout the 1780s, but Madison referred to the power in his writings as "Publius" and in his speech submitting the Bill of Rights. Thus, the decision to use the state legislatures and interposition to protect individual liberty was a natural one. With fears of prosecution under the Sedition Act, however, both Jefferson and Madison drafted their resolutions anonymously. In November of 1798, John Taylor of Caroline submitted the Virginia Resolution to his state's assembly and John Breckinridge delivered his to the Kentucky legislature.

Both resolutions opened by expressing the constitutional theory that Federalists had promised during ratification and that Republicans maintained throughout the 1790s. "That the several States composing, the United States of America, are not united on the principle of unlimited submission to their general government."[112] Instead, the Constitution was a "compact" in which "each state acceded as a state, and is an integral party, its co-states forming to itself, the other party." Thus, when the states compacted together to form the Constitution, they were constituting "a general government for special purposes, delegated to that government certain definite powers, reserving, each State to itself, the residuary mass of right to their own self-government."[113] The Alien and Sedition Acts and the "forced construction of the constitutional charter," as the Virginia Resolution called it, violated this basic premise, and now threatened the liberty of Virginia's and Kentucky's citizens. The measures were the latest, and most dangerous, reliance upon "implications . . . to expound certain general phrases . . . so as to destroy the meaning and effect, of the particular enumerations which necessarily explains and limits the general phrases."[114]

The Virginia Resolution recalled that when the state had ratified the Constitution it had "expressly declared" that the federal government had no power over the liberty of the press. This understanding was eventually "annexed" to the Constitution via the Tenth Amendment.[115] Jefferson reinforced this idea. Restating the arguments he first expressed in his "Opinion on the Bank," Jefferson noted that the Tenth Amendment was foundation upon which the entire constitutional structure rested. Since the Constitution did not provide the federal government with the power over alien friends and sedition, it was therefore "reserved to the states" to determine what constituted licentious speech or publication. Had the

Constitution stopped with the Tenth Amendment, that would have been enough, Jefferson argued, but the First Amendment's explicit language doubly reinforced the reservation. Yet, the Alien and Sedition Acts were attempting to undermine this foundation by removing the power from the state and placing it in the hands of the executive.[116] The "uniting of the legislative and judicial powers to those of the executive," the Virginia Resolution stated, "subervt[ed] the general principles of free government." Not only did the measures threaten state sovereignty, but by allowing the president to decide arbitrarily which alien to deport, the Alien Act also deprived alien friends the basic right to a trial by jury while the Sedition Act undermined the "only effectual guardian of every other right."[117]

The Virginia Resolution also noted how both measures were further steps in the "obvious tendency" of the federal government to acquire nondelegated powers. The purpose behind these steps was to "consolidate the states by degrees, into one sovereignty" in order to "transform" republican government into an "absolute, or at best a mixed Monarchy."[118] Jefferson agreed, adding that "in questions of power then let no more be heard of confidence in mind, but bind him down from mischief by the chains of the Constitution." This was the only way to stop the federal government from:

> seizing the rights of the States, and consolidating them in the hands of the General Government, with a power assumed to bind the States (not merely as the cases made federal) but, in all cases whatsoever, by laws made, not with their consent, but by others against their consent: that this would be to surrender the form of government we have chosen, and live under one deriving its powers from its own will, and not from our authority.[119]

Jefferson's language in this passage was a restatement of the colonies' arguments during the imperial crisis. His reference to binding the states in "all cases whatsoever" harkened to Parliament's language in the Declaratory Act while his references to the "consent" of the states was reminiscent of the arguments posed by Dickinson and Adams in the 1760s and 1770s. The issue of a consolidated empire wielding absolute sovereignty had forced the colonies to assert their sovereignty then, and had now reemerged with the Federalists in 1798. Only with a reassertion of state sovereignty could the states defend individual liberty.

To preserve the constitutional structure of the "compact, to which the states are parties," and protect the liberties of their citizens, demanded that the states interpose themselves between the federal government and the people. All the states, the Virginia resolution argued, were "duty bound, to interpose for arresting the progress of the evil, and for maintaining within their respective limits, the authority, rights and liberties appertaining to them."[120] Thus, the Alien and Sedition Acts were "altogether void and of no force." The states had to intervene because the federal government could not be trusted. Its discretion and not the plain language of the Constitution would be "the measure of its power." The responsibility for determining the constitutionality of a measure, therefore, resided only with the states. Since they created the federal government, "each party has an equal right to judge for itself" whether a measure violated that compact and to determine "the mode and measure of readdress."[121] Yet, the states should not use interposition casually. States should exercise it only "in case of deliberate, palpable, and dangerous excise of other posts, not granted by the said compact." Finally, interposition would mean little if the other states did not voice their concern as well, it required uniting "Co-states [in] recurring to their natural right in cases not made federal" to "concur in declaring these acts void and of no force."[122] Thus, both resolutions called upon the other states to join them in the efforts of protecting liberty and the constitutional order.

The Kentucky and Virginia Resolutions were the most important expressions of the Republicans' constitutionalism of the 1790s. Scholars often consider the resolutions as nothing more than Jefferson and Madison's desperate search to find some way to attack the Alien and Sedition Acts. Under this treatment, the resolutions were political expedients created out of thin air.[123] Most treatments of the Kentucky and Virginia Resolutions ignore the influence that the past several decades had upon resolutions. They focus, instead, on how southern antebellum secessionists relied upon the Jefferson and Madison's work to justify secession, thereby implying that a taint to the idea since the resolutions were of intellectual importance to southern defenses of slavery and disunion. This is reading historical events, thoughts, and actions of one period back into those of another.[124]

The Kentucky and Virginia Resolutions expressed neither new ideas nor a radical constitutionalism.[125] They were the most eloquent, concise, and clearest expression of Revolution's state sovereignty-centered constitutionalism. Jefferson and Madison's arguments on the compact nature of the Constitution, state sovereignty, and interposition expressed ideas first articulated during the Revolution. State sovereignty, recall, fueled the creation of the Burke Amendment, while State Sovereigntists applied the Burke Amendment and interposition in their fight with the Nationalists over implied powers and the Treaty of Peace. When Anti-Federalists called for a state sovereignty amendment during ratification, they sought it in order to protect both their states and the liberties of their citizens. Madison explained and defended this reasoning when introducing what became the Tenth Amendment, and Republicans made repeated assertions to these ideas throughout the 1790s. The Kentucky and Virginia Resolutions simply expressed well-established ideas. They did not introduce a new and radical concept to American constitutionalism. Instead, they were conservative defenses of the established constitutional order against the truly radical constitutionalism of the Federalists.

Although Jefferson and Madison had hoped the other states would rally to the resolutions, they were disappointed. Not only did states fail to rally to Kentucky and Virginia, but most of the New England states passed resolutions of their own denouncing the Kentucky and Virginia Resolutions. New Hampshire and Rhode Island, for example, both held that "the state legislatures [were] not the proper tribunals to determine the constitutionality of the law of the general government," that was the duty of the federal courts.[126] The most powerful denunciation came from Massachusetts. Its state legislature agreed with the other New England states in that the federal judiciary was the proper body to decide the issue of constitutionality. The state went on to add that if the states determined the constitutionality of measures, it would be reducing the Constitution to a "mere cypher [*sic*]—to the form and pageantry of authority, without the energy of power." Massachusetts then went further to declare that the Alien and Sedition Acts were constitutional because "certain powers [were] granted in general terms by the people to their General Government, for the purpose of their safety and protection."[127] Thus, explicit authority to pass the Alien and Sedition Acts did not matter because "this protection is and has been for nine years past uniformly found in the principles and usages of the Common Law." Had the Constitution explicitly denied the government the power to pass the Alien and Sedition Acts it would have "essentially failed" in "answering the great ends for which the people of the United States" formed the Constitution as expressed in the preamble.[128]

The rejection of the Virginia and Kentucky Resolutions by ten of the fourteen states was not the dismissal of the constitutional ideas contained within those documents, although scholars often portray it as such. All of these states had been vocal proponents of state sovereignty throughout the entire founding era, including the 1790s. It was Massachusetts and its congressional representatives that pushed the strongest for what became the Eleventh Amendment, even providing the language for the amendment. Rather, the states dismissed the Kentucky and Virginia Resolutions because of the heightened partisan atmosphere resulting from the French Revolution and crisis with France. All of the states that published condemnations of Jefferson and Madison's work were Federalist strongholds. They feared that endorsing interposition, especially from Republican bulwarks like Kentucky and Virginia, would be a tacit endorsement of the French Revolution.[129] New Hampshire expressed this in its resolution. The state noted that if it had to render a decision on the constitutionality of the Alien and Sedition Acts, it would vote to confirm them as "highly expedient" because of "the present critical situation of our country."[130] Massachusetts, once again, was even more expressive of this connection to the Franco-American crisis. The "unjust and ambitious conduct of the French Government into warlike preparations" had forced the federal government to protect itself. With "thousands of Aliens, whom we doubt not, were ready to co-operate in any external attack" made it necessary for the government to protect itself from all external and "domestic violence." The prosecution of sedition became necessary to cease the "scandalous misrepresentation" of federal measures that would aid the French in their invasion. In other words, stopping a licentious press also thwarted the spread of the licentiousness Federalists saw in the French Revolution.[131]

The rejection of the Virginia and Kentucky Resolutions frustrated Madison. Having reentered the Virginia legislature in 1799, he took the responsibility of responding to the various state resolutions attacking the Virginia and Kentucky Resolutions.[132] In 1800, he penned Virginia's response to those resolutions. Known as the "Report of 1800," it was an extended restatement and defense of the ideas contained within the Virginia Resolution. Madison opened by clarifying that when the word "state" was used in relation to the constitutional structure it meant "the people composing those political societies, in their highest sovereign capacity."[133] Hence, when Madison noted that the Constitution was "formed by the sanction of the states" operating in their "sovereign capacity" what he meant was that people of the states, in agreeing to the Constitution, exercised their respected but separate popular sovereignties.[134]

From this definition of the people of the several states flowed the ideas of interposition. Madison defended interposition as the "plain principles, founded in common sense, illustrated by common practice, and essential to the nature of compacts." Since the people of the states formed the Constitution, there was no tribunal above their authority. Even the federal judiciary, which Federalists claimed was the only body to determine constitutionality of federal measures, was a creature of that agreement and, as such, did not possess authority greater than that of the states. Thus, interposition was an attempt to stave off the "danger of degeneracy to which republics are liable" by returning the "fundamental principles . . . and political doctrines . . . which characterized the epoch of our revolution."[135] The resolution was not a blanket endorsement of interposition, Madison noted. A state could not interpose for "light and transient" reasons. Rather, as the Virginia Resolution notion, it was a "last resort" intended for "dangerous" threats against the reason "which the Constitution was established." Even then, that danger had to be of an "evil" nature so as to cause doubt about the continuation of government, its principles, or the liberties of the people.[136]

Madison devoted nearly half of his report to refuting the idea of a federal common law, claiming in pointed terms that "this stage of our political history furnishes no foothold for the patrons of this new doctrine."[137] In attempting to demonstrate the fallacy of the Federalists' idea,

Madison offered perhaps the best and most succinct explanation of the constitutional settlement of the Revolution. He wrote that:

> [t]he fundamental principle of the Revolution was, that the colonies were co-ordinate members with each other, and with Great Britain, of an empire, united by a common executive sovereign, but not united by any common legislative sovereign. The legislative power was maintained to be as complete in each American parliament, as in the British parliament. And the royal prerogative was in force in each colony, by virtue of its acknowledging the king for its executive magistrate, as it was in Great Britain, by virtue of a like acknowledgment there. A denial of these principles by Great Britain, and the assertion of them by America, produced the Revolution. . . . The assertion by Great Britain of a power to make laws for the other members of the empire *in all cases whatsoever*, ended in the discovery that she had a right to make laws for them *in no cases whatsoever*. Such being the ground of our Revolution, no support nor color can be drawn from it, for the doctrine that the common law is binding on these states as one society. The doctrine, on the contrary, is evidently repugnant to the fundamental principle of the Revolution. [138]

The Constitution, he finished, "does not contain a sentence or syllable that can be tortured into a countenance of the idea, that the parties to it were, with respect to objects of the common law, to form one community." To insist that the authority of Congress contained the authority of the common law would be an admission that Congress was "co-extensive with the objects of the common law" since the common law touched all elements of governance. Congress' authority would, "therefore be no longer under the limitations marked out in the Constitution. They would be authorized to legislate in all cases whatsoever." [139] An unlimited federal government was not what Virginia, or the other states, had agreed to when they adopted the Constitution. In fact, "in all the contemporary discussion and comments which the Constitution underwent" during ratification, this interpretation was rejected explicitly in favor of the idea that the states retained all the power not authorized to the Constitution, and was confirmed with the Tenth Amendment. [140]

Madison's "Report of 1800," which was more explicit about the constitutional settlement of the Revolution than either the Kentucky or Virginia Resolutions, was among the last explicit statements on the debates over the Alien and Sedition Acts. Several months after the report, President Adams reported that attempts to achieve a treaty of peace with France were successful. With peace achieved, the furor over the Alien and Sedition Acts and the idea of a federal common law subsided as thoughts turned to the presidential election of 1800. Jefferson's contentious victory in that heated contest ended not only the Alien and Sedition Acts—Jefferson would pardon those prosecuted under the Sedition Act—but also the constitutional arguments over the nature of the Constitution in the American constitutional system.

Those debates, which had raged since the presentation of the Constitution in 1787, pitted two opposite and competing visions of what the Constitution represented. The Federalists, building off the ideas of Nationalists, expressed a belief that the federal government was a complete sovereign possessing the powers necessary to fulfill the promises stated in the preamble. The Constitution's enumeration of powers were not limitations, but expressions of how to fulfill that greater sovereignty. The Alien and Sedition Acts and a federal common law were the culmination of those beliefs. The Republicans, however, viewed the Constitution from the vantage point of the constitutional order established by the Revolution. The order was one where the states were sovereign and the federal government limited by expressed powers. The Constitution had no greater purpose beyond that which was stated, and it had no authority past its enumeration. They believed they had confirmed this idea during ratification and the adoption of the Tenth and Eleventh Amendments. Their reliance upon interposition in the Kentucky and Virginia Resolutions to stop the ideas contained in the Alien and Sedition Acts drew upon well-established ideas of how state sovereignty was to operate in the constitutional system. The Republicans' victory in 1800 appeared to confirm that understanding.

NOTES

1. Aaron N. Coleman, "'A Second Bonaparty?': A Reexamination of Alexander Hamilton during the Franco-American Crisis, 1796–1800," *Journal of the Early Republic* 28 (Summer 2008): 183–214.

2. Ibid.; Stanley Elkins and Eric McKitrick, *The Age of Federalism: The Early American Republic, 1788–1800* (New York: Oxford University Press, 1993), 336–41; James Rogers Sharp, *American Politics in the Early Republic: The New Nation in Crisis* (New Haven: Yale University Press, 1993), 92–137; and Gordon Wood, *Empire of Liberty: A History of the Early Republic, 1789–1815* (New York: Oxford University Press, 2009), 89.

3. Coleman, "Second Bonaparty," 190.

4. The best treatments of this division are Sharp, *Politics in the Early Republic*, 69–91, and Wood, *Empire of Liberty*, 174–208.

5. Coleman, "Second Bonaparty?," 197.

6. Ibid., 200.

7. John Adams, Special Session Message, May 16, 1797, *A Compilation of the Messages and Papers of the Presidents, 1789–1897*, ed. James D. Richardson (10 vols., Washington, DC, 1901), 1: 224–25.

8. John Adams to the Inhabitants of Providence, R. I., Apr. 30, 1798, and Adams to the Young Men of Boston, M.A. in *The Works of John Adams*, Charles Francis Adams, ed. (10 vols., Boston, MA, 1850–1856), 9: 184, 194.

9. Coleman, "Second Bonaparty?," 203.

10. James Morton Smith, *Freedom's Fetters: The Alien and Sedition Laws and American Civil Liberties* (Ithaca: Cornell University Press, 1956), 35–49. This book remains the standard text on the details surrounding the writing and debates of the Alien and

Sedition Acts. Also see William Watkins, *Reclaiming the American Revolution: The Kentucky and Virginia Resolutions and Their Legacy* (New York: Palgrave, 2008), 27–55.

11. The texts of the Alien and Sedition Acts are conveniently located in the appendices of ibid., 435–42.

12. Ibid., 102–103. During congressional debates, Federalists read numerous expects from the *Aurora*. For examples of those see John Allen, Speech of July, 5 1798, in *Annals of Congress*, 5th Congress, 2nd Session, 2093–94.

13. For text of the Sedition Act see ibid., 441–42.

14. Harrison Gray Otis, Speech of June 19, 1798, in *Annals*, 5th Congress, 2nd Session, 1989.

15. Otis, Speech of July 10, 1798, in ibid., 2148.

16. William Blackstone, *Commentaries on the Laws of England*, 4 vols., Stanley Kurtz, ed. (Oxford: The Clarendon Press, 1765; reprint, Chicago: University of Chicago Press, 1979), 4: 150–53.

17. This is not to claim that only the Federalists were influenced by Coke or Blackstone. Jefferson, for example, considered Coke fundamental reading for all good republicans while St. George Tucker, a devout Republican, published an Americanized version of Blackstone in 1801. As will be shown further in the chapter, it was the application of the common law that separated Federalists from Republicans.

18. James Wilson, "Lectures on Law, Chapter XII: The Common Law," in Kermit Hall and Mark David Hall, eds., *Collected Works of James Wilson*, 2 vols. (Indianapolis: Liberty Fund, 2008), 2: 779 [hereafter, Wilson, *Collected Works*].

19. Peter and Nicholas Onus, *Federal Union, Modern World: The Law of Nations in an Age of Revolution, 1776–1814* (New York: Madison House, 1993); Andrew C. Lenner, *The Federal Principle in American Politics, 1790–1833* (Lanham: Rowman and Littlefield, 2001). For the importance of law of nations thinking in Anglo-American political thought see Lee Ward, *The Politics of Liberty in England and America* (Cambridge: Cambridge University Press, 2010). Alison LaCroix, *The Ideological Origins of American Federalism* (Cambridge: Harvard University Press, 2010) has connected law of nations writing to the formation of federalism in the late colonial period.

20. Wilson, "Lectures on Law, Chapter IV: Law of Nations," in Wilson, *Collected Works*, 1: 526–49; Zephaniah Swift, *A System of the Laws of the State of Connecticut in Six Books* (Windham: John Byrne, 1796); James Kent, "Dissertation being the Preliminary Part of a Course of Law Lectures" (New York: George Forman, 1795); Alexander Addison, "Analysis of the Report of the Committee of the Virginia Assembly on the Proceedings of Sundry of the Other States in Answer to Their Resolutions" (Raleigh: Hodor and Boylan, 1800). For an in-depth discussion of these writers and their writings on the common law and law of nations see Lenner, *The Federal Principle*, 1–34, 10–31, especially.

21. Wilson "Lectures on Law," in Wilson, *Collected Works*, 2: 8.

22. Swift, *System of Law*, 41.

23. Addison, "Analysis of the Report," 30.

24. Wilson, "Law Lectures," in Wilson, *Collected Works*, 1: 391–92.

25. Ibid., 397.

26. Kent, "Dissertation," 51–52.

27. Wilson, "Law Lectures," in Wilson, *Collected Works*, 1: 400.

28. The Henfield case originated from President Washington's 1793 Proclamation of Neutrality. In the proclamation, Washington noted at any American caught violating neutrality would be subjected to the "punishment or forfeiture" as determined by the law of nations. When officials caught Henfield attempting to become a French privateer, the federal government prosecuted him on grounds that he violated the proclamation and law of nations. After losing in the district court, Henfield appealed to the circuit court. The case can be found in *United States v. Henfield*, 11 F. Cases, 1099, 1793.

29. James Wilson, "Charge to the Grand Jury" in *United States v. Henfield*, in Maeva Marcus, ed., *The Documentary History of the Supreme Court*, 8 vols. (New York: Columbia University Press, 1986–2007), 2: 414.

30. *United States v. Worrall*, April Term, 1798 ,report in James Alexander Dallas, *Reports of the Cases Ruled and Adjudged in the Courts of Pennsylvania, Before and Since the Revolution*, 4 vols. (Philadelphia: 1790–1799), 3: 384–96.

31. Remarks by Rawle, in *United States v. Worrall*, in Dallas, *Reports*, 3: 386.

32. Ibid., 392.

33. Samuel Peters, "Opinion," in ibid., 395–96.

34. A lively debate exists in the legal academy over the existence of a federal common law of crime. See Stuart Jay, "Origins of Federal Law of Crime: Part One," *University of Pennsylvania Law Review* 133 (June 1985): 1003–116; and the essays by Kathryn Preyer, "Jurisdiction to Punish: Federal Authority, Federalism and the Common Law of Crimes in the Early Republic"; Robert C. Palmer, "The Federal Common Law of Crime"; and Stephen B. Presser, "The Supra-Constitution, the Courts, and the Federal Law of Crimes: Some Comments on Palmer and Preyer," all in *Law and History Review* 4 (Autumn 1986): 223–335. This book does not take a particular side in the argument, expect to argue implicitly that the idea of a federal common law violates the tenants of an Constitution of limited and enumerated powers.

35. William Gordon, Speech, June 19, 1798, in *Annals*, 5th Congress, 2nd Session, 1983–84.

36. Theodore Goodloe Harper, Speech, June, 19, 1798, in *Annals*, 5th Congress, 2nd Session, 1990.

37. Charles Lee, "Defense of the Alien and Sedition Law: Shewing Their Entire Consistency with the Constitution of the United States, and the Principles of Our Government" (Philadelphia; John Ward Fenno, 1798), 20.

38. Ibid.

39. Ibid., 5.

40. Thomas Evans, "An Address to the People of Virginia Respecting the Alien and Sedition Laws" (Richmond: Augustine Davis, 1798), 14.

41. Ibid.

42. Ibid., 15.

43. Ibid.

44. Harrison Gray Otis, Speech, June 19, 1798, in *Annals*, 5th Congress, 2nd Session, 1986.

45. Evans, "An Address," 14–15. Interestingly, Hamilton did not support the Alien and Sedition Laws. For most of the Quasi-War, Hamilton advocated policies based upon moderation. See Coleman, "Second Bonaparty?," *passim* and 209–210 for Hamilton's hesitation towards the Alien and Sedition Acts.

46. Ibid.

47. The classic statement on this point is Leonard Levy, *Emergence of a Free Press* (New York: Oxford University Press, 1987).

48. John Phillip Reid, *The Concept of Liberty in the Age of the American Revolution* (Chicago: University of Chicago Press, 1987), 32–37. Michal Jan Rozbicki, *Culture and Liberty in the Age of the American Revolution*, (Charlottesville: University of Virginia Press, 2011) has argued that the concept and application of liberty during this period was stratified and class based. While eighteenth century Americans held a more restrictive concept of egalitarianism than Americans of the twenty-first century do, his argument reads our modern conceptions of liberty and egalitarianism back into those of the past. He fails to take into account that Americans of Revolution certainly did not believe their fundamental English liberties—such as trial by jury—was confined only to elites. That elites had more privileges than most was accepted unconsciously in deferential culture. The key is how the Revolution changed this assumption, and unleashed what Bernard Bailyn has called the "Contagion of Liberty." See Bailyn, *Ideological Origins of the American Revolution* (Cambridge: Harvard University Press, 1965; 1991), 230–320, and Gordon Wood, *The Radicalism of the American Revolution* (New York: Knopf, 1991).

49. Harrison Gray Otis, Speech, July 10, 1798, in *Annals*, 5th Congress, 2nd Session, 2150.

50. John Allen, Speech, July, 5 1798, in *Annals of Congress*, 5th Congress, 2nd Session, 2094.

51. Theodore Goodloe Harper, in ibid., 2102.

52. John Allen, in ibid., 2094.

53. Ibid., 2098.

54. Ibid., 2097.

55. Ibid.

56. Lee, "Defense," 25.

57. Evans, "An Address," quoting Blackstone, *Commentaries*. Also see ibid.

58. Evans, "An Address," 43–44.

59. Ibid., 40–41; also see Addison, "Analysis," 31.

60. Otis, Speech, in *Annals*, 5th Congress, 2nd Session, 2146.

61. Addison, "Analysis," 29.

62. Ibid., 30–31.

63. Otis, Speech, July 10, in *Annals*, 5th Congress, 2nd Session, 2148.

64. Addison, "Analysis," 45.

65. Otis, Speech, July 10, in *Annals*, 5th Congress, 2nd Session, 2146.

66. John Allen, Speech, July 5 1798, in *Annals of Congress*, 5th Congress, 2nd Session, 2101.

67. Lee, "Defense," 40.

68. John Mercer, "Speech in the Virginia House of Delegates," December 15, 1798, in *Debates in the House of Delegates upon the Alien and Sedition Acts* (Richmond: Nicholson, 1798; 1818).

69. Thomas Jefferson to Edmund Randolph, August 18, 1799, in Julian P. Boyd, ed., *The Papers of Thomas Jefferson*, 38 vols. to date (Princeton: Princeton University Press, 1950–) 31: 168–71 [hereafter, Jefferson, *Papers*].

70. Edward Livingston, Speech, July 10, 1798, in *Annals*, 5th Congress, 2nd Session, 2154.

71. Jefferson to Randolph, August 18, 1799, in Jefferson, *Papers*, 31: 168–71.

72. The following section is influenced by Andrew C. Lenner, "Separate Spheres: Republican Constitutionalism in the Federalist Era," *American Journal of Legal History* 41 (April 1997): 250–81.

73. Quote taken from ibid., 257.

74. James Madison's "Helvidius" essays encapsulated the Republicans' fear over what this use of the executive prerogative meant for the constitutional system. Yet, nowhere in his essays did Madison challenge the idea that the federal government was sovereign over international relations. For Madison's essays against the Neutrality Proclamation see Morton J. Frisch, ed., *The Pacificus-Helvidius Debates: Toward the Completion of the American Founding* (Indianapolis: Liberty Fund, 2007).

75. Thomas Jefferson to James Monroe, July 14, 1793, in Jefferson, *Papers*, 26: 501–503.

76. Jefferson to Edmund Genet, June 17, 1793, in Jefferson, *Papers*, 26: 298–99.

77. This is shared by Lenner, "Separate Spheres," 266.

78. James Barbour, Speech in the Virginia House of Delegates, Dec 17, 1798, in *Debates in the House of Delegates upon the Alien and Sedition Laws* (Richmond: Nicholson, 1798; 1818), 55.

79. Albert Gallatin, Speech, May 3, 1798, in *Annals*, 5th Congress, 2nd Session, 1582.

80. Albert Gallatin, Speech, June 18, 1798, in *Annals*, 5th Congress, 2nd Session, 1977.

81. Ibid.,

82. Ibid., 1982.

83. Jefferson to John Taylor, June 4, 1798, in Jefferson, *Papers*, 30: 388–89.

84. Samuel Chase, "Opinion in *Worrall v. United States*," in Dallas, *Reports*, 3: 393–95.

85. Jefferson, "Petition to the Virginia House of Delegates," August 7–September 7, 1797, in Jefferson, *Papers*, 29: 499–504.

86. David N. Mayer, *The Constitutional Thought of Thomas Jefferson* (Charlottesville: University of Virginia Press, 1993), 199.

87. Jefferson, "Petition," in Jefferson, *Papers*, 29: 499–504.

88. Ibid.

89. Jefferson to Monroe, September 7, 1797, in Jefferson, *Papers*, 29: 526–27.

90. Ibid.

91. John Taylor to Jefferson, June 25, 1798, in Jefferson, *Papers*, 30: 430–35.

92. Ibid.

93. Jefferson to Taylor, June 4, 1798, in ibid., 387–90.

94. Ibid.

95. Ibid.

96. Gallatin, Speech, July 9, 1798, in *Annals*, 5th Congress, 2nd Session, 2137.

97. Ibid., July 10, 1798, 2158.

98. Ibid., 2160.

99. Wilson Cary Nicholas, July 10, 1798, in ibid., 2139–40.

100. George Mason, July 10, 1798, in ibid, 2149–50.

101. Broadside of Albemarle Co. Petition to the Senate and House of Representatives of the United States, 1798. Also see the "Address" by "Alpha" in *The New York Gazette and Daily Advertiser* February 11, 1799, and Bradburn, *Citizenship Revolution*, 190–91.

102. John Page, "Address to the Freeholders of Gloucester County" (Richmond: John Dixon, 1799), 33.

103. Clyde Wilson, "Foreword," in Clyde Wilson, ed. St. George Tucker, *View of the Constitution of the United States with Selected Writings* (Indianapolis: Liberty Fund, 1999), iv–xxi [hereafter, Tucker, "Of the Unwritten, or Common Law of England].

104. Tucker, "Of the Unwritten, or Common Law of England," 317–46.

105. Ibid., 343.

106. Ibid..

107. Ibid., 346, 349. Emphasis in the original.

108. Ibid., 345.

109. Ibid., 355.

110. Ibid.

111. Ibid., 356.

112. Although the Kentucky and Virginia Resolutions have been printed numerous times, and can be found in Jefferson, *Papers*, 30: 529–67 and David B. Mattern, J. C. A. Stagg, Jeanne K. Cross, and Susan Holbrook Perdue., eds., *The Papers of James Madison*, 17 vols. (Chicago: University of Chicago Press and Charlottesville: University Press of Virginia, 1961–1991), 17: 185–91 [hereafter, Madison, *Papers*], for ease of reference, however, citations to both resolutions will be from Lance Banning, *Liberty and Order: The First Party Struggle* (Indianapolis: Liberty Fund, 2004), 233–36. Quote is from the Kentucky Resolution, 233.

113. Ibid, 233.

114. Virginia Resolution, ibid., 236.

115. Ibid., 237.

116. Kentucky Resolution, ibid., 233–34.

117. Virginia Resolution, ibid., 237.

118. Ibid.

119. Kentucky Resolution, 236–37.

120. Virginia Resolution, ibid., 236–37.

121. Kentucky Resolution, ibid., 233–34.

122. Ibid.

123. Adrianne Koch and Harry Ammon, "The Virginia and Kentucky Resolutions: An Episode in Jefferson's and Madison's Defenses of Civil Liberties," *William and Mary Quarterly* 5 (1948): 147–76; Sharp, *American Politics in the Early Republic*, 194; Andrew Bernstein and Nancy Isenberg, *Madison and Jefferson* (New York: Random House, 2012), 337. For three excellent counterarguments see Douglas Bradburn, *The Citizenship Revolution: Politics and the Creation of the American Union, 1774–804* (Charlottesville:

University of Virginia Press, 2009), 169–206; and K. R. Constantine Gutzman, "The Virginia and Kentucky Resolution Reconsidered: 'An Appeal to the Real Laws of Our Country," *Journal of Southern History* 66 (August 2000): 473–96; and Kurt Lash, "James Madison's Celebrated Report of 1800: The Transformation of the Tenth Amendment," *Loyola Legal Studies Papers 2005–30* (November 2005): 1–46.

124. Elkins and McKitrick, *Age of Federalism*, 720; Richard E. Ellis, *The Union at Risk: Jacksonian Democracy, States' Rights, and the Nullification Controversy* (New York: Oxford University Press, 1987), 1–13; Wood, *Empire of Liberty*, 269; Pauline Maier, "The Road Not Taken: Nullification, John C. Calhoun, and the Revolutionary Tradition in South Carolina," *The South Carolina Historical Magazine* 82 (Jan. 1781): 1–19.

125. On this point also see Bradburn, *The Citizenship Revolution*, 192–200, especially, 194; Gutzman, "The Virginia and Kentucky Resolutions Reconsidered," 483; Banning, *The Jeffersonian Persuasion: Evolution of a Party Ideology* (Ithaca: Cornell University Press, 1978), 264–66.

126. Resolutions of Rhode Island and New Hampshire in Banning, ed., *Liberty and Order*, 237–38. For a more detailed account of the rejections see Bradburn, *Citizenship Revolution*, 197–98. The Federalist minority in Virginia also produced a resolution condemning the Virginia Resolution. See "An Address of the Minority in the Virginia Legislature to the People of that State Containing a Vindication of the Constitutionality of the Alien and Sedition Acts" (Richmond: Augustine Davis, 1799).

127. Massachusetts General Court, "Report on the Virginia Resolutions," (Boston: Young and Minns, 1799).

128. Ibid.

129. On this point, I must thank Michael Schwarz for pointing out this context to me.

130. New Hampshire Resolution, in Banning, *Liberty and Order*, 238.

131. Massachusetts General Court, "Report on the Virginia Resolutions."

132. "Editor's Note to the Report of 1800," in Madison, *Papers*, 17: 303–304.

133. James Madison, "Report of 1800," in ibid., 7: 303–51. Quote is on 309.

134. Ibid.

135. Ibid., 309–10.

136. Ibid., 310.

137. Ibid., 327.

138. Ibid., 327–28.

139. Ibid., 328.

140. Ibid.

Conclusion

In his inaugural address of March 4, 1801, Thomas Jefferson explained how Americans were "all republicans, we are all federalists." In nearly all the published forms of this important phrase, Jefferson's use of republican and federalists are capitalized. In Jefferson's handwritten note, however, those terms were lowercased.[1] Although this change might not seem important, the distinction is significant. Jefferson was not referring to the political divisions that had emerged during the 1790s between his Republican Party and the Federalists. Rather, he was referring to the constitutional disposition of Americans. They were republicans because they adhered to self-government and they were federalists due to their belief in the division of powers between the federal and state governments. In this phrase, Jefferson was restating an American understanding of their constitutionalism that stretched back to their colonial experience, and was maintained and protected during the Revolution, the Articles of Confederation, and, finally, with the Constitution and the Tenth Amendment.

As Jefferson realized, maintaining the constitutional settlement of state sovereignty under the new Constitution had not been easy. The forces of consolidation, led most ably by Alexander Hamilton and expressed through his economic program and the Alien and Sedition Acts, had not only challenged the constitutional settlement but had come close to overturning it. Thus, when Jefferson and the Republicans swept the Federalists out of power in 1801, they had reason to see those results as "real a revolution in the principles of our government as that of [17]76 was in its form; not effected indeed by the sword, as that, but by the rational and peaceable instrument of reform, the suffrage of the people."[2] Through the elections of 1800, Americans had rejected the idea of sovereignty resting with the general government in much the same way that Americans of 1776 had rebuked the notion of King-in-Parliament. Both 1776 and 1800 were affirmations of the American commitment to a state sovereignty constitutional order.

Although the Republicans were victorious in keeping state sovereignty the focus of American constitutionalism, once in power, the great challenge that lay before them was maintaining that order. The task was not easy, especially given the dramatic change that occurred within the Republican Party itself. As the popular support for Federalists waned in the early nineteenth century and former Federalist supporters, particularly in urban areas in the middle states, joined the ranks of the Republicans, the party struggled to keep its constitutional bearings.[3] Further complicating the task was the growing foreign crises that started in Jefferson's second term and eventually led to war with Britain in 1812. Although this book leaves it to others to trace and detail the development of the constitutional settlement past the election of 1800, it is fair to say that despite the challenges the Republicans did a remarkable job of staying true to the constitutional settlement they claimed they represented and defended. This was especially true during the War of 1812 when Federalists used state sovereignty as an excuse not to support the war effort.

At the same time, the Republican ascendency may have swept the Federalists from power in the elective branches, but it did not completely "sink federalism into an abyss from which there shall be no resurrection," as Jefferson had hoped.[4] The Federalists still controlled the federal courts. Heading that branch would be the great Virginian Federalist John Marshall. Through force of personality, and his permanent tenure on the Supreme Court, Marshall nearly single handedly preserved the Federalists' constitutional vision in the early years of Republican dominance. When President Madison appointed the lukewarm Republican Joseph Story to the bench in 1811 (against Jefferson's advice), the duo embarked in a series of cases that took direct aim at state sovereignty.[5]

The most important of these Marshall Court decisions came in the 1819 case of *McCulloch v. Maryland*. Perhaps the most important Supreme Court case in American history, the Court's opinion was a classic statement of the Federalists' constitutionalism. In the decision written by Marshall, the Court dismissed the idea that the people of the states created the Constitution. Instead, it embraced the Federalist idea that a national popular sovereignty had created the Constitution, and that in adopting the Constitution, they also ratified the idea that the general government possessed implied powers through the necessary and proper clause. The establishment of the Bank of the United States was one of those implied powers, and thus, the bank was constitutional. In a paraphrase of Hamilton's "Opinion on the Bank," Marshall noted that the necessary and proper clause permitted a broad range of federal powers beyond those enumerated. As long as "the end be legitimate, let it be within the scope of the constitution, and all means which are appropriate, which are plainly adapted to that end, which are not prohibited, but consist with the letter and spirit of the constitution, are constitutional." The purpose of the necessary and proper clause, moreover, was "to enlarge, not to diminish the powers vested in the government. It purports to be an additional power, not a restriction on those already granted." Finally, there was little the states could do to stop this use of federal power. Relying upon the supremacy clause, Marshall noted that it explained the relationship between federal government and the states and ensured that the states could not control the national government. Marshall dismissed the

Tenth Amendment as useless, too. Since it did not contain the word "expressly" in it, it did not offer a limitation upon federal power. Its only purpose, he claimed, was to "quiet the excessive jealousies" in favor of state sovereignty.[6]

The *McCulloch* decision signified that the Nationalist challenge to the Revolution's constitutional settlement had not been fully vanquished. Although Jefferson, Madison, and other Republicans, especially John Taylor of Caroline and Spencer Roane, attacked the *McCulloch* decision as well as the rest of the Court's "aggressive nationalism" that it displayed in the period of 1811 to 1823, Marshall's actions on the bench did much to preserve the Federalists' constitutionalism.[7] That preservation would prove important in the decades following the *McCulloch* case as issues over the role of the federal government in economic affairs split the Republicans into the more state sovereignty oriented Jacksonian Democrats and the Nationalist Republicans, or Whigs, who took Hamiltonianism as their inspiration. After nearly thirty years of general acceptance of state sovereignty as the foundation of constitutional system, the clash between state sovereignty and national power was renewed with striking vigor in the Nullification Crisis of 1832–1833.

At the same time, other fissures were appearing in the constitutional settlement. As the United States became increasingly sectional in decades following the Missouri Crisis of 1819, state sovereignty also became a weapon to support sectional arguments. As southerners perceived threats to slavery and their agricultural society from a growing market-oriented North, they would draw upon the Revolution's constitutional settlement to defend those institutions. At the same time, the North would also employ state sovereignty and interposition to attack the Fugitive Slave Act of 1850. Yet, it would be the connection between state sovereignty and slavery, made most forcibly by John C. Calhoun, that would permanently stain the idea of state sovereignty.

The deathblow to Revolution's constitutional settlement came from Abraham Lincoln and the Republican Party. Built from the ashes of the Whig Party, the Republican Party's constitutional vision was distinctly nationalist. The union that Lincoln claimed to be preserving in 1861 was not a union of where the people of the several states had compacted together to form the Constitution. Instead, and in a direct recall of the old Federalist argument, it was a perpetual union of the whole American people that predated even the War for Independence.[8] When this national popular sovereignty created the Constitution, they vested the national government with full sovereignty. Thus, it was a Federalist-cum-Republican vision of the sovereignty of national government that emerged triumphant during the Civil War, and became enshrined in the Fourteenth Amendment. The result was a new constitutional settlement of sovereignty resting wholly with the federal government and the relegation of all arguments of state sovereignty to defenses of slavery, racism, and discrimination. It is this second American constitutional settlement that governs America today.

The stain that Calhoun and others left upon state sovereignty does not need to remain permanent, however—although it should not be forgotten. Too often, scholars read the arguments of the antebellum period back into founding. This leads scholars to see any form of state sovereignty as an unintentional mistake or aberration corrected only with the outcome of the Civil War and subsequent constitutional developments. This book has attempted to challenge that prevailing understanding of state sovereignty's origins. It has sought to recover the understanding and arguments made by eighteenth-century Americans and to appreciate on their terms, and not ours or any other periods, just how and why they intimately connected liberty with state sovereignty. By doing so, it has revealed a fuller and more accurate picture of the why Revolutionary Americans made state sovereignty the foundation of their constitutional settlement.

NOTES

1. Thomas Jefferson, "Inaugural Address," March 4, 1801, in Julian P. Boyd, ed., *The Papers of Thomas Jefferson*, 38 vols. (Princeton: Princeton University Press, 1950–2011), 33: 149–152, and "Editor's Note: First Inaugural Address," 134–38.

2. Jefferson to Spencer Roane, September 6, 1819, in Paul L. Ford, ed., *The Writings of Thomas Jefferson*, 12 vols. (New York: G. P. Putnam and Sons, 1904–1905), 12: 136.

3. Andrew Shankman, *Crucible of American Democracy: The Struggle to Fuse Egalitarianism and Capitalism in Jeffersonian Pennsylvania* (Lawrence: University Press of Kansas, 2004).

4. Jefferson to Levi Lincoln, October 25, 1802, in Jefferson, *Papers*, 38: 565–67.

5. Aaron N. Coleman, "James Madison's Domestic Policies, 1809–1817: Jeffersonian Factionalism and the Beginnings of American Nationalism," in Stuart Leibiger, ed., *A Companion to James Madison and James Monroe* (Malden, MA: Wiley-Blackwell, 2013): 198–99.

6. *McCulloch v. Maryland*, 17 U.S. 316 (1819).

7. See the essay exchange between Spencer Roane and John Marshall over the implications of the *McCulloch* decision in Gerald Gunther, ed., *John Marshall's Defense of McCulloch v. Maryland* (Stanford: Stanford University Press, 1969); Richard Ellis, *Aggressive Nationalism: McCulloch v. Maryland and the Foundation of Federal Authority in the Young Republic* (New York: Oxford University Press, 2007); Adam Tate, "A Historiography of States' Rights: John Taylor of Caroline's *New Views of the Constitution*." *Southern Studies: An Interdisciplinary Journal of the South* 18 (Spring 2011): 10–28.

8. Kenneth M. Stampp, "The Concept of a Perpetual Union," *Journal of American History* 65 (June 1978): 5–33; Donald A. Faber, *Lincoln's Constitution* (Chicago: University of Chicago Press, 2003).

Bibliography

PRIMARY SOURCES

Newspapers

The Boston Gazette.
The Independent Gazetteer; or The Chronicle of Freedom.
The New Jersey Gazette.
The New York Gazette and Daily Advertiser.
The Pennsylvania Packet.

Pamphlets and Edited Collections

A Collection of the Acts or Laws passed in the State of Massachusetts Bay, relative to the American Loyalists and Their Property, n.e. (London: John Stockdale, 1785).

Adams, Charles Francis, ed. *The Works of John Adams.* 10 vols. Boston: Little, Brown, and Company 1850.

Addison, Alexander. "Analysis of the Report of the Committee of the Virginia Assembly on the Proceedings of Sundry of the Other States in Answer to Their Resolutions." Raleigh: Hodor and Boylan, 1800.

Ames, Seth, ed., *The Work of Fisher Ames.* 2 vols. Indianapolis: Liberty Fund, 1983.

American Museum: Or Repository of Ancient and Modern Fugitive Pieces Prose and Poetical. Philadelphia: Mathew Carey, 1787.

Annals of Congress, 1st Congress, 1st Session.

Annals of Congress, 5th Congress, 2nd Session.

Anonymous. "An Address of the Minority in the Virginia Legislature to the People of that State Containing a Vindication of the Constitutionality of the Alien and Sedition Acts." Richmond: Augustine Davis, 1799.

Bailyn, Bernard, ed. *Debates on the Constitution.* 2 vols. New York: Library of America, 1993.

Ballagh, James, ed. *The Letters of Richard Henry Lee.* 2 vols. New York: Macmillan, 1914.

Banning, Lance, ed. *Liberty and Order: The First American Party Struggle.* Indianapolis: Liberty Fund, 2004.

Blackstone, William. *Commentaries on the Laws of England.* Edited by Stanley Kurtz. 4 vols. Oxford: The Clarendon Press, 1765; reprint, Chicago: University of Chicago Press, 1979.

Bland, Richard. "An Inquiry into the Rights of the British Colonies." Williamsburg: n.p., 1766.

———. "The Colonel Dismounted: Or the Rector Vindicated." Williamsburg: Joseph Royle, 1764.

Bodin, Jean. *On Sovereignty: Four Chapters from "The Six Books of the Commonwealth.* Edited and Translated by Julian H. Franklin. Cambridge: Cambridge University Press, 1992.

Bowling, Kenneth and Helen E. Viet, eds. *The Diary of William Maclay and Other Notes on Senate Debates, March 4, 1789–March 3, 1971.* Baltimore: John Hopkins University Press, 1988.

Broadside of Albemarle Co. Petition to the Senate and House of Representative of the United States, 1798.

Carey, George W. and James McClellan, eds. *The Federalist: The Gideon Edition.* Indianapolis: Liberty Fund, 2001.

Clark, Walter, ed. *State Records of North Carolina.* 26 vols. Raleigh: P. M. Hale, 1896–1907.

Cushing, Alonzo, ed. *The Writings of Samuel Adams.* 4 vols. New York: G. P. Putnam, 1904–1908.

Dallas, James Alexander, ed. *Reports of the Cases Ruled and Adjudged in the Courts of Pennsylvania before and since the Revolution.* 4 vols. Philadelphia: T. Bradford, 1790–1800.

Debates in the House of Delegates upon the Alien and Sedition Acts. Richmond: Nicholson, 1798; 1818.

The Documentary History of the First Federal Congress. 18 vols. to date. Edited by Helen Viet, Charlene Bangs Bickford, Kenneth Bowling, and William Charles DiGiacomantonio. Baltimore: The Johns Hopkins University Press, 1977–.

The Documentary History of the Supreme Court of the United States, 1789–1800. 7 vols. to date. Edited by Maeva Marcus et al. Columbia: Columbia University Press 1986–.

Documentary History of the Ratification of the Constitution. 26 vols. to date. Edited by Merrill Jensen, John P. Kaminski, et al. Madison: University of Wisconsin Press, 1976 –.

Elliot, Jonathan, ed. *The Debates in the Several Conventions on the Adoption of the Constitution* 5 vols. Washington, DC: n.p., 1836.

Evans, Thomas. "An Address to the People of Virginia Respecting the Alien and Sedition Laws." Richmond: Augustine Davis, 1798.

Farrand, Max, ed. *The Records of the Federal Convention.* 4 vols. New Haven: Yale University Press, 1911.

Fitch, Thomas. "Reasons Why the British Colonies in America, Should not be Charged with Internal Taxes." New Haven, CT: n.p., 1764.

Force, Peter, ed. *The American Archives* 6th series. Series 4, volume 1. Washington, DC: St. Clair Clarke and Peter Force, 1837.

Ford, Paul L. ed. *The Writings of Thomas Jefferson* 12 vols. New York: G. P. Putnam and Sons, 1904–1905.

Ford, Timothy. "An Enquiry into the Constitutional Authority of the Supreme Federal Court." Charleston: Young, 1792.

Ford, Worthington C., ed. *Journals of the Continental Congress.* 34 vols. Washington, DC: Government Printing Office, 1904–1937.

Fortesque, Sir John. *On the Laws and Governance of England.* Edited by Shelley Lockwood. Cambridge: Cambridge University Press, 1997.

Frisch, Morton J. ed. *The Pacificus-Helvidius Debates: Toward the Completion of the American Founding.* Indianapolis: Liberty Fund, 2007.

Frohnen, Bruce, ed. *The American Republic: Primary Sources.* Indianapolis: Liberty Fund, 2002.

Giunta, Mary A., ed. *The Emerging Nation: A Documentary History of the Foreign Relations of the United States under the Articles of Confederation, 1780–1789.* 3 vols. Washington, DC: Government Printing Office, 1996.

Gunther, Gerald ed. *John Marshall's Defense of McCulloch v. Maryland.* Stanford: Stanford University Press, 1969.

Goebel, Julius Goebel, ed. *The Law Practice of Alexander Hamilton: Documents and Commentary* 3 vols. New York: Columbia University Press, 1964.

Hall, Kermit and David Hall, eds. *The Collected Works of James Wilson.* 2 vols. Indianapolis: Liberty Fund, 2007.

Harris, Jr., Thomas Harris and John McHenry, eds. *Maryland Reports being a Series of the Most Important Laws Cases.* 4 vols. New York and Annapolis: Wiley, 1809–1818.

Hicks, William. "The Nature and Extent of Parliamentary Power Considered." New York: n.p., 1765.

Henning, William, ed. *Statutes at Large: Being a Collection of all the Laws of Virginia from the First Session of the Legislature, in the Year 1619*. 13 vols. New York, Richmond, and Philadelphia, 1819–1823.

Hopkins, Stephen. "The Rights of the Colonies Examined." In *American Political Writings*. Edited by Charles Hyneman and Donald Lutz, 45–61. 2 vols. Indianapolis: Liberty Fund, 1983.

Journal of the Honorable House of Representatives of His Majesty's Province of the Massachusetts Bay in New England. Boston: Edes and Gill, 1769.

Journals of the Votes and Proceedings of the General Assembly of New York. New York: Gaine, 1769.

Kent, James. "Dissertation being the Preliminary Part of a Course of Law Lectures." New York: George Forman, 1795.

Kurland, Philip and Ralph Learner, eds. *The Founders Constitution*. 5 vols. Indianapolis: Liberty Fund, 2000.

Ledyard, Isaac. "Mentor's Reply to Phocion's Letter." New York: Kollock, 1784.

Lee, Charles. "Defense of the Alien and Sedition Law: Shewing Their Entire Consistency with the Constitution of the United States, and the Principles of Our Government." Philadelphia: John Ward Fenno, 1798.

Lence, Ross M., ed. *Union and Liberty: The Political Philosophy of John C. Calhoun*. Indianapolis: Liberty Fund, 1992.

Lutz, Donald S., ed. *The Colonial Origins of the American Constitution: A Documentary History*. Indianapolis: Liberty Fund, 1998.

Madison, James. *Notes of the Debates in the Federal Convention of 1787*. Edited by Adrienne Koch. Columbus: Ohio University Press, 1966; reprint, New York: W. W. Norton, 1987.

Magna Charta

Massachusetts General Court. "Report on the Virginia Resolutions." Boston: Young and Minns, 1799.

McCulloch v. Maryland 17 U.S. 316 (1819).

McDonald, Forrest, ed. *Letters from a Farmer in Pennsylvania (John Dickinson) and Letters from the Federal Farmer (Richard Henry Lee)*. Indianapolis: Liberty Fund, 1992.

Montesquieu, Charles de. *The Spirit of the Laws*. Edited by Anne M. Cohler, Basia C. Miller, and Horld S. Stone. Cambridge: Cambridge University Press, 1989, 112–130.

Moore, Maurcie. "The Justice and Policy of Taxing the American Colonies in Great Britain, Considered." In *Not a Conquered People: Two Carolinians View Parliamentary Taxation*. Edited by William S. Price. Raleigh: North Carolina Department of Archives and History, 1975.

New Jersey General Assembly for the Year 1784. Trenton: Isaac Collins, 1784.

Page, John. "Address to the Freeholders of Gloucester County." Richmond: John Dixon, 1799.

Parson, Jonathan. "A Consideration of Some Unconstitutional Measures, Adopted and Practices in this State." Newburyport, MA: John Mycall, 1784.

Pennsylvania General Assembly. Philadelphia: Hall and Sellers, 1784.

Prince, Carl E., ed. *Papers of William Livingston*. 5 vols. Trenton: New Jersey Historical Commission, 1979–1987.

Richardson, James D. *A Compilation of the Messages and Papers of the Presidents, 1789–1897*. 10 vols. Washington, DC: Government Printing Press, 1901.

Sheehan, Colleen and Gary L. McDowell eds. *Friends of the Constitutions: The Writings of the "Other" Federalist*. Indianapolis: Liberty Fund, 1998.

Sheppard, Steven, ed. *The Selected Writings of Sir Edward Coke*. 3 vols. Indianapolis: Liberty Fund, 2003.

Sherman, Roger. "Remarks on a Pamphlet, Entitled, 'A Dissertation on the Political Union.'" New Haven, CT: n.p., 1784.

Smith, Meriwether. "Observations on the Fourth and Fifth Articles of the Preliminaries for a Peace with Great Britain designed for the Information and Consideration of the People of Virginia." Richmond: Dixon and Holt, 1783.

Smith, Paul H., ed. *Letters to Delegates to Congress 1774–1789*. 25 vols. Washington, DC: Library of Congress, 1976–2000.

Storing, Herbert ed. *The Complete Anti-Federalists*. 7 vols. Chicago: University of Chicago Press, 1979.

Sullivan, James. "Observations on the Government of the United States." Boston: Samuel Hale, 1791.

Swift, Zephaniah. *A System of the Laws of the State of Connecticut in Six Books*. Windham: John Byrne, 1796.

Taylor, John. "An Argument Respecting the Constitutionality of the Carriage Tax." Richmond: Augustine Davis, 1795.

———. "An Enquiry into the Principles and Tendency of Certain Public Measures." Philadelphia: Dobson, 1794.

———. "An Examination of the Late Proceedings in Congress Respecting the Official Conduct of the Secretary of the Treasury." Richmond: n.p., 1793.

The Papers of Alexander Hamilton. 26 vols. Edited by Harold C. Syrett and Jacob E. Cooke. New York: Columbia University Press, 1956–1981.

The Papers of Benjamin Franklin. 37 vols. to date. Edited by Leonard Labree et al. New Haven, CT: Yale University Press, 1953–.

The Papers of George Washington: Confederation Series. 5 vols. Edited by W. W. Abbot et al. Charlottesville: University of Virginia Press, 1992–1997.

The Papers of George Washington: Presidential Series. 17 vols. to date. Edited by Dorothy Twohig et al. Charlottesville: University of Virginia Press, 1987–.

The Papers of James Iredell. 2 vols. Edited by Don Higginbothom. Raleigh, NC: Division of Archives and History Department of Cultural Resources, 1976.

The Papers of James Madison. 17 vols. Edited by William T. Hutchinson and William M. E. Rachal et al. 17 vols. Chicago: University of Chicago Press, 1962, 2: 303–304.

The Papers of Thomas Jefferson. 38 vols. Edited by Julian P. Boyd et al. Princeton, NJ: Princeton University Press, 1950–.

Thomas, P. D. G., ed. "Parliamentary Diaries of Nathaniel Ryder, 1764–7." *Camden Miscellany*. vol. XXIII 4th series volume 7 (1969).

Thompson, C. Bradley, ed. *Revolutionary Writings of John Adams*. Indianapolis: Liberty Fund, 2000.

Tucker, St. George. *View of the Constitution of the United States with Selected Writings*. Edited by Clyde Wilson. Indianapolis: Liberty Fund, 1999.

Viet, Helen E., Kenneth R. Bowling, and Charlene Bangs Bickford, eds. *Creating the Bill of Rights: The Documentary Record from the First Federal Congress*. Baltimore: Johns Hopkins University Press, 1991.

Vernier, Richard B., ed. *The Revolutionary Writings of Alexander Hamilton*. Indianapolis: Liberty Fund, 2008.

Virginia Legislative Assembly, Petitions, 1782–1789

Webster, Noah. "Sketches of American Policy." Hartford, CT: Hudson and Goodwin, 1785.

Webster, Pelatiah. "A Dissertation on the Political Union and Constitution of the Thirteen United States." Philadelphia: Bradford, 1783.

Zucker, Michael, and Derek Webb, eds. *The Anti-Federalist Writings of the Melancton Smith Circle*. Indianapolis: Liberty Fund, 2009.

The Works of the Right Honorable Edmund Burke. 2 vols. N. E. London: Holdsworth and Ball, 1803.

SECONDARY SOURCES

Allen, David Grayson. *In English Ways: The Movement of Societies and the Transferal of English Local Law and Custom to Massachusetts Bay in the Seventeenth Century*. New York: W. W. Norton, 1983.

Amar, Akhil. *The Bill of Rights: Creation and Reconstruction*. New Haven, CT: Yale University Press, 2000.

Ammerman, David. *In the Common Cause: The American Response to the Coercive Acts of 1774*. Charlottesville: University of Virginia Press, 1974.

Bailyn, Bernard. *Ideological Origins of the American Revolution*. Cambridge: Harvard University Press, 1967; 1991.

Banning, Lance. *Jefferson and Madison: Three Conversations from the Founding*. New York: Rowman and Littlefield, 1995.

———. *The Jeffersonian Persuasion: Evolution of a Party Ideology*. Ithaca, NY: Cornell University Press, 1978.

———. *The Sacred Fire of Liberty: James Madison and the Founding of the Federal Republic*. Ithaca, NY: Cornell University Press, 1995.

Barnett, Randy E. *Restoring the Lost Constitution: The Presumption of Liberty*. Princeton, NJ: Princeton University Press, 2005.

Bradburn, Douglas. *The Citizenship Revolution: Politics and the Creation of the American Union, 1774–1804*. Charlottesville: University of Virginia Press, 2009.

Beer, Samuel. *To Make a Nation: The Rediscovery of American Federalism*. Cambridge, MA: Harvard University Press, 1993.

Berger, Raoul. *Federalism: The Founders' Design*. Norman: University of Oklahoma Press, 1987.

———. "The Founders' Views—According to Jefferson Powell" *Texas Law Review* 67 (1988–1989): 1033–1096.

———. *Government by Judiciary: The Transformation of the Fourteenth Amendment*. Cambridge, MA: Harvard University Press, 1977; reprint, Indianapolis: Liberty Fund, 1997.

———. "Jack Rakove's Rendition of Original Meaning." *Indiana Law Journal* 72 (Issue 3, 1997): 619–649.

Berns, Walter. "The Meaning of the Tenth Amendment." In *A Nation of States: Essays on the Federal System*. Edited by Robert A. Godwin, 126–148. Chicago: Rand McNally, 1961.

Bernstein, Andrew and Nancy Isenberg. *Madison and Jefferson*. New York: Random House, 2010.

Bilder, Mary Sarah. *The Transatlantic Constitution: Colonial Legal Culture and Empire*. Cambridge, MA: Harvard University Press, 2008.

Bowling, Kenneth. "Dinner at Jefferson's: A Note on Jacob E. Cooke's 'The Compromise of 1790.'" *William and Mary Quarterly* 28 (October 1971): 629–648.

———. "'A Tub to the Whale:' The Founding Fathers and Adoption of the Federal Bill of Rights." *Journal of the Early Republic* 8 (Autumn, 1988): 223–251.

Buel, Richard J. *Securing the Revolution: Ideology in American Politics, 1789–1800*. Ithaca, NY: Cornell University Press, 1972.

Burgess, Glenn. *Absolute Monarchy and the Stuart Constitution*. New Haven, CT: Yale University Press, 1996.

———. *The Politics of the Ancient Constitution: An Introduction to English Political Thought, 1603–1642*. University Park: Pennsylvania State University Press, 1992.

Bradford, M. E. *Original Intentions: On the Making and Ratification of the United States Constitution*. Athens: University of Georgia Press, 1993.

Brewer, John. *The Sinews of Power: War, Money, and the English State, 1688–1783*. Cambridge, MA: Harvard University Press, 1990.

Brooks, Robin. "Alexander Hamilton, Melancton Smith, and the Ratification of the Constitution in New York." *William and Mary Quarterly* 24 (1967): 339–358.

Brunhouse, Robert L. *The Counter-Revolution in Pennsylvania, 1776–1790*. Harrisburg: Pennsylvania Historical Commission, 1942.

Brunsman, Denver. "James Madison and the *National Gazette* Essays: The Birth of a Party Politician." In *A Companion to James Madison and James Monroe*. Edited by Stuart Leibiger, 143–158. Malden, MA: Wiley-Blackwell, 2013.

Casto, William R. *The Supreme Court in the Early Republic: The Chief Justiceships of John Jay and Oliver Ellsworth*. Columbia: University of South Carolina Press, 1995.

Carey, George W. *In Defense of the Constitution*. Indianapolis: Liberty Fund, 1997.

Carmical, Jr. Oline. "Plans of Union, 1643–1783: A Study and Reappraisal of Projects for Uniting the English Colonies in North America." PhD Dissertation: University of Kentucky, 1975.

Carp, E. Wayne. *To Starve the Army at Pleasure: Continental Army Administration and American Political Culture, 1775–1783*. Chapel Hill: University of North Carolina Press, 1984.

Clark, Bradford R. "The Eleventh Amendment and the Nature of the Union." *Harvard Law Review* 123 (June 2010): 1817–1918.

Coleman, Aaron N. "Debating the Nature of State Sovereignty: Nationalists, State Sovereigntists, and the Treaty of Paris (1783)." *Journal of the Historical Society* 12 (September 2012): 309–340.

———. "James Madison's Domestic Policies, 1809–1817: Jeffersonian Factionalism and the Beginnings of American Nationalism." In *A Companion to James Madison and James Monroe*. Edited by Stuart Leibiger, 192–206. Malden, MA: Wiley-Blackwell, 2013.

———. "'A Second Bonaparty?:' A Reexamination of Alexander Hamilton during the Franco-American Crisis, 1796–1800." *Journal of the Early Republic* 28 (Summer 2008): 183–214.

Cooke, Jacob E. "The Compromise of 1790" *William and Mary Quarterly* 27 (November, 1970): 523–545.

DePauw, Linda Grant. *The Eleventh Pillar: New York State and the Federal Constitution*. Ithaca, NY: Cornell University Press, 1966.

Dellinger, Walter and H. Jefferson Powell. "The Constitutionality of the Bank Bill: The Attorney General's First Constitutional Law Opinions." *Duke Law Journal* 44 (1994): 110–133.

Diamond, Martin. "What the Framers Meant by Federalism." In *A Nation of States: Essays on the American Federal System*. Edited by Robert A. Goldwin, 24–41. Chicago: Rand McNally, 1961.

Dickinson, H. T. "The Eighteenth-Century Debates over the Sovereignty of Parliament." *Transactions of the Royal Historical Society* 26 (1976): 189–210.

Dickinson, O. M. *The Navigation Acts and the American Revolution*. Philadelphia: Pennsylvania University Press, 1951.

Dougherty, Keith L. *Collective Action Under the Articles of Confederation*. Cambridge: Cambridge University Press, 2001.

Edling, Max M. *A Revolution in Favor of Government: Origins of the U.S. Constitution and the Making of the American State*. Oxford: Oxford University Press, 2003.

Elkins, Stanley, and Eric McKitrick. *The Age of Federalism: The Early American Republic, 1788–1800*. New York: Oxford University Press, 1993.

Ellis, Richard. *Aggressive Nationalism: McCulloch v. Maryland and the Foundation of Federal Authority in the Young Republic*. New York: Oxford University Press, 2007.

———. *The Union at Risk: Jacksonian Democracy, States' Rights, and the Nullification Crisis*. New York: Oxford University Press, 1987

Faber, Donald A. *Lincoln's Constitution*. Chicago: University of Chicago Press, 2003.

Ferguson, E. James. "The Nationalists of 1781–1783 and the Economic Interpretation of the Constitution." *Journal of American History* 56 (September 1969): 241–261.

———. *The Power of the Purse: A History of American Public Finance, 1776–1790*. Chapel Hill: University of North Carolina Press, 1961.

Goebel, Julius. *History of the Supreme Court of the United States: Antecedents and Beginnings to 1801*. Volume 1 of the *Oliver Wendell Holmes Device: History of the Supreme Court*. 12 vols. to date. New York: The Macmillan Company, 1971.

Greenberg, Janelle. *The Radical Face of the Ancient Constitution: St. Edward's 'Laws' in Early Modern Political Thought*. Cambridge: Cambridge University Press, 2006.

Greene, Jack P. *Peripheries and Center: Constitutional Development in the Extended Polities of the British Empire and the United States, 1607–1788.* Athens: University of Georgia Press, 1986.

———. *The Constitutional Origins of the American Revolution.* Cambridge: Cambridge University Press, 2010.

Gregg, Gary L., ed. *Vital Remnants: America's Founding and the Western Tradition.* Wilmington, DE: ISI Books, 1999.

Gutzman, Kevin, R. C. "Edmund Randolph and Virginia Constitutionalism." *The Review of Politics* 66 (Summer 2004): 469–497.

———. *James Madison and the Making of America.* New York: St. Martin's Press, 2012.

———. *Virginia's American Revolution: From Dominion to Republic, 1776–1840.* Lanham, MD: Lexington Books, 2007.

———. "The Virginia and Kentucky Resolution Reconsidered: An Appeal to the Real Laws of Our Country." *Journal of Southern History* 66 (August 2000): 473–496.

Hendrickson, David. *Peace Pact: The Lost World of the Founding.* Lawrence: University of Kansas Press, 2003.

Heideking, Jurgen. *The Constitution before the Judgement Seat: the Prehistory and Ratification of the American Constitution.* Edited by John P. Kaminiski and Richard Leffler. Charlottesville: University of Virginia Press, 2012.

Hickock, Eugene W. "The Original Understanding of the Tenth Amendment." In *The Bill of Rights: Original Meanings and Current Understandings.* Edited by Eugene W. Hickock, 455–464. Charlottesville: University of Virginia Press, 1991.

Hobson, Charles. "The Tenth Amendment and the New Federalism of 1789." In *The Bill of Rights: A Lively Heritage.* Edited by Jon Kukla, 153–163. Richmond: Library of Virginia, 1988.

Holt, Wythe. "'To Establish Justice:' Politics, the Judiciary Act of 1789, and the Invention of the Federal Courts." *Duke Law Journal* 38 (1989): 1421–1531.

Holton, Woody. *Unruly Americans and the Origins of the American Constitution.* New York: Hill and Wang, 2008.

Jaffa, Harry. "The Case for a Stronger National Government." In *A Nation of States: Essays on the American Federal System.* Edited by Robert A. Goldwin, 106–124. Chicago: Rand McNally, 1961.

Jensen, Merrill. *The Articles of Confederation: An Interpretation of the Social-Constitutional History of the American Revolution, 1774–1781.* Madison: University of Wisconsin Press, 1940; 1970.

———. *The New Nation: A History of the United States during the Confederation.* New York: Vintage Books, 1950.

Kaminski, John. "New York: The Reluctant Pillar." In *The Reluctant Pillar: New York and the Adoption of the Federal Constitution.* Edited by Stephen L. Schechter, 48–117. Lanham, MD: Rowman & Littlefield, 1985.

———. "Rhode Island: Protecting State Interest." In *Ratifying the Constitution.* Edited by Michael Allen Gillespie and Michael Lienesch, 368–390. Lawrence: University of Kansas Press, 1989.

Kammen, Michael. *Deputyes & Libertyes: The Origins of Representative Government in Colonial America.* New York: Knopf, 1969.

Kenyon, Cecila M. "The Anti-Federalists on the Nature of Representative Government." *William and Mary Quarterly* 12 (January 1955): 3–45.

Kettner, James. *Development of American Citizenship, 1608–1870.* Chapel Hill: University of North Carolina Press, 1978.

Koch, Adrianne and Harry Ammon. "The Virginia and Kentucky Resolutions: An Episode in Jefferson's and Madison's Defenses of Civil Liberties." *William and Mary Quarterly* 5 (1948): 147–176.

Kohn, Richard. *Eagle and the Sword: The Federalists and the Creation of the Military Establishment in America, 1783–1802.* New York: The Free Press, 1975.

Labinski, Richard. *James Madison and the Struggle for the Bill of Rights.* New York: Oxford University Press, 2006.

LaCroix, Alison. *The Ideological Origins of American Federalism.* Cambridge, MA: Harvard University Press, 2010.

Lash, Kurt. "James Madison's Celebrated Report of 1800: The Transformation of the Tenth Amendment." *Loyola Legal Studies Papers 2005–30.* (November 2005): 1–46.

———. "Leaving the *Chisholm* Trail: The Eleventh Amendment and the Background Principle of Strict Construction." *Loyola Legal Studies Paper 2008–18* (June: 2008): 1–83.

———. "The Original Meaning of an Omission: The Tenth Amendment, Popular Sovereignty and "Expressly" Delegated Power." *Loyola Legal Studies Paper 2007–31* (October 2007): 1–54.

Leder, Lawrence H. *Liberty and Authority: Early American Political Ideology.* Chicago: Quadrangle Books, 1968.

Lenner, Andrew C. *The Federal Principle in American Politics, 1790–1833.* Lanham, MD: Rowman & Littlefield, 2001.

———. "Separate Spheres: Republican Constitutionalism in the Federalist Era." *American Journal of Legal History* 41 (April 1997): 250–281.

Levy, Leonard. *Emergence of a Free Press.* New York: Oxford University Press, 1987.

———. *Original Intent and the Framer's Constitution.* New York: Macmillian, 1988.

———. *Origins of the Bill of Rights.* New Haven, CT: Yale University Press, 2001.

Lofgren, Charles A. "The Original Understanding of Original Intent?" In *Interpreting the Constitution: The Debate over Original Intent.* Edited by Jack N. Rakove, 117–150. Boston: Northwestern University Press, 1990.

———. "The Origins of the Tenth Amendment: History, Sovereignty, and the Problem of Constitutional Intention." In *Constitutional Government in America: Essays and Proceedings from Southwestern University Law Review's First West Coast Conference on Constitutional Law.* Edited by Ronald K. L. Collins, 331–357. Durham, NC: Carolina Academic Press, 1980.

Lutz, Donald S. *The Origins of American Constitutionalism.* Baton Rouge: Louisiana State University Press, 1988.

Maier, Pauline. *Ratification: The People Debate the Constitution, 1787–1788.* New York: Knopf, 2010.

———. "The Road Not Taken: Nullification, John C. Calhoun, and the Revolutionary Tradition in South Carolina." *The South Carolina Historical Magazine* 82 (January 1781): 1–19.

Massey, Calvin R. "State Sovereignty and the Tenth and Eleventh Amendments." *University of Chicago Law Review* 56 (1989): 61–151.

Marcus, Maeva, and Natalie Wexler, "The Judiciary Act of 1789: Political Compromise or Constitutional Interpretation." In *Origins of the Federal Judiciary: Essays on the Judiciary Act of 1789.* Edited by Maeva Marcus, 13–39. New York: Oxford University Press, 1992.

Marsten, Jerrilyn Greene. *The King and Congress: The Transfer of Political Legitimacy, 1774–1776.* Princeton, NJ: Princeton University Press, 1987.

Mayer, David N. *The Constitutional Thought of Thomas Jefferson.* Charlottesville: University of Virginia Press, 1993.

McDonald, Forrest. *Alexander Hamilton: A Biography.* New York: Norton, 1979.

———. *E Pluribus Unum: The Formation of the American Republic, 1776–1790.* Boston: Houghton Mifflin, 1965.

———. *Imperium in Imperio: States' Rights and the Union.* Lawrence: University of Kansas Press, 2000.

———. *Novus Ordo Seclorum: The Intellectual Origins of the Constitution.* Lawrence: University of Kansas Press, 1987.

———. *The Presidency of George Washington.* Lawrence: University of Kansas Press. 1974.

——— and Ellen Shapiro McDonald. *Requiem: Variations on Eighteenth-Century Themes.* Lawrence: University of Kansas Press, 1988.

Middlekauff, Robert. *The Glorious Cause: The American Revolution, 1763–1789.* New York: Oxford University Press, 1982; 2005.

Miller, F. Thornton. *Juries and Judges Versus the Law: Virginia's Provincial Legal Perspective, 1783–1828.* Charlottesville: University of Virginia Press, 1994.

Miller, John C. *The Federalist Era, 1789–1801.* New York: Harper and Row, 1960.

Miller, Joshua. "The Ghostly Body Politic: The Federalist Papers and Popular Sovereignty." *Political Theory* 16 (1988): 99–119.

Morgan, Edmund. "Colonial Ideas of Parliamentary Power, 1764–1766." *William and Mary Quarterly* 5 (July 1948): 311–341.

———. *Inventing the People: The Rise of Popular Sovereignty in England and America.* New York: W. W. Norton, 1988.

Morris, Richard B. *The Forging of the Union, 1781–1789.* New York: Harper, 1987.

———. "The Forging of the Union Reconsidered: A Historical Refutation of State Sovereignty Over Seabeds. " *Columbia Law Review* 74 (1974): 1056–1093.

Nettles, Curtis P. "The Origins of the Union and the States." *Proceedings of the Massachusetts Historical Society* 62 (1963): 68–83.

Oakeshott, Michael. *Lectures in the History of Political Thought.* Edited by Terry Nardin and Luke O'Sullivan. Exeter: Imprint Academics, 2005.

———. *On History and Other Essays.* Indianapolis: Liberty Fund, 1999.

———. *On Human Conduct.* Oxford: Oxford University Press, 1975.

Onuf, Peter. "Federalism, Democracy, and Liberty in the New American Nation." In *Exclusionary Empire: English Liberty Overseas, 1600–1900.* Edited by Jack P. Greene, 132–159. Cambridge: Cambridge University Press, 2009.

——— and Nicholas Onuf. *Federal Union, Modern World: The Law of Nations in an Age of Revolution, 1776–1814.* New York: Madison House, 1993.

———. "James Madison's Extended Republic." *Texas Tech Law Review* 21 (1990): 2375–87.

———. *The Mind of Thomas Jefferson.* Charlottesville: University of Virginia Press, 2007.

———. *The Origins of the Federal Republic: Jurisdictional Controversies in the United States, 1775–1787.* Philadelphia: University of Pennsylvania Press, 1983.

Palmer, Robert C. "The Federal Common Law of Crime." *Law and History Review* 4 (Autumn 1986): 223–335.

Pocock, J. G. A. *The Ancient Constitution and the Feudal Law: A Study of English Historical Thought in the Seventeenth-Century.* Cambridge: Cambridge University Press, 1957.

———. *The Machiavellian Moment: Florentine Political Thought and the Atlantic Tradition.* Princeton, NJ: Princeton University Press, 1975.

Powell, H. Jefferson. "The Modern Misunderstanding of Original Intent." *The University of Chicago Law Review* 54 (Autumn, 1987): 1513–1544.

———. "The Original Understanding of Original Intent." In *Interpreting the Constitution: The Debate over Original Intent.* Edited by Jack N. Rakove, 53–150. Boston: Northeastern University Press, 1990.

Presser, Stephen B. "The Supra-Constitution, the Courts, and the Federal Law of Crimes: Some Comments on Palmer and Preyer," *Law and History Review* 4 (Autumn 1986): 223–335.

Preyer, Kathryn. "Jurisdiction to Punish: Federal Authority, Federalism and the Common Law of Crimes in the Early Republic." *Law and History Review* 4 (Autumn 1986): 223–335.

Purcell, Jr., Edward A. *Originalism, Federalism, and the American Constitutional Enterprise.* New Haven, CT: Yale University Press, 2007.

Rakove, Jack. "American Federalism: Was there an Original Understanding?" In *The Tenth Amendment and State Sovereignty: Constitutional History and Contemporary Issues.* Edited by Mark Killenbeck, 107–130. Lanham, MD: Rowman & Littlefield, 2001.

———. *Beginning of National Politics: An Interpretative History of the Continental Congress.* New York: Knopf, 1978.

———. "Making a Hash of Sovereignty Parts I and II." *Green Bag* 2 and 3 (1998 and 1999): 35–44 and 51–59.

———. "On Understanding the Constitution: A Historian's Reflections (and Dissent)." In *Principles of the Constitutional Order: The Ratification Debates.* Edited by Robert L. Utley, Jr. and Patricia B. Gray, 33–49. Lanham, MD: University Press of America, 1989.

———. *Original Meanings: Politics and Ideas in the Making of the Constitution.* New York: Knopf, 1996.

Reid, John Phillip. *Constitutional History of the American Revolution,* abridged ed. Madison: University of Wisconsin Press, 1996.

———. *Constitutional History of the American Revolution: The Authority to Legislate* Madison: University of Wisconsin Press, 1991.

———. *The Concept of Liberty in the Age of the American Revolution.* Chicago: University of Chicago Press, 1987.

———. *The Rule of Law: The Jurisprudence of Liberty in the Seventeenth and Eighteenth Centuries.* DeKalb: Northern Illinois Press, 2004.

Richards, Leonard L. *Shay's Rebellion: The American Revolution's Final Battle.* Philadelphia: University of Pennsylvania Press, 2003.

Ritz, Wilfred J. *Rewriting the History of Judiciary Act of 1789: Exposing Myths, Challenging Premises, and Using New Evidence.* Edited by Wythe Holt and L. H. LaRue. Norman: Oklahoma Press, 1990.

Robbins, Caroline. *The Eighteenth-Century Commonwealthman: Studies in the Transmission, Development, and Circumstance of the English Liberal Thoughts from the Restoration of Charles II until the War with the Thirteen Colonies.* Cambridge, MA: Harvard University Press, 1959; reprint, Indianapolis: Liberty Fund, 2004.

Rozbicki, Michal Jan. *Culture and Liberty in the Age of the American Revolution.* Charlottesville: University of Virginia Press, 2011.

Rutland, Robert Allen. *The Birth of the Bill of Rights, 1776–1791.* Bicentennial Edition. Boston: Northeastern University Press, 1955; 1991.

Schwarz, Michael. "The Great Divergence Reconsidered: Hamilton, Madison, and U.S.-British Relations, 1783–1789." *Journal of the Early Republic* 27 (Fall 2007): 407–436.

———. "The Origins of Jeffersonian Nationalism: Thomas Jefferson, James Madison, and the Sovereignty Question in the Anglo-American Commercial Dispute of the 1780s." *Journal of Southern History* 79 (August 2013): 569–579.

Shain, Barry Alan. *The Myth of American Individualism.* Princeton, NJ: Princeton University Press, 1996.

Shankman, Andrew. *Crucible of American Democracy: The Struggle to Fuse Egalitarianism and Capitalism in Jeffersonian Pennsylvania.* Lawrence: University of Kansas Press, 2004.

Sharp, James Rogers. *American Politics in the Early Republic: The New Nation in Crisis.* New Haven, CT: Yale University Press, 1993.

Smith, James Morton. *Freedom's Fetters: The Alien and Sedition Laws and American Civil Liberties.* Ithaca, NY: Cornell University Press, 1956.

Stampp, Kenneth M. "The Concept of a Perpetual Union." *Journal of American History* 65 (June 1978): 5–33.

Stuart, Jay. "Origins of Federal Law of Crime: Part One." *University of Pennsylvania Law Review* 133 (June 1985): 1003–1116.

Stourzh, Gerald. *Alexander Hamilton and the Idea of Republican Government.* Stanford: Stanford University Press, 1970.

Somerville, J. P. *Politics and Ideology in England, 1603–1640.* New York: Longman, 1986.

Tate, Adam. "A Historiography of States' Rights: John Taylor of Caroline's *New Views of the Constitution.*" *Southern Studies: An Interdisciplinary Journal of the South* 18 (Spring 2011): 10–28.

———. *Conservatism and Southern Intellectuals, 1789–1861.* Columbia: University of Missouri Press, 2005.

———. "James Madison and State Sovereignty, 1780–1781." *American Political Thought: A Journal of Ideas, Institutions, and Culture* 2 (Fall 2013): 174–197.

Trenholme, Louise Irby. *The Ratification of the Federal Constitution in North Carolina.* New York: AMS Press, 1967.

Tubbs, J. W. *The Common Law Mind: Medieval and Early Modern Conceptions.* Baltimore: Johns Hopkins University Press, 2000.

Vazquez, Carlos Manuel. "What is Eleventh Amendment Immunity?" *Yale Law Journal* 106 (1997): 1683–1806.

Ward, Lee. *The Politics of Liberty in England and America.* Cambridge: Cambridge University Press, 2010.

Warren, Charles. "New Light on the History of the Judiciary Act of 1789." *Harvard Law Review* 27 (November 1923): 49–132.

Watkins, William. *Reclaiming the American Revolution: The Kentucky and Virginia Resolutions and Their Legacy.* New York: Palgrave, 2008.

Watson, Alan D. "States' Rights and Agrarianism Ascendant." In *The Constitution and the States: The Role of the Original Thirteen in the Framing and Adoption of the Federal Constitution.* Edited by Patrick Conley and John P. Kaminski, 251–268. Madison: Madison House, 1988.

Wood, Gordon. *Creation of the American Republic, 1776–1787.* Chapel Hill: University of North Carolina Press, 1970.

———. *Empire of Liberty: A History of the Early Republic, 1789–1815.* New York: Oxford University Press, 2009.

———. "Federalism from the Bottom Up: A Review of Alison LaCroix, *Ideological Origins of American Federalism.*" *The University of Chicago Law Review* 78 (2011): 705–732.

———. *The Radicalism of the American Revolution.* New York: Knopf, 1991.

Index

Macon, Nathaniel, 220
Madison, James, 51, 147, 152, 171–172, 201, 215, 237; amendments to Articles, 54; appoints Joseph Story, 236; attacked by Alexander Hamilton, 174–175; Bank of the United States, 157, 159–161; Bill of Rights, 128–135; criticism of, 134; Constitutional Convention, 82–84, 86–88; Constitution, private assessment, 95; implied powers rejected, 50, 53–54; "National Gazette essays," 172–174; Judiciary Act, 137; popular sovereignty, 100; "Publius," 103–104; Report of 1800, 227–228; "Vices of the Political System," 80–81; Virginia Convention, 110; Virginia Resolution, 223–226
Magna Charta , 23
Maier, Pauline, 10
Marshall, John, 110, 201, 236–237
Martin, Luther: Anti-Federalists writing, 96–97; defends state sovereignty, 84–85, 88; supremacy clause, 88, 89
Mason, George, 110
Massachusetts, 21, 32, 34; condemns Parliament, 27, 31; condemns Kentucky and Virginia Resolution, 226; Constitution of 1780, 137; ratification of Constitution, 99, 101, 107–108, 110, 112, 190; reaction to Economic conditions, 68, 69; response to Shay's Rebellion, 72–73; supports sovereignty immunity amendment, 192, 193; Treaty of Peace, 58
Maclay, William: Alexander Hamilton's program, 150; Judiciary Act, 134, 138, 139
McCulloch v. Maryland, 236–237
McDonald, Forrest, 7, 9
"Mercantile" party, (Rhode Island), 115–116
Monroe, James: amendments to Articles, 74–75, 79; state immunity amendment, 192; Thomas Jefferson writes to, 217

Montesquieu, 30, 97
Morris, Gouverneur, 83, 84, 88
Morris, Richard, B., 4
Morris, Robert, 134, 147; Constitutional Convention, 79; financial program, 47–48, 50, 148; implied powers, 50; Superintendent of Finance, 47
Mutiny Act, 31–32

National Gazette, 172; James Madison's essays in, 172–174
Nationalist (Faction), 203; accept state sovereignty, 45, 49, 86, 90, 95, 96, 99, 104, 105, 156; Burke Amendment, 45; Confederation as weak, 67–68, 70, 71, 72, 75, 80, 90, 210; Constitution and, 89, 104; Constitutional Convention, 82–83, 85, 86–87, 154; constitutional reform, calls for, 75–77, 78–79, 81–82; Federalist during ratification, 99–101, 111, 115; Federalist Party and, 130; implied powers, 48–53, 209, 225; *McCulloch* decision, 237; origins, 40–43, 44; Shays' Rebellion, 72–74; response to crisis of 1780s, 46–48; Treaty of Peace, 55–57, 188, 225
Nationalists' interpretation, 3–7, 73
necessary and proper clause: Alien and Sedition Act debate, 207–208, 215, 220, 221; Anti-Federalists condemn, 97–99, 110; Bank of the United States debate, 154–156, 159–160, 162–163, 166; *McCulloch* decision, 236; state sovereignty amendment to protect against, 132; supremacy clause and, 97–99
Neutrality Proclamation, 200, 205, 214
New Hampshire, 68, 107, 114, 127; condemns Kentucky and Virginia Resolution, 226
New Jersey Plan, 85–87
Nicholas, Wilson Cary, 220
Noel, John, 183
nomocratic: Bank of the United States debate, 154; Burke Amendment, 44, 45; colonial argument, 29, 30; definition, 9; Eleventh Amendment,

About the Author

Aaron N. Coleman is associate professor of history and higher education at the University of the Cumberlands where he teaches in both the History and Leadership Studies departments. A native of Inez, Kentucky, Aaron obtained his BS in history from Cumberland College (now University of the Cumberlands), his MA in history from the University of Louisville, and PhD in American history from the University of Kentucky. Aaron has published articles in several history journals and contributions to edited volumes, as well as a number of book reviews. He lives in Williamsburg, Kentucky, with his wife, Dr. Emily Coleman, and their two children, Alex and Lorelei.